Never Give Up on Your Dream

Never Give Up on Your Dream

MY JOURNEY

WARREN MOON
WITH DON YAEGER

DA CAPO PRESS
A Member of the Perseus Books Group

Designed by Trish Wilkinson
Set in 11-point Janson by the Perseus Books Group

Library of Congress Cataloging-in-Publication Data

Moon, Warren.
    Never give up on your dream : my journey / Warren Moon, with Don Yaeger. — 1st Da Capo Press ed.
      p.   cm.
    Includes bibliographical references and index.
    ISBN 978-0-306-81824-0 (alk. paper)
    1. Moon, Warren. 2. Quarterbacks (Football)—United States—Biography. 3. African American football players—Biography. I. Yaeger, Don. II. Title.
GV939.M595A3 2009
796.332092—dc22
[B]   2009007834

First Da Capo Press edition 2009

Published by Da Capo Press
A Member of the Perseus Books Group
www.dacapopress.com

10 9 8 7 6 5 4 3 2 1

To my mom, Pat Moon, who sacrificed her life after my father passed to make a happy, healthy environment for me and my sisters.

To Felicia Fontenot and my children, who provided the best support system a husband, father, and athlete could have as a professional.

To my wife, Mandy, thanks for your continued loving support and understanding throughout this process.

And finally to all my mentors, and African American QBs before and after me, who gave me the motivation and inspiration to become the player and person I am.

Thank you all!

Contents

Prologue: Motor City Madness

The weather in Detroit on the afternoon of February 4, 2006, was everything you would expect. It was gray and cold, twenty degrees tops, and a driving snowstorm was blanketing the city. Cars were slowing on Interstate 75, but I was throwing caution to the wind, barreling full speed toward downtown.

Then it happened. It was one of those life-changing events that I will never forget.

My cellular phone, set to vibrate, started buzzing. I recognized the number but was paralyzed for a moment. The caller had news for me—but would it be history or would it be heartache?

My mind was swirling much like the heavy snowflakes that pelted the windshield of my rental car. Sitting behind the wheel— my wife Mandy next to me in the passenger seat—I was not sure what awaited me this particular Saturday.

I was an emotional mess.

Yes, me, Harold Warren Moon, the quarterback who was always so cool, calm, and confident on and off the football field, nick-named Pops as a youth because of my mature demeanor as the only man in a home filled with seven women, was a bundle of frayed, exposed nerves.

I always thought I had to be perfect during every stage of my life, without flaw and emotion. But I had no idea what was going on— other than it was snowing like crazy, I was breaking the speed limit, and Mandy was sitting next to me, so composed and so supportive.

My insides were twisted like a sailor's knot.

A news conference was scheduled in downtown Detroit to introduce the 2006 class of the Pro Football Hall of Fame, and I was awaiting word on whether or not I had been inducted. The news conference was the last place I wanted to be if it didn't happen.

Former Dallas Cowboys wide receiver Michael Irvin had attended the 2005 news conference when he first became eligible for induction. It didn't work out that year for Michael though he was eventually inducted in 2007, and I didn't want to be around if it didn't work out for me.

The significance of my eligibility was historic—if inducted, I would become both the first and only African American and the first and only undrafted quarterback in the Pro Football Hall of Fame.

The pressure, suspense, and anticipation surrounding this induction class had been building. Even in retirement my worth was again being debated and dissected on television, on radio, and in newspapers.

Over the course of my career, I had soldiered through, dealing with racism, living in two countries, and playing for a countless number of teams that didn't believe I could play quarterback, let alone reach this point in my life. And here I was in a rental car, on my way to the Hall of Fame selection announcement at the Renaissance Center, and I was still unsure if I belonged.

It seems funny now, though it wasn't funny at the time, that my cell phone would not stop ringing as we sped toward Detroit. Family and friends must have had my number on speed dial, calling in rapid-fire succession to wish me luck, asking if I had heard any news, leaving me wonderful, heartfelt messages. One of those emotional messages was from my sister Kim, who told me how proud she was and how much she loved me, no matter what happened.

I appreciated the calls—I truly did—because I am a guy who replies to all my voicemails. But now I was just trying to get everyone off the phone as politely and quickly as possible to clear the line for the Pro Football Hall of Fame.

Twenty-eight years ago, I had waited on a call that never came from the NFL. Now here I was, weaving in and out of traffic in a Michigan snowstorm, rushing to tell loved ones, "Thanks, but I really, really need to hang up now."

Earning entry into the Hall of Fame—unless purchasing an eighteen-dollar ticket at the front window for daily admission—is extremely difficult. The Pro Football Hall of Fame's forty-four-person Board of Selectors is charged with the task of making sure that new inductees are the finest players the game has produced. If the Board of Selectors doesn't believe you are worthy enough to be an inductee, you are out of luck.

The board consists of one media representative from each pro-football city, with two from New York because both the Giants and Jets play in the Big Apple. A thirty-third member is a representative of the Pro Football Writers of America, and there are eleven at-large delegates. Each year, the Board of Selectors meets the day before the Super Bowl to elect a new class. To be elected, a nominee must receive at least 80 percent support from the board, and at least two but no more than six candidates are chosen annually.

John McClain, a veteran sportswriter with the *Houston Chronicle* who I had gotten to know during my days playing with the Houston Oilers, is a member of the Pro Football Hall of Fame Selection Committee. He also serves on the Senior Selection Committee, a nine-person committee that reviews nominees from the pre-1984 era.

McClain had told me not to get my hopes up, saying there were members of the committee who didn't believe I should be elected into the Hall of Fame in 2006. Maybe down the road, but not now. Although I was one of fifteen finalists determined earlier by the committee, McClain said dissenting opinions ranged from "He couldn't win the big game" to "He was a product of the run-and-shoot offense that inflated his statistics while he played with the Oilers."

For the umpteenth time in my life, the odds were stacked against me. Not only had no African American quarterbacks or undrafted quarterbacks been inducted, it was my first year of eligibility. Previously, only fifty-six players in the Hall of Fame's history had gained entry in their first year of eligibility; a player can only be considered after five seasons have passed since his retirement. Many great players in the Hall of Fame have had their patience tested by the selection process.

For lack of a better description, it was McClain who served as the "lead defense attorney," presenting my case to his fellow selectors on the morning of February 4. McClain also had presentation support on my behalf from John Clayton of *ESPN*, Jarrett Bell of *USA Today*, and Tony Grossi of *Cleveland's Plain Dealer*.

In his five-minute presentation, McClain reminded his colleagues how our defense at Houston had struggled protecting playoff leads in the fourth quarter and that my playoff statistics were as productive as my regular-season numbers. He pointed out that I had thrown for personal bests in touchdowns and passing yardage in a conventional offense in Minnesota. He stressed that when I was playing in Seattle, at age forty, my numbers were better than 90 percent of the quarterbacks in the NFL.

McClain also showed that my numbers were better than Dan Fouts, who, like me, had never won a Super Bowl but was elected into the Hall of Fame in 1993. McClain offered tributes from players such as Rod Woodson and coaches such as Marty Schottenheimer of the Kansas City Chiefs. Clayton, Bell, and Grossi each stood for a few minutes after McClain and told the committee why they also believed I belonged in the Hall of Fame now, and not later.

The presentation might sound like a dog-and-pony show, but it's so important. The Hall of Fame itself has no say whatsoever as to who is or is not elected to membership. In order for a finalist to be inducted, he really has to have a good presentation because it has become so political. You have to have the right alliances with the important and powerful selectors in that room. You have to make them believe, and once you do, their influence can sway others.

If you have Peter King of *Sports Illustrated* on your side, if you have John Clayton of *ESPN* on your side, if you have certain guys on your side, then you have a chance to receive the 80 percent of votes needed to gain entry. If you don't, if those guys don't believe in you, it obviously becomes more difficult, if not impossible, because many other selectors follow their lead.

McClain had a good presentation for me, but it was all about things that I had accomplished. It was just a matter of people knowing it. Unless these selectors know you and cover you, they *really* don't know your career. Sure, they know your numbers and your accomplishments, but they *really* don't know you. John did a good job of making his fellow selectors more knowledgeable. I am sure he didn't have to work too hard to convince some people of my worth, but in other cases, for some people, he did.

While McClain felt better about my chances following the meeting, I still believed that I was a long shot.

Talk about confidence. Aside from me, everyone in the Moon family and most of my friends were so sure I would be inducted the first time around that I wouldn't have been surprised if somebody had already carved a sculpture of my bust and delivered it personally from our childhood home in the midcity district of Los Angeles to the Hall of Fame in Canton, Ohio.

Truthfully, I believed I would be inducted one day because of my production and longevity: twenty-three seasons in professional football, including seventeen in the NFL after playing in the Canadian Football League. However, I had heard the word *no* so many times and had had to wait at nearly every turn in my life and career, so I thought the induction would happen later rather than sooner.

I wish I'd shared in everyone's confidence as Mandy and I headed for a news conference that was scheduled to start four minutes earlier at 2:00 P.M.

I still hadn't heard a peep and I wondered how in the world I was going to console all those people who believed I would be inducted.

What would I tell them?

My telephone rang for what seemed like the millionth time.

It was around 2:04 when Joan, a secretary in the NFL office, called to say she had gotten me the extra tickets I had requested for the league's tailgate party before the Super Bowl game between Pittsburgh and Seattle. I told Joan thanks and how much I appreciated her help.

And then Joan casually added, "By the way, congratulations, Warren." I asked, "For what?" Joan said she saw on the NFL Network that I had been inducted into the Hall of Fame.

"Nobody has told me that," I answered, confused.

At that same time, another caller buzzed in.

It was McClain. He had telephoned me an hour earlier in my hotel room in nearby Dearborn, saying he thought it would be a good idea for Mandy and I to drive into Detroit to be available for the news conference if I was inducted. After initially hesitating, Mandy and I agreed, figuring we could always turn around if the news wasn't good.

McClain was now on the phone, telling me that, yes, what Joan had said was true. I had been inducted into the Hall of Fame.

"The Hall of Fame"—four simple words that easily roll off the tip of your tongue. Unless you are tongue-tied.

The reality and power of that statement hit me like a blindside tackle. McClain needed my reaction for his story, and I honestly have no idea what I told him. My world stopped. I turned my head and looked at Mandy and, at that moment, everything came pouring out of me.

In rapid succession, the challenges in my life flashed before me.

There were coaches at every level, from youth to professional, who believed I couldn't play the quarterback position because of my skin color. I lost my father at age seven to heart and liver ailments due to alcoholism, forcing me to become the man of our home, a responsibility I took seriously as I looked after my mother and six sisters.

I dealt with everything during my amateur and professional careers, from the *N* word to death threats, hate mail, guards, guns, never wanting to talk about it because I didn't want to bring any more attention to my situation. I didn't receive a scholarship out of high school—Arizona State rescinded its offer for me to play quarterback after the school signed two white quarterbacks.

I wasn't drafted out of the University of Washington and was forced to begin my professional career across the border in Canada. Still, I went from being undrafted and unwanted to signing the most lucrative contract at that time in NFL history at $5.5 million with the Houston Oilers in 1984. When I finally made it to the NFL as a twenty-eight-year-old rookie, and despite passing more than 70,000 yards professionally, critics pointed to my inability to win a Super Bowl for my team and city.

Not only did I take each snap and play the game for myself and for my teammates, I always carried the extra burden that I had a responsibility to play the game for others of my race. Honestly, I probably would have been a much better player if I didn't have that burden. But you know what? I carried that burden proudly.

And I have had to deal with apologies that were overdue by decades. Some of those who acted maliciously and out of pure hate now feel sorry. People have approached me in the years since I led the University of Washington out of obscurity and on to a 1978 Rose Bowl victory—grown men, crying, asking for forgiveness.

You have to understand that I was a guy who bottled up his emotions and never shared them. It makes sense that once the dam broke, it let loose a flood. I was a grown man, forty-nine years old, but I started crying like a baby.

I thought about my family, about every African American quarterback who played the game, and about the racism, ignorance, and doubt—no, make that the *shit*—that I dealt with throughout my career.

I bowed my head, covering my face with my right hand. I had lost control emotionally, but Mandy made sure we didn't lose control of the car that was speeding down the highway in a February blizzard. She calmly grabbed the steering wheel for me as I tried to regain my composure.

My closest friends are the first to say they were surprised by my reaction that day. I am always so stoic, so quiet, so mature. After the movie *Star Wars* aired in 1977, many of my friends actually started to call me Yoda, the wisest and most powerful Jedi of all time, who was always completely unshakable and totally unemotional.

Of course, I just wanted to be a quarterback on the football field. And just moments before, I had been informed in a rather unusual fashion that I was a Hall of Fame quarterback. My youth coach Bernard Parks, the former chief of the Los Angeles Police Department and current member of the L.A. city council, said two years after my induction that if somebody had told him I had broken down and cried over any situation, Hall of Fame or not, it must have been a "unique situation."

Well, this was a unique situation.

All these years I had kept things buried deep inside, carefully tucked between my heart and soul. Suddenly, with one telephone call on a snowy afternoon, these memories surfaced like a volcano. Maybe it was therapeutic in a way, the start of an essential healing process.

Despite my hardships and successes, there was no guarantee I would be elected into the Hall of Fame on that first ballot. I was always confident in my athletic ability, but years of being questioned and second-guessed has a way of peeling away tiny layers of your self-esteem.

Later that evening I met with my dear friend and business partner Leigh Steinberg at his annual Super Bowl party. It was crowded, and there were a number of celebrities and players who made quick appearances, including Pittsburgh quarterback Ben Roethlisberger, who led the Steelers to a 21–10 victory over my Seattle Seahawks in Super Bowl XL the following day. Leigh said the telephone call from the Pro Football Hall of Fame allowed me to cleanse myself of past bitterness that I had buried inside and never expressed. He called it liberating.

When I finally found Leigh, we embraced and cried together.

Leigh and I had gone through a lot together. I hired Leigh as my agent out of the University of Washington, and we became close friends. We had known each other for nearly thirty years. I had loaned him money to make the down payment on his first home. Another time I rolled a big-screen television into his house because I liked the way he had negotiated my contract.

The relationships that grow over time between clients and agents are much more than business relationships. They are friendships with a lot of love and caring. Steinberg has probably represented more NFL players than anyone else, but I always thought I was his main priority.

It turns out that twenty-seven minutes earlier a spokesperson had actually left a voicemail, which I hadn't accessed on my overloaded cell phone, to officially inform me of my induction. But it was my friends who first told me the news, just as it has always been my friends and family who were the first to be there in all of my triumphs and all of my failures.

By the time Mandy and I made it to the hotel for the press conference, I had regained control of my emotions. Or at least I thought I had. As I walked into the lobby, I saw McClain, who was in a conversation with Elvin Bethea. Bethea was an outstanding defensive end with the Houston Oilers who had been inducted into the Hall of Fame three years earlier in 2003. I had no idea at the time, but I was the tenth player from the Oilers to receive that telephone call, and first after Bethea. Bruce Matthews's induction in 2007 pushed Houston's total to eleven, a respectable showing considering the Chicago Bears, one of the NFL's oldest and most prestigious franchises, have a league-high twenty-six enshrinees in the Pro Football Hall of Fame.

Although I normally shook hands with McClain when our paths crossed, this time we embraced, and I told him thank you. I was just so thrilled.

I was part of an incredible class that also included quarterback Troy Aikman, linebacker Harry Carson, head coach John Madden, defensive end Reggie White, and tackle Rayfield Wright. Their accomplishments were impressive.

I was so proud to share the stage with these guys.

My unprecedented journey, capped by my enshrinement into the Pro Football Hall of Fame, is about struggle, empowerment, and perseverance. It's about race, stereotyping, and overcoming roadblocks that were first placed in front of me as a child. In fact, those roadblocks exist to this day, as African Americans strive for equality in every phase and every part of life, from athletics to business.

As much as I would like to think my induction into the Hall of Fame has taken African American athletes over an important hurdle, there are still important hurdles in front of us. Turn on just about any major sports program, and you're likely to see African American athletes excelling. Baseball's Ryan Howard, football's Donovan McNabb, basketball's LeBron James, and golf's Tiger Woods are all exceptional athletes.

The combined revenues of the sports industry is more than 213 billion dollars. While African Americans continue to dominate on the field—nearly 80 percent of NFL rosters are African American—there remains a gross disparity in the numbers of black and nonblack people in decision-making positions in all areas and at all levels of the industry: ownership, management, coaching, and scouting.

Many have called my induction into the Hall of Fame, the venue that guarantees football immortality, an extraordinary achievement. Those same people believed that if the system worked for me—an African American who tore down barriers—it doesn't need to be fixed. I disagree.

The battle to integrate the quarterback position has stirred passions for many years. Actually, the debate raged on long after every other position in the four major professional sports—football, basketball, baseball, and hockey—had been opened to African American athletes.

I want to think that race is no longer an issue when it comes to African American quarterbacks. I feel the players are being judged solely on performance. While strides must continue to be made, there's new, young blood within organizations, people who understand whether a guy can play or not. There are player-personnel directors who have played, there are scouts who have played the game, and there are African Americans in those positions, as well, who are now judging all these players the same way.

When I was inducted into the Hall of Fame, I felt it was an achievement that nobody could ever take away from me, regardless of what others thought of me as a player. That's all I had heard the last month leading up to the vote: "Does Warren Moon belong?" Everyone had their opinions, which is fine, because that's what this world is all about, expressing your opinion.

I always felt, however, that at some point, somewhere down the line, I would be inducted into the Hall of Fame. But to make it in my first year of eligibility—there were only fifty-six players who had previously accomplished that feat. That number, to me, says it all.

As of February 2009, that number increased to sixty-three, with the additions of Bruce Smith and Rod Woodson. The 2009 class—Smith, Woodson, Bob Hayes, Randall McDaniel, Derrick Thomas, and owner Ralph Wilson—will be enshrined in August.

As Mandy and I drove toward Detroit on the snowy Hall of Fame election day, I knew our ride, and my story, was *really* just beginning.

1

Man of the House

The stereotypical athlete is a manly man who loves power tools and fixing things and working on cars, but that's not me.

My father, Harold Moon, was a wonderful man who died from liver and heart ailments when I was only seven. He struggled with alcoholism, but that's not what I remember most about him. In my mind, he will always be the silly guy who tickled us kids until we nearly had to pee. Maybe that's not the most picturesque memory, but that's what stuck with me.

I think my father was wise in a way I didn't realize until years later. He had ideals and instilled those ideals in us. We lived in Los Angeles, and every Saturday night, after we were finished playing in the backyard, Dad would make us listen to opera on the radio. He wanted us to be introduced to as much as possible, to various aspects of life and all kinds of cultural experiences. He wanted us to be as well rounded as possible. At the same time, though, every time someone black would come on television (which wasn't very often then), my parents would call all of us kids in to watch it so that we would know that we were a part of that world, as well.

My parents took us to parks and museums and the beach—we loved the beach. They were all for any kind of free activity that would give us variety or educate us or expose us to culture or new experiences. My dad really loved golf and used to try to teach me to play a bit, too. He enjoyed the excitement and variety of life and was determined to impart that passion for learning to his children.

Dad and my mother, Pat Moon, met during college in 1944. They were both in school in Atlanta; she was at Spellman, and he was at Morris Brown. They were introduced by some mutual friends, and it was love at first sight. I remember that she used to say that Dad just struck her as interesting and unusual. She thought he was just different from the Atlanta boys she knew.

For one thing, Dad was a good talker. He loved to tell stories, and he could tell them better than anyone I know. The man loved words—he loved the way he could mold them to fit his purposes, how he could make everyday language bow to his will and create the effect he wanted. I remember Mom telling me that he used to always carry a book of words around with him, either a dictionary or thesaurus, and would look up words he didn't know so that he could increase his vocabulary, or he'd try to find more interesting and vivid words to help tell his stories. She said he was just fluent in a way that other young people weren't.

Dad's love of language was really important for my mother, for whom education had been stressed her whole life. My grand-parents only had basic schooling in a rural town and did mostly do-mestic work as adults—there just weren't the same opportunities for their generation. When they moved to Atlanta, their neighbor-hood was situated near Westfair Court, which runs through the college district where Claude, Spellman, Morehouse, and Atlanta University were all located. Morris Brown was just over the hill from the group. Mom saw college students every day, and they were always pointed to as the picture of success and what she should be aiming for.

Mom and Dad married and moved to Dad's hometown, Detroit—neither one had graduated, but they figured they could get on just fine. Dad had a job with a glass company, and then the babies started to come. Before Mom and Dad met, he actually had the opportunity to invest six hundred dollars in a local record company started by one of his friends. You probably recognize both names—Motown Records and Berry Gordy. But Dad didn't have the extra cash at the time. That missed opportunity haunted my father later in life as Mo-town, the first record label owned by an African American and to feature African American artists, gained worldwide commercial and artistic success.

After a few years up north, they ended up moving back down to Atlanta because the cold was really hard on my oldest sister, who had developed a serious recurring cough in the winter. When Dad read about job opportunities in California, and how it was supposedly more open for African Americans than a number of other places, they decided to head out west to Los Angeles.

I was the first child in my family born on the West Coast. Mom still speaks proudly of the fact that I was delivered by a physician named Dr. Weeks, who was the only African American doctor on the board at the general hospital and the two Catholic hospitals. I was kind of a difficult pregnancy for her, so she wanted to have me at a private hospital because the care there was supposed to be better. Unfortunately, a number of hospitals in Los Angeles were still segregated in 1956, though that was starting to change.

I didn't really know or appreciate any of this about my parents and their work and sacrifice for us kids until later. The main thing I was aware of was that without a father during my formative years, I had to be the man of the house. All of a sudden, at seven years old, I was surrounded by seven women—my mother and six sisters, with the kids' ages ranging from two to seventeen. Three sisters were older, three sisters were younger, and I was the only male in the house. My mother disliked that phrase—"man of the house"—thinking that it put too much pressure on me. But it was a role that I took very seriously.

But with Dad gone, I never learned how to replace spark plugs, change the oil filter, or replace a flat tire on the family car. I had to look for direction from athletic coaches who believed and had faith in me. I played whatever sport was in season, and my coaches were the ones who gave me the opportunity to learn from my mistakes and excel.

I rode my bicycle everywhere in my younger days, avoiding trouble and temptation, determined to get to practice on time and not to get distracted by anything else along the way. My old coaches still remember me with that bike, years later. I rode it to and from practice every day, rather than relying on a parent to pick me up. I was very serious about it—it gave me a sense of responsibility and independence so that I could step up and be the man who I felt I needed to be.

I wanted to grow big, strong, and be fiercely protective of my mother and six sisters. My mother was always big on manners and she taught me to always hold doors for women and to stand until all those present were seated. Our neighbors used to laugh at the sight of me standing next to the car as the rest of my family piled in, but that was just how I was taught. That was how Mom said a gentleman should behave.

It seems funny now, looking back, that even as I was working hard at learning what I thought a man should be, I was also learning a lot about things that were traditionally considered women's work. I guess that's to be expected growing up in a house with six sisters and no father.

My mom was always encouraging me to sew, press my clothes, and cook. In fact, she got me into the habit of baking cookies every Thursday night as a way to relax before my football game the next day. She was also the most organized woman I have ever known and raised my sisters and me to be the same way—to keep us put together and our house clean. Lorenzo Romar, the University of Washington men's basketball coach, even teases me that I'm the only guy he knows who on the way home from a road trip stops at the store for window cleaner so I can straighten up when I get back to the house.

Mom was really an incredible lady dedicated to teaching her children what they needed to know in order to take care of themselves and never be reliant on anyone else. She worked nights from eleven P.M. to seven A.M. The hours were terrible, but she was proud that she was providing for us, so she never complained. After Dad died, she knew she needed to get a stable job that would create a steady income for the family, so she studied to become a registered nurse. I remember her telling us afterwards that one of the proudest moments of her life was looking out and seeing all six of her children in the audience at her graduation ceremony.

Yet even with the demanding schedule she had, dinner was always on the table at night, and clean clothes and breakfast always waiting for the seven of us kids before we left for school. As hard as she worked to make sure we knew how to do everything required for running a house, she still took that responsibility on herself. She taught us to do those things for ourselves not to get out of doing them herself, but so we would be capable adults. I've always been grateful for this.

We really didn't have very much—just a tiny two-bedroom house for seven children in mid-town Los Angeles—so the house was always crowded. The one bathroom belonged to the women, or at least that was how it always seemed. We had one television, too, which we also shared. If I wanted to watch *The Rat Patrol* but it was Mom's time for the TV, we'd watch soap operas or *The Lawrence Welk Show*.

The voice coming from our stereo usually belonged to Billy Eckstine or to Nat King Cole or to Harry Belafonte. If I didn't like the music, I could always take the tops off Mom's empty wine bottles to emcee for my sisters, imitating the Supremes and the Jackson Five. We weren't half bad, either.

Mom always kept the house immaculate. I mean, you couldn't find a crumb or a speck of dust if you looked for it. And even though I know looking back that we didn't have much (I'm sure I knew it even then), I always think of my childhood as a time of having enough.

I don't know how she did it, but we always had a hot meal and clean clothes. They may not have been the newest or finest clothes, but they were always cleaned, ironed, and laid out for us the night before. Mom found a way to make ends meet so that none of us kids ever felt like we were lacking. And she never complained about not having enough to work with—she just found a way.

We went on welfare briefly while my father was sick, but it was only for a few months, and Mom never went back on it, even though we were eligible. The only assistance she accepted was Medicare, because she couldn't afford health care for seven children. But her pride was very important to her, and she later said that going down to the Medicare office was one of the most degrading experiences of her life. There were other times when Mom received money—she told us it was our "ice cream money"—from a rich family she knew in Atlanta.

All Mom wanted for us was to have happy childhoods. She had a happy childhood, even though her mother died when Mom was thirteen years old. My grandmother was one of eight sisters, so Mom had seven aunts to give her plenty of love, and they did. Mom traveled a lot between New York, Florida, and Georgia, so she experienced and saw a lot of nice things. We didn't have a lot, but Mom made sure we appreciated what we had.

That's why, as my kids say, I'm such a miser now. Nothing went to waste in my house, and I still insist that they use every last ounce out of everything in a jar. Whether it's ketchup, mayonnaise—anything, I make them pull out a spatula and scrape the sides. I walk around the house constantly turning off lights to save electricity. Whenever I walk into an empty room with a light on, I can still hear my mother say, "Is anyone using this light? No? Then why are you burning electricity?" It's funny how those little things stay with you.

Mom wanted us to have the same advantages as any other kids. Outside of the house, I worked at a succession of jobs and played every sport possible. I was a paperboy, I worked in restaurants, and I was a clerk for the Veterans Administration in high school. I also had fun in our neighborhood. We played hide-and-seek and built soapbox racers from shopping carts.

My friends and I played with an electric tabletop football game, where the little players buzzed along the game board. I covered the running backs with adhesive tape for added size. I also learned to make the little springboard quarterback throw a spiral with the white cotton ball.

Even then I knew that football—and being a quarterback—was my main game.

When I was twelve, Mom started dating again and met a great guy named Tom Robinson. And even though he wasn't into cars or mechanical things, it was so exciting for me to have a kind of father figure in my life again.

Tom was a chef, and he used to take me into work with him. I'd sit in the back of the restaurant, and he'd teach me what went into each dish and little secrets about how to tweak each recipe to make it come out perfectly. Pretty soon, I started to work for him, doing food preparation and eventually even preparing some of the dishes myself.

I loved talking with Tom, learning to do something none of the other guys I knew could do. It made me feel special, like I was in on some kind of secret. Any money I earned I brought home for the family. The same was true of my older sisters and their baby-sitting money. Everything we earned went for the family.

The thing I loved more than anything else, though, was football, and I discovered this love thanks to my mother.

Mom did more than just teach us how to look after ourselves. She encouraged us to develop our talents, and she recognized the unique challenges that each one of us was facing. For me, that challenge was a lack of male leadership, so she pointed me toward sports as a way to interact with other boys and to have some male role models.

I really admire that she had the foresight to see that athletics would be a good place for me to learn what I wasn't able to learn at home. My mother is an amazing woman—smart, strong, kind, hardworking. She taught me everything I know . . . except about sports. She didn't know the first thing about athletics, but she knew that it was a place where I could learn how to be a man, and so she did whatever needed to be done to get me involved.

I probably first touched a football when I was six or seven years old. I know my dad and I used to play catch with a baseball in the yard, but we didn't play football much that I can remember. Football was something I discovered right around the time that my dad died. My best friend next door was named Charles Hatcher, and he had a big yard where we used to play tackle football, slamming into each other and crashing to the ground. I'm sure it wasn't safe, but it sure was fun. We had little uniforms you could buy in a box, and we imagined we were professionals, just hitting and running as hard as we could. It was every little boy's dream.

It's strange how the wonderful and the terrible can sometimes get jumbled in your mind. Some of my very best and very worst memories are from the football field. I remember storming into the house one day, bruised and out of breath and absolutely beaming from a particularly tough day of football with Charles, and noticing that everyone was upset. A couple of my sisters were crying and my mother looked completely crushed. They told me Dad had just had a heart attack and died.

Just a minute or two before, while I was out having the time of my life, my father was next door, taking his last breath. I couldn't believe it; he was only thirty-eight, and he was *my dad*. That's not supposed to happen while you're running around in the yard next door. That's not supposed to happen when you're seven years old and he's the only man in your life. He wasn't supposed to die.

I am not sure what triggered Dad's drinking problem. I know he was beaten up pretty bad during a riot in Detroit when he was a kid. I know that bothered Dad. He lived in an area where Italian Americans and African Americans lived side by side, and everyone got along and the kids played and rode bikes together. I am not sure of the events surrounding the riot, but I know after Dad was beaten up he started to have migraine headaches, and at some point he may have turned to alcohol as a form of self-medication.

Dad wasn't physical or really verbally abusive with anyone in the house when he drank, but I knew to stay out of his way. He would sit there and drink by himself. It just wasn't a good thing.

It wasn't long after the funeral that my mother sat me down and told me that I was now the man of the house. It was six sisters and me, so I had to be the one who made sure the house was locked up at night and to make sure the trash cans were out when trash day came. I had new responsibilities, and I took them all on full-bore, maybe even more than I needed to at times. I wasn't afraid to boss my older sisters around.

I became very serious very quickly because I felt like I had to be successful.

It didn't take long after mom enrolled me in my first football program at nearby Baldwin Hills Park for me to realize what kind of coach I wanted to play for. I hated the ones who yelled, and I liked the ones who were strict and worked us hard, but who would also ask for our opinions—because I tend to be pretty opinionated. I may not have anything worth offering, but for me, just to know that I have an opportunity to be heard makes such a difference.

In the end, though, I just wanted to be coached. I wanted someone to tell me what I was doing right and what I was doing wrong. I didn't just want a pat on the shoulder and someone saying, "It's just a game." I wanted to be taught, corrected, and improved on. I wanted them to instill the discipline that made me a better athlete. I craved that kind of experience and the expectations that went along with it, even as a little guy.

In the Pop Warner youth football league, my coaches were Bernard Parks and Joe Rouzan. Rouzan was a Los Angeles policeman, and he epitomized, in my mind, everything that an L.A. policeman should be. He appeared to be gigantic, seemingly seven feet tall (in reality, he's closer to six foot three); his legs seemed enormous, bulging with muscles and stretching down from his shorts to running socks crammed into tennis shoes. He wore that getup at every practice.

My sisters were good to help me out with my football practice, too. Patsy still rolls her eyes and claims I came close to working her to death with throwing. And Kim was a track star, so she used to run with me for conditioning. I'm glad my sisters were willing to work with me like that because when I hit junior high, my school didn't have an athletics program beyond physical-education class.

My sisters looked out for me in other ways, too, especially at Christmas. I probably believed in Santa Claus longer than my buddies, but that was okay. On Christmas Eve, one of my sisters would climb out on the roof and walk around, and they'd tell me I needed to get to bed, because Santa wouldn't deliver the toys if I was awake.

Of course, my sisters couldn't help me in football when I got to high school. That was a whole different story.

At the time, we lived on the line that divided the zone for Los Angeles High School from that of Dorsey High School, so we got to choose which school to attend. My sisters all chose to go to Dorsey, but I was different. I wanted to go to Alexander Hamilton High School in West Los Angeles even though it was outside our district.

Hamilton High was known for its academics and athletics, but the rules stated that we had to stay with the schools for which we were zoned. But Hamilton had the football team I wanted to play with, and Coach Jack Epstein was the man I wanted to play for, so I used Mom's boyfriend Tom's address for me instead of our home address. Since Tom lived so close to the school, when district administrators realized the problem—they initially wanted to pull me out and transfer me back to one of the schools I was zoned for—I was granted one of the permits allotted to students out of district.

I was able to stay at Hamilton and develop with the team there. I've always been so grateful that we were able to find a way to make it work, because it seemed like all the other boys in my neighborhood landed in trouble. Some just drank and smoked and others ended up in and out of jail.

Instead of going to parties in the evenings, I was either coming home late from football practice to help around the house and attend to my homework, or I'd be baking cookies to relax before the next day's football game.

My mom always made me divide those cookies with my sisters. I'd insist, "They're my cookies!" and she'd answer, "And you baked them with my ingredients, so you'd better share!" Because I went to school elsewhere and had enough to keep me busy in my free time, I just never managed to get mixed up with the wrong crowd.

Even as I was finding my identity as an athlete and working to avoid anything that would pull me away from that goal, I think my coaches were struggling with what to do with me as a player.

I didn't hit my growth spurt until pretty late, so I wasn't really defense material. (I wasn't really any kind of material at all for basketball, which was what I really wanted to try.) In Pop Warner, the coaches would move us from position to position so we could try out each part of the line; even when I was little, though, I think my Pop Warner coaches knew where they would have to put me. And sure enough, by the time I hit high school, Coach Epstein was willing to take a chance on me as quarterback.

Why? I wish I could say that it was because of my amazing arm or my cool head under pressure, but I think it probably came down—at least at first—to one real reason: I was bossy.

It started not long after Dad died. I went through a very bossy phase for several years. My teachers and coaches all noticed it, and my family *definitely* noticed it. In my mind, I was trying to fill the father role, and a father was in charge and the head of the family. Apparently, though, it just came across as a headstrong, stubborn kid who had to have things his way.

Mom will tell you how, when I was smaller, she'd get me ready for school and then I'd go outside and sit on the curb. I was supposed to be walking with my sisters because I was still pretty young, but instead I'd just sit and insist I wasn't going. So I'd get a spanking. Then I'd just walk down one block and sit again. So I'd get spanked again. Once I got big enough to walk to school by myself, I'd still sometimes go through that routine and wait for my sisters to give up and just walk on before I'd follow them.

I always felt that I needed to tell the girls what to do because I was the man of the house, but they failed to see things that way. When a guy stopped by the house to date one of my sisters, I asked him his intentions. Mom failed to see things that way, too. She appreciated the spirit and seriousness with which I took on the role, but she also recognized that some headstrong behavior would not be tolerated in her house. I seem to recall a lot of spanking during that bossy phase.

My coaches, though, were able to channel that bossiness into something positive. They recognized that a player who is confident in his decisions and assertive in his execution is one that can earn and hold on to the respect of his teammates.

And that's how Warren Moon, quarterback, was born. A stubborn kid with a serious sense of responsibility and a dedication to football was shaped by smart coaching, tough drills, hands-on demonstrations, and intense discipline, and by a mother determined to keep him on the right path.

My mother is an amazing woman, who was very wise to have foreseen how necessary sports would be for me after my dad passed away. I know he'd be proud. I just wish he could have seen me play. He wanted me to be a leader, to be the man of the house.

When I hit the gridiron, I was.

2

Discovering Football

I began playing football at age ten at Baldwin Hills Park in the Pop Warner association. I played on some teams that were very, very talented. On my first team there, I played with another guy who is a member of the Pro Football Hall of Fame, former Green Bay Packer and Buffalo Bills receiver James Lofton.

Our program also produced a number of other pros, such as Wendell Tyler, Butch Johnson, and Keyshawn Johnson. I didn't play football to break barriers. I played because I loved it from the first moment I competed at an organized level.

Actually, I loved to throw the football any chance I got. When I was nine years old, I entered the local Punt, Pass & Kick competition. Punt, Pass & Kick is a national skills competition sponsored by the NFL and Pepsi for boys and girls ages eight to fifteen and was started in 1961. What makes it so much fun is that it gives the winners of the local competitions an opportunity to compete in an NFL stadium. It was a big deal in the neighborhood, and I was excited about the chance to compete.

I knew I would do well in the competition because I could throw the football probably fifty yards when I was nine years old. I threw it a lot farther than any of my friends. I could kick the football pretty good, too, and I actually ended up being our punter at Hamilton High School a few years later.

I won our local competition at age nine and advanced to the area event at the Los Angeles Coliseum. I was so pumped because the Coliseum is where the University of Southern California Trojans played their home football games. I couldn't wait to get on the field that I saw so many times on television.

When I arrived at the Coliseum, however, Punt, Pass & Kick officials wouldn't let me compete because the representative who had organized our local competition hadn't shown up. I was devastated. I walked around the entire Coliseum, inside and outside, over and over, and looked for that guy. I never found him—or ever saw him again, for that matter. I will always remember that day because I believed I would have won my age bracket at the Coliseum and won my age bracket at the national level, too. I wasn't cocky, but I knew what I could do with a football in my hands.

When I watched the national finals on television and saw the winning total—the combined distances and accuracy scores for each event—it wasn't as high as my total from my local event. To this day, I don't know why our local representative didn't show. It is more than forty years after the fact and it still bothers me! That was the last time I participated in the competition. I never had any more interest in it once I started Pop Warner football at Baldwin Hills the following year, when I turned ten.

Even at that young age, however, I discovered that I had the ability to put aside any bad memories and move on. A lot of the negative things that have happened in my life, I've been able to put aside and not think about anymore. I don't know if that was always good, but it helped me move on.

Baldwin Hills Park is in west Los Angeles, between West Jefferson Boulevard and Rodeo Road. Interstate 10 is a few miles north of the community center, which actually serves south Los Angeles. The facility features basketball courts, a baseball diamond, an indoor gymnasium and weight room, picnic tables, a children's play area and, of course, a football field.

I lived just south of Adams Street, so I rode my bicycle back and forth to the community center and really never ran into any trouble. I knew what areas to avoid, and I minded my own business.

Baldwin Hills Park was affiliated with Pop Warner football, which gained popularity in the late 1960s and is still a very strong league today. There are more than 300,000 boys and girls, ages five through sixteen, participating in Pop Warner programs in the United States. Teams in Japan and Mexico also have joined Pop Warner in recent years.

When I played at Baldwin Hills, the Pop Warner program involved three hundred to four hundred kids. The entry fee was thirty to forty dollars, and that basically paid for your insurance to participate in the league. The money to fund the program and equipment such as helmets, jerseys, and pads was raised by parents and players. There wasn't any federal money, city money, or grants earmarked for the league. The money was raised by car washes, hot-dog sales, advertising, shirt and hat sales, family support, and different activities. It seemed like we held as many fund-raising events as we played games.

I was skinny, but I was also a little taller than most kids my age. It didn't matter, though. I was excited about playing Pop Warner football and, even then, I knew I wanted to be a quarterback full time. My first year, however, I played primarily flanker and linebacker. To show you how much talent we had, James Lofton played defensive end. Imagine a Moon-to-Lofton connection in Pop Warner? That would have been wild. Even when lined up away from the center, I always knew I wanted to be a quarterback.

I liked it because I was in control on the field. I was the guy who made things happen, I was the guy everyone relied on. Even at a young age I challenged myself to make big plays and make good decisions. I wasn't the fastest player, but I was fast enough. I wasn't the biggest player, but I was big enough. My secret weapon? I had a good arm, and I knew I could throw the football longer, harder, and straighter than anyone I knew.

Honestly, I had looked at my mother and my sisters and decided that I probably wouldn't grow tall enough to be a pro basketball player, though basketball was one of my favorite sports. Baseball was fun, but it was also a bore at times. I thought my arm could take me all the way to professional football. That was my goal.

Pop Warner football features nine divisions of play, all of which are determined by a strict age-weight scale. The division for the youngest and lightest is Tiny Mite, for players ages five through seven who weigh between thirty-five and seventy-five pounds. I first played in the Junior Midget Division for players ten through twelve years old who weighed between eighty-five and one hundred and thirty-five pounds.

I loved to put on that uniform. I don't know if I felt invincible when I buckled my chinstrap, but I was confident, and I wanted to make things happen on the field.

That's when Bernard Parks first saw me play.

Parks is one of the best-known local figures to have coached at Baldwin Hills. In 2008, Parks served his second term as Los Angeles City Council member for the Eighth Council District. One of the most densely populated areas in South Los Angeles, Parks represents more than 250,000 people.

Before being elected to the Los Angeles City Council, Parks spent thirty-eight years as a police officer. Beginning his career with the police department at a time when patrol cars were just recently integrated, he rose through the ranks of one of the nation's largest municipal law enforcement agencies to become chief of police in 1997. As police chief, Parks implemented some of the most rigorous police reforms ever proposed in the history of the police department, including the institution of an officer-accountability policy. Parks also made it easier for the community to file complaints against problem officers by streamlining the citizen complaint system. Under Chief Parks, the City of Los Angeles saw homicides fall by 45 percent, rape assault drop by nearly 20 percent, and robbery decline by over 45 percent.

Parks dedicated many years to overseeing youth activities in the district. He coached Baldwin Hills youth football for ten years, from 1970 to 1980. Parks also attended night school and still found time to coach football twice a week and on Saturdays. He has mentored many players who became successful community and business leaders.

During my Hall of Fame induction speech, I described Parks as "a guy who instilled values in me at a very young age, showed me discipline, and taught me hard work and dedication."

Parks and his wife, Bobbie, are involved in numerous community groups, such as the Challengers Boys & Girls Club, the Los Angeles Urban League, and the Brotherhood Crusade. He is also a lifetime member of the National Association for the Advancement of Colored People (NAACP). Parks has been recognized as a long-time voice for minority communities, and his footprints were added to the International Civil Rights Walk of Fame in Atlanta in 2006.

A number of other police officers coached Pop Warner football when I played in the league. The adults thought that was a good thing because it helped ease tension from the impression that players and people in general had that police officers only drove around and arrested people. I got to see these men in a different light as a player. They drove players to the games, they coached them, they talked to them. I know some of the players that Parks coached in the 1970s are back at Baldwin Hills coaching their sons today.

As Parks got to know me, he learned my friends called me Pops because of my maturity. I always looked my coaches and adults in the eye when I talked to them. I always made sure to be polite and respectful. That's the way I was taught at home. Like mostly everyone else, Parks was initially impressed by my strong arm. I developed that strength by throwing the football with my sisters in the front yard and across West Boulevard to my friends on the other side of the street. That's how we played catch—throwing over the traffic. Throw it short and there's a good chance the football was lost for good. As I got older, Parks always told me I threw the prettiest pass he had ever seen.

We practiced twice a week for Pop Warner football and played our games on Saturdays at Jackie Robinson Stadium at nearby Rancho Cienega Park. Games between the different Pop Warner divisions lasted all day. I used to think that stadium was so huge with its aluminum bleachers on both sides. There also was a softball field and baseball field adjacent to the stadium, so there always was a steady stream of people and action.

Parks never had to worry about me missing a practice or a game. After school, I jumped on my bicycle and rode it the two or so miles to Baldwin Hills for practice. I was very independent. I had a lot of friends, but I guess you could call me a loner. I didn't hang out with a bunch of other kids, but I always kept busy.

After practice, I'd climb back on my bike and head home. I didn't stick around afterwards like some of the other kids who would run around the park. I mean, I got along well with the other kids, but I didn't have time to hang out. I had to get home to start my homework and help around the house. I didn't have time to waste. I had responsibilities that I knew I had to attend to. Coach Parks seemed to understand that I was a different kind of kid, and he spoke to me in a way that I really respected because I felt like he understood that football wasn't just a game to me.

I took the game—and the opportunity—seriously.

Since Baldwin Hills was located in the heart of the black community, we helped break down barriers in the early 1970s as we traveled into white neighborhoods and played all-white teams. We played games in Mission Viejo, Long Beach, Irvine, and Inglewood. Parks has said he couldn't recall a white kid playing in Baldwin Hills during the time he coached Pop Warner football.

The bulk of the black players played for Baldwin Hills and, at that time, the city's black population was pretty well localized in the Crenshaw, Dorsey, Lock, and Summit areas of Los Angeles. But, honestly, at that age, skin color didn't matter. All of us wanted to play football.

I had a number of Pop Warner coaches as I progressed through the divisions. And some of these coaches would get upset if you made a mistake. There was one instance that I can still recall clear as day, when I threw an interception late in a close game and one of my coaches was infuriated with me. As I came off the field, he said, "Warren, you stink." That ticked me off, and I couldn't understand why he would say that, but his criticism certainly made me work harder.

Bernard Parks had all these drills we worked on, and he constantly reminded me as quarterback never to throw late on a square out, to keep my head up in the pocket, and always look down field. He constantly drilled me on the finer points of the game and the finer points of being a quarterback.

Parks knew I could run the team and take control in the huddle. When the coaches gave me a play, I made sure my teammates got into the right positions. I understood what the coaches wanted to run. We had a very complicated offense, and our head coach, Joe Rouzan, also a police officer and the former city manager of Inglewood, California, sometimes made up plays the day of the game.

We would practice twice during the week, and we'd be under the goal posts ready to begin warm-ups when Rouzan would say, "Warren, come over here. We are going to do this and this." It was almost like drawing a new play in the dirt. Rouzan was very spontaneous, but he was very offensive minded. He called these plays Wiggle Right and Wiggle Left, and we'd have to adapt and learn the play on the spot. But I enjoyed making those adjustments.

Coach put us through drills during the week that made us think. We had to understand the game and the issues of the game, like penalties. I knew all the penalties and what they meant. There were times when I ran over to the sidelines and I'd talk to the coaches about the penalty and the game situation and offer my suggestion. The coaches welcomed the input. I really enjoyed being prepared. And our coaches drilled the heck out of us, too.

Stretches, up-downs, toe-raisers, leg lifts, jumping jacks, sprints—we were ten years old, and we thought we were going to die. Anyone who has ever tried to exhaust a group of ten-year-old boys can understand what an undertaking that must have been, but Rouzan and Parks succeeded. We never won any championships at the lower levels in Pop Warner because the league was so competitive, but we never had a bad team. The competition made everyone a better player.

I never told anyone at that time that my goal was to be a professional quarterback. But there was a certain intensity that I carried, and I always wanted to improve myself. I did it in a quiet manner, but I always had that desire to be the best, even in youth football.

Plus, kids develop physically at different rates. The guy who couldn't figure out how to put his shoes on when he played as a Mighty Mite all of a sudden became a real football player at the Midget level. Speed was very important at the youngest levels of Pop Warner. If you could run, you had a chance to be very good. I was tall and gangly, but everyone could tell from my long arms and legs, and the size of my feet, that I had the chance to grow into my frame as I got older. I may not have been the greatest athlete in Pop Warner, but I held my own. I ran okay, and of course, my arm was strong.

One thing about Pop Warner football players was that they were significantly farther along than kids entering high school who didn't play in the league. If a Pop Warner alum didn't play their first year in high school, as a sophomore, the likelihood was that there were other issues than just his football skills. Some of the players in Pop Warner football were five- and six-year veterans of football when they got to high school.

When Parks served as the athletic director at Baldwin Hills, he was also concerned about the practice habits of teams and coaches. He watched out for coaches who put players through drills and exercises that might be harmful. We had some tough practices, but my time at Baldwin Hills was a great learning experience.

The Baldwin Hills Youth Foundation celebrated the organization's fiftieth anniversary in October 2008. Vera Ford, BHYFA past president and board member, reminded the large homecoming crowd that BHYFA is the only youth football organization to have two members in the NFL Hall of Fame, me and James Lofton.

Lofton attended George Washington High School in Los Angeles and played quarterback and safety and also ran track. He won the long jump at the 1974 California State Track & Field Championships with a jump of twenty-four feet, three-and-a-half inches after placing sixth in this meet the year before.

James signed with Stanford, where he was a record-setting receiver and a national champion in the long jump. Lofton was drafted by the Green Bay Packers with the sixth pick of the 1978 NFL Draft and played sixteen seasons. He was named to the NFL Pro Bowl eight times (seven with the Packers and one with the Buffalo Bills) and played in three Super Bowls during his career with the Bills. Lofton was inducted into the Pro Football Hall of Fame in 2003.

Ford also told the homecoming crowd that many former Baldwin Hills players were playing and coaching in collegiate, high school, and youth sports. Sons of actor Denzel Washington, singer Ray Charles, singer Tina Turner, Rams running back Dick Bass, and former baseball standout Darryl Strawberry also played at Baldwin Hills.

Two of the organization's better-known players also have inspirational stories.

One was Michael Stennis, whose parents were founders of the popular Golden Bird Fried Chicken franchise in Los Angeles. Stennis, who died in 2003 at the age of forty-five from colon cancer, was the first African American quarterback at the University of Hawaii. He began his active athletic career with the Baldwin Hills Park Football Association and was a star player at Palisades High School, which recently divided scholarship money between a community-service award, a performing-arts award, and an athletic scholarship and was given in the name of Michael Stennis, class of 1976. Stennis was the one-time president of the Magic Johnson Foundation and along with his wife founded the Stennis Family Foundation.

Eric Scroggins, a former linebacker at USC who helped the Trojans win a national championship and was the defensive player of the game in a season-shaping victory over 1978 co–national champion Alabama, also played at Baldwin Hills. In January 2007, Eric was diagnosed with Lou Gehrig's disease, a progressive, usually fatal malady caused by the degeneration of motor neurons, the nerve cells in the central nervous system that control voluntary muscle movement. In 2006 Scroggins founded Eric's Vision, an adjunct foundation that supports a research initiative focused on finding treatments and a cure for Lou Gehrig's disease.

In addition to developing young male athletes, thousands of girls have passed through the Baldwin Hills cheerleading program. Currently playing in the Orange County Junior All-America League, the program's youth are exposed to players from a wide variety of ethnic communities.

The program's motto is Building Champions. Baldwin Hills played an important role in my youth, but the Baldwin Hills experience is about much more than winning on the football field. Sure, football can be a great conduit to opening the world to young people and helping them grow as individuals. But Baldwin Hills also wants to help educate youth and encourage them to make a difference.

I took the advice to heart. I wanted to make a difference, too.

3

Finally, a Starting Quarterback

Our neighborhood was in a school district that sent kids to either Los Angeles High or Dorsey High: inner-city, predominately black schools. I was supposed to go to Dorsey, but my mother said there was a huge gang presence and she didn't want me to get taken in. I wanted to attend Hamilton, a school with racial balance and one with a solid reputation for both education and football. But there was one problem: I wasn't zoned to attend Hamilton.

So I registered under the address of the gentleman my mom was dating, Tom Robinson, who lived in the Hamilton school district. I rode the city bus from near our house and then walked the two miles or so to school.

My deception wasn't immediately discovered, and I was eventually given one of the handful of permits allotted to students from out of the district. Starting school at Hamilton, for the first time in my life I dealt every day with whites, Asians, and blacks. The school also had a large Jewish enrollment. My makeup didn't change, though the scenery had. I was quiet, calm, and reserved. I didn't make any trouble, and nobody gave me any trouble.

Jack Epstein, Hamilton's head football coach, happened to be in the school's attendance office when I arrived with my mother that first year to meet with one of the counselors. My mother raised me to be courteous, so at least I made a favorable first impression. I wish I could say the same about my prep football career, which started slowly.

Actually, a simple fact made my life suddenly very complex.

I played on Hamilton's B reserve football team my first year in high school, as a sophomore. It was basically the program's jayvee team for the younger and smaller players. I was tall but lean at age fifteen. But I was excited about the opportunity to play football for the first time at the high school level. I had always been honest with myself about my abilities and the abilities of those around me, and that season wasn't any different.

I was the best quarterback on our B team.

Even so, I was benched in favor of another quarterback. A white quarterback. In fact, I played only when my team was way behind or far out in front. That's when I experienced a man named Mel Klein, our B-team coach, who didn't believe I could play quarterback. Even at that age, my competitiveness was burning inside of me. I wanted to prove to myself and to Coach Klein that I was and could be the best quarterback on the field. All I wanted was an opportunity.

Coach Klein knew how well I could throw the football. My teammates knew I was dependable. We would spread the field and send out five receivers. I had four or five pass plays scripted exclusively for me, to use against a defense that usually knew I wanted to pass the football.

Was Coach Klein a racist? I am not sure, but I do know he wasn't fair. He may have received pressure from the chiefly white parents' booster club at Hamilton High, or he simply didn't believe in me for some reason. Honestly, I felt no remorse when Coach Klein died years later while jogging around the high school track with Coach Epstein. That might sound harsh, but it was the truth. Don't get me wrong. I was sorry that he died, but I felt no remorse because of the way he treated me that season. He just wouldn't have anything to do with me.

We played our jayvee games on Thursday nights, while the varsity played on Fridays. Coach Epstein made as many jayvee games as he could. He usually sat in the stands and scribbled notes. He didn't think much of me until he saw me play late one game. We were either ahead by forty points or behind by forty points, but I had the chance to show off my arm strength. I overthrew one of my receivers on a long bomb by twenty yards, but Coach Epstein smiled to himself and later said that steam shot out of the back of the ball. I threw a beautiful, tight spiral that sliced the sky. Coach Epstein had no idea why I wasn't playing all the time, but he was amazed that I wasn't the team's starter.

I had obviously made another favorable impression on Coach Epstein, who believed in me right away regardless of my skin color. He caught up with me after the game and told me point blank that I was going to be the starting quarterback on his varsity team next season. My eyes lit up, I was so thrilled. I was going to be the starting quarterback! That was great, but I also knew I had to remain committed and get better.

From the time my father died, my whole maturity level changed. When Coach Epstein told me I was going to be his starting quarterback the next season, I knew I had to work to get better. But Coach Epstein gave me the motivation and inspiration when he said that I could play the position. When my father died, I went from being a young kid to a teenager. I still had fun, but while other kids were out messing around, I worked or practiced football. I knew I wanted to be a quarterback, and that drove me to obsessive lengths. I wanted to take it as far as I could.

I built my own regimen, just like in the army. And I stayed busy, too. I think that's another reason why I became successful. Not only did I play in organized football, baseball, or basketball leagues when I had free time, I was also involved in Vacation Bible School in the summertime. I was part of the Boys and Girls Club, too; being so involved kept me from hanging out in the neighborhood which was teeming with gangs.

Gang members threatened my life many times over winning a football game starting in high school. I've never talked about it before publicly; I've just held it inside for many years. I was always able to endure those things somehow and keep going. It wasn't easy. I'm sure there are a lot of kids out there who have worse lives right now, but I don't think mine was the typical daily life of most kids growing up.

Of course, football was my main focus. It helped keep me stay on the right path. Coach Epstein promised me an opportunity to start at quarterback, and I wasn't going to waste it.

I never felt like I was a great athlete in high school. I figured I was a good athlete, and maybe an above-average athlete for the quarterback position, but as far as being able to play other positions, I usually felt like I wasn't fast enough or strong enough to play in college. At the high school level I was good enough to play wide receiver or defensive back, but looking at the next level, I felt like I was best suited to play quarterback. Because I wanted to become a better quarterback, I worked with a pulley-cable system I attached to the fence around the track at my high school to do arm-strengthening exercises. Nowadays kids use rubber bands to do the same thing. I didn't start to use the rubber bands until college, because nobody was using them when I was in high school.

I also got into a very light weight-lifting program in high school. I don't think weight lifting should be a main focus for young kids. I think it should be something that progresses over three or four years, because kids are still growing as young teenagers. Some guys, however, naturally develop more quickly than others, so it all depends on how your body is growing.

I was and am a big believer in doing drills with your own body weight—doing push-ups for your chest, dips for your triceps, a lot of sit-ups for your core. It was during my sophomore season at Hamilton that I started lifting weights. I expanded the program slowly, so that by the time I was a senior, I was into a full-fledged program.

I did a lot of working out by myself, but I think it's always good to train with a partner. If your partner is as motivated as you are, the two of you can push one another to make sure you're getting as much as you can out of each drill. Make sure your partner is as

motivated as you are because you don't want to have to drag someone along every time you go work out.

Nobody ever had to drag me to work out.

I met Felicia Hendricks in chemistry class when we were sopho-
mores. When she first spoke to me, she asked for a pencil because
we had a big test that day. I had three pencils sharpened and lined
up on my desk, and Felicia wanted to borrow one because she had
forgotten hers. I asked her how she could forget a pencil when she
knew we had a test. That was just the way I was. It didn't make any
sense to me that she didn't bring a pencil.

Although I gave her a hard time—and let her borrow a pencil—
we grew to like each other, and we spent a lot of time together in
high school. She thought I was different from the other guys she
knew. We were pretty much inseparable, though we really never
talked about being boyfriend-girlfriend. When I left Felicia's home at
night and pedaled the two miles to my house, I always made a point
to telephone her when I got home to let her know I arrived safely.

Gangs had started their lethal rise in Los Angeles in the early
1970s. The Bloods and the Crips and all the others were not afraid
to intimidate and hurt people. It was 1973, my senior season, and
we were set to play our neighborhood rival Crenshaw High that
Friday night. A Crenshaw player had told Felicia that if Hamilton
won, I was going to be killed. This Crenshaw player was a known
gang member, so I took the threat seriously. But I also handled it
in my own way.

When Felicia pointed out the guy on the street that week, I approached him, introduced myself, and wished the guy good luck in
the game. I didn't want to fight the guy. I just thought that was the
best way to diffuse the situation. But I wasn't a fool, either. I told
my Mom, Coach Epstein, and the appropriate authorities about
the threat. I really never thought anything would happen, but I
also wanted to be careful.

Coach Epstein had the stadium on Friday night encircled by
police. We won the game and the threat proved to be just that—a

threat. Still, as a precautionary measure, I hitched a ride with my mother back home from the game that night, while my best friend drove my car.

Felicia and I hooked up later that night, and we went to a victory party at somebody's house. Of course, it's just the way I am, but I couldn't believe it when Felicia kicked off her shoes to dance. Why in the world would she take off her shoes? This wasn't her house. Somebody could steal the shoes, or they could be lost. Felicia told me not to worry, that nobody would take her shoes.

Everyone was dancing, and at some point in the festivities, some kids from Crenshaw arrived. I immediately stopped dancing, thinking they might be there for me. They weren't, but that didn't mean there wasn't going to be trouble. A Hamilton kid was dancing with a Crenshaw kid's girl, and a fight quickly ensued.

I grabbed Felicia's hand and we headed out the door. Down the street, we heard the sound of gunshots coming from the house, so we dived to the sidewalk together. It was also at that moment when Felicia realized she had forgotten her shoes back at the house. She wanted to go back and get them. Wrong. I told her we weren't going back to get them, that maybe next time she would listen to me.

That's why everyone called me Daddy Warren or Pops. You always had to be prepared.

I may have been a C student in high school, but Coach Epstein knew I had the smarts to excel in the classroom if I put my mind to it. I was serious, but I was also a happy-go-lucky kid. I spent a lot of time shooting hoops or talking to Felicia when I should have been in class. Coach Epstein also knew I had the smarts to make good decisions on the football field.

Coach Epstein always said his quarterbacks had to be smarter than him. He had a system where he checked the math and English scores of all his incoming football players, dating back to grammar school. Coach Epstein believed those scores helped him determine a player's potential on the football field—especially his quarterbacks—because decisions had to be made in tenths of a second, under pressure. Coach felt I was one of his top kids in that regard.

Although I still didn't have the preferred size or speed for football, my secret weapon was my arm. As Coach Epstein promised, I was his starting quarterback as a junior. By the time I was a senior at Hamilton, I was one of the top high school quarterbacks in Los Angeles, even at five feet eleven and 165 pounds. I led my team to the city playoffs and was named to the all-city team in 1973.

In the league championship game against Pacific Palisades High, I threw a pass sixty yards in the air that ended as an eighty-five-yard touchdown pass on the game's first play. In our last regular-season game against Venice High School in knee-deep mud, I engineered a game-winning drive on quick completions and runs in the fourth quarter. My best game as a senior was a 16-for-23 effort, good for 289 yards and two touchdowns. I was also named our team's MVP.

I was good enough to be a Division I prospect, but nobody wanted me as a quarterback. They wanted me to be a wide receiver or a defensive back. Coach Epstein couldn't understand why not one school stepped up and offered me a scholarship as a quarterback. Honestly, I couldn't understand it, either.

A high school all-star game was held at the Rose Bowl at the end of my senior season. I didn't even receive an invitation to play. But I went and sat in the stands anyway with my good friend, Clyde Walker, and I watched the game in a slow burn. Clyde had watched me go through workouts during the summer with players from USC and UCLA, and he knew I had the talent to play with anyone. I just sat there and watched that all-star game without saying a word, knowing full well I belonged in that game. Was it because I was a black quarterback? Was it because I played for a city school against quarterbacks from those heralded programs in the suburbs? Was it something else?

Whatever it was, it left me with an uneasy feeling of injustice.

When I graduated from high school, the only colleges willing to let me play quarterback were small ones, such as Cal Poly Pomona,

San Jose State, and Cal Poly San Luis Obispo. Some Pacific-10 Conference teams were interested in me, but only as a defensive back or wide receiver. That was unacceptable. Arizona State extended an offer for me to play quarterback, but rescinded it after signing two white quarterbacks. It wasn't cockiness or overconfidence, but I felt like I was a Division I quarterback. That was the only position I'd played since I was ten years old.

A fire burned deep inside of me, too. I guess it was my own inner confidence and stubbornness. I always played with that chip on my shoulder—I had something to prove all the time. It always seemed like I couldn't do it the regular way, the normal way, like everybody else, to compete for the position and the best guy wins. It just didn't work that way for me. Something or someone got in the way. Whether it was people who didn't believe in me like that high school coach, or just me being stubborn and saying, "I'm going to do what I want to do." It started with my mother, who raised me to believe that I could do whatever I wanted to do. I wasn't going to deviate from that mindset.

I also judged myself against others. When I looked at my peers, day in and day out, whether I was playing in a summer passing league or during the season, I knew that I was as good as if not better than all the guys. But why wasn't I able to play quarterback, or why weren't people going to give me the opportunity to play quarterback at the next level? I knew it had to do with a little bit more than just my ability. These were the times we lived in, and that was something I was going to have to overcome.

I also had a couple of role models, like Roman Gabriel, who was the quarterback of the Rams at the time and was the first Asian American to start as an NFL quarterback. Jimmy Jones was an African American quarterback at USC in the early 1970s. Those were guys who I looked up to, and I felt, watching them, that there would be an opportunity for me to play the quarterback position down the road. My thing with playing quarterback, I just wanted to look for a team that wanted me. If somebody wanted me, that's where I wanted to be. If you didn't want me, okay. I didn't want to be with you, either.

So I decided to stay in Los Angeles and attend West Los Angeles Community College, a two-year school where Coach Epstein had been named the offensive coordinator.

Coach Epstein wanted me.

West L.A. College is located just east of Sepulveda and Jefferson and overlooks Culver City, Marina Del Rey, and greater West Los Angeles. On a clear day, from the highest point on campus, you can see the Pacific Ocean.

I also had a clear view of what I wanted to accomplish at West L.A. I didn't want to go to a community college in the first place, but it was just something I felt I had to do in order to get to a major college. My intention was to play one season and move on.

Coach Epstein barely recognized me when I arrived on campus my freshman season in the fall of 1974. I had grown three inches, to six feet two, and added twenty pounds to my frame. Coach Epstein wanted to continue to do what we had done together at Hamilton—pass the football and win games—so he installed a four-receiver set, and that's exactly what we did. Our receivers coach, Ron Price, also coached at Hamilton High, so it was an easy transition for me.

Although we were projected to finish near the bottom in the Western States Conference, we won the conference and went to the state playoffs. Our offense was like a pinball machine—we lit up the scoreboard. We basically outscored our opponents. I was selected as the conference player of the year. I had seventeen, nineteen, and twenty-four completions in three games. I threw for 293 yards, 321 yards, and 367 yards in three games. I threw for four touchdowns each in two games. I had a great sophomore receiver named Leon Garrett, who was also all-state and caught eighty passes that season. One of my best games was against College of the Canyons, when I threw for four touchdowns, two to Leon. Once the playoffs started, though, we got smoked because we were one-dimensional, all offense and not much defense.

Just weeks into the season, I was convinced more than ever that I should be in a major college, not in a community college. Plus, I started to get some Division I offers, and I knew I didn't want to waste another year there. But it was tough, because my head coach wanted me to stay two years and fulfill my commitment. I understood his position, but I also felt it was his responsibility to place his players in a major college program. Whether that happens after one or two years shouldn't matter, because some players are good enough to leave after one year. That's the point I tried to make to him. I was ready to leave, and I had really never wanted to attend junior college, but circumstances dictated my decision.

Although we eventually worked it out so that I could leave, he didn't let schools come in and recruit me during the season. But I had a part-time job in the athletic department to make some extra money, and I was able to get into the team's film library without any problems. So I used to go into our film library at night, take a game film—no, make that "borrow" a game film—and send it off to the schools I wanted to talk to. I'd send a message with the tape that said it was important to return it as soon as possible. Why? So I could get it back into the film library before the coaches knew it was gone. I always had to do a little something extra to draw attention to myself and prove that I could play quarterback.

It was difficult for me to concentrate on school that year because I just wanted to get through it and get out of there. I used my one season as a stepping stone to get to a major college. I never expressed that to anyone at the beginning, but my high school coaches, Epstein and Price, had known that was my primary reason for attending junior college. After my high school graduation, they'd said, "Why don't you come with us? Have a good year, and maybe you will get the offer you want." And that's how it worked out, too.

Most of my interest was from West Coast teams. It would have been nice to stay in my hometown of Los Angeles, but UCLA was running and winning with the wishbone offense under Pepper Rodgers, and Vince Evans was the quarterback at USC. I knew I didn't fit into the wishbone offense, which was geared for the running game, and I wasn't interested in a redshirt season behind

Vince. I wanted to go somewhere I'd have the opportunity to play right away and throw the football. I just couldn't see myself sitting a whole season, not playing, or only handing off the football.

I was intrigued by the University of Washington in Seattle, which was one of the first schools to express a serious interest in me. The Huskies had a new coach in Don James, who was hired in December 1974 after coaching four seasons at Kent State. James coached future NFL great Jack Lambert and future college head coaches Nick Saban (now with Alabama) and Gary Pinkel (now with Missouri). Huskies assistant coach Jim Mora, who recruited in San Diego and Orange County, had seen me on film, and he told Chick Harris, the Huskies' defensive back coach who recruited in the Los Angeles area, to talk with me. It also helped that my star receiver, Leon Garrett, had been offered a scholarship to Washington and had accepted.

Mora was a strong advocate for bringing me to Seattle. I thought the University of Washington would be a good place for me to come in and compete right away because the new coaching staff there promised everyone a fair opportunity to compete. I also wanted to stay close to my family, on the West Coast, so they could see me play. And I was still in a relationship with Felicia, who was attending San Jose State and had been able to catch two or three of my junior-college games.

Although Washington had a returning starter at quarterback in senior Chris Rowland, I was assured that I would be given a fair chance to win the quarterback job as soon as I hit campus. Coach James told me that every player on the team was starting even, including his incoming recruiting class. James stressed to me that no returning player had any type of job security and every position was wide open.

I believed him.

4

Washington Bound

After I'd spent one season in junior college, coach Don James gave me the opportunity to play major-college football at the University of Washington. James later said a former colleague advised him against recruiting a black player at quarterback, but he saw something in me that a lot of other people didn't see. It wasn't easy, though.

Washington had a black quarterback as a backup, Cliff McBride. Cliff told me not to come to Washington because he didn't think I'd get a chance to play. I had also heard from athletic-department personnel about racial tension in the program.

The Huskies also returned their starting quarterback, senior Chris Rowland. Rowland was a hometown favorite, a popular Seattle native who had led the Huskies in passing yards in consecutive seasons and had once thrown an NCAA-record thirty-one pass attempts in one quarter. And Chris was white. Many Washington fans didn't approve when I was named the starting quarterback to open the 1975 season.

Coach James stuck with me through some extremely tough times at Washington early in my career. I was booed relentlessly by our hometown fans. I tried to not let it bother me, to keep a calm face and a cool demeanor, but it still hurt. But James never wavered, saying I graded out better than his other quarterbacks. In the huddle I had to look into ten sets of eyes and on each play prove to my teammates that I was capable of leading them to victory.

After we had gone 11–11 in my first two seasons as a starter, we turned the corner during my senior year, 1977, and the boos turned into applause. I was named one of three team captains, and by that time, I had come to understand that taking abuse and criticism was a part of life, particularly for an athlete.

I couldn't have planned for a better moment of revenge during our emotional home victory over fourteenth-ranked USC on November 12, 1977. We were beating the Trojans 28–10 and holding on to the ball in the final minutes, when a hole opened, and I ran seventy-one yards for a touchdown. Our fans chanted, "War-ren, War-ren, War-ren," as I reached the end zone.

Many of those same fans who stood and cheered for me at that moment had booed and hated me for the past two years. A voice in the back of my head told me to give the fans the bird, to flip them off, to give them the digital salute. *Go ahead and do it*, the voice said. *You will feel better, and they deserve it.* But that wasn't the right thing, the classy thing, to do. I maintained my composure and enjoyed the moment. I wanted fans to judge me on what I did on the field and in my life. I didn't want pointing my middle finger at them to be part of that judgment.

Again, in all those different situations, there's a lot involved that I was never able to talk about, or never did talk about, a lot that was involved in those situations. I just dealt with them. I never wanted to feel like I was complaining or whining or making excuses. I'm just not that type of person. I always wanted it to seem like everything was okay, and that I would endure, no matter what.

I flipped the football to the referee and headed to the sidelines with a wide smile.

In December 1974, Don James was hired by UW athletic director Joseph Kearney to succeed Jim Owens as head coach. Owens, who had coached at UW for eighteen years, was very successful early in his career. He led the Huskies to back-to-back ten-win seasons in 1959 and 1960, to a win at the Rose Bowl and a national title in

1960, according to the Football Writers Association, and again to the Rose Bowl in 1964. Owens had also, however, had four losing seasons in his last seven years there, including a 1–9 mark in 1973 and a 5–6 record in 1974, before he was replaced by James, who had had a successful coaching stint at Kent State.

James took a big chance on me, because they had never had an African American starting quarterback at the University of Washington. James believed in me, and we went through some very lean years during that time, and he stuck with me. He is one of the guys that I respect probably as much as any person I've ever played with or played for.

Yet my decision to attend Washington didn't have a thing to do with my skin color. My mother raised her children to believe there were good people in all races. She never wanted to put a lot of blame on race, even though the race issue was always there. When Coach James was in our home when he recruited me in the spring of 1975, he looked at me and told me I would be given the opportunity to compete for the starter's role. He said the starter's role wasn't promised; I had to earn it. That's all I needed to hear. My decision was based on the promise of opportunity.

It didn't matter to me that the University of Washington, and Seattle itself, was predominately white. Even when McBride told me not to come to Washington, I didn't know if he was telling me that because he didn't want to compete against me or if he was really serious about the program's racial tension. I knew there had been a lot of racial problems in the athletic department, but it seemed to have gotten better under Coach James.

All I wanted was the chance to compete on the field, anyway. And James gave me that chance to earn the starter's role.

Chris Rowland was a prized six-feet-three, 220-pound recruit when he selected UW over Washington State and Stanford. He picked the Huskies because they had a drop-back style, which favored a quarterback with a good arm, in place a season earlier for Sonny Sixkiller. As a sophomore, in 1973, Rowland worked his way into the starting lineup and threw five touchdown passes against

Cal and four more against Washington State. But in 1974, Coach Owens switched offenses to the run-heavy veer, and midseason Rowland was lost to a broken ankle. In two seasons, Chris had thrown for nearly 1,400 yards and twenty touchdowns, with thirty-four interceptions.

When Coach James replaced Coach Owens, however, he was bent on making dramatic changes. Because of the situation with Rowland and me, James evaluated every single snap and every single practice film and graded both of us during preseason drills. After two weeks of practice, I was named the starter for our season opener at Arizona State. I know Chris wasn't happy, but we were teammates, and we were roommates on the road that season. We had a young team and James preached patience, but we also wanted to win. That didn't happen in our opener at Arizona State; we lost 35–12.

The hail of boos pelted me almost immediately in our home opener against eighth-ranked Texas and their prized running back Earl Campbell on September 30, 1977. My teammates got to know me during preseason practice and they knew my abilities because they saw me play every day. But they had no idea how I would hold up under adversity. And we faced plenty of adversity against the Longhorns.

Texas was a good team, and we had a tough time stopping the Longhorns' wishbone offense. We hung in there as long as we could but just couldn't get anything going, and our fans started to boo. They put their hearts into it, too. I got our signals from the sidelines and, as I ran into the huddle, the boos poured down from the stands. I looked each of my teammates in the eye, and I had to make them have confidence in me and believe that I could march us down the field.

I should have won an Oscar. It was the ultimate acting job to go into that huddle and show them that this crap, all this booing, didn't bother me. Of course, it did. I am only human. I didn't want to be booed by our own fans. I had never experienced that before.

First of all, I had never played in front of 56,000 fans. All of a sudden it sounded like everyone in the stadium was booing me. I had to pull it together and stay composed. I had seen it happen when I watched games on television, but you never really put yourself in the other guy's shoes as far as being booed and heckled. It's part of the game. And then, later on, when I started to hear some of the racist things that were being said about me in the stands, I started to wonder. I didn't know if the booing was because of the way I played, or was it because of the color of my skin? I really didn't know.

We lost to Texas 28–10 and stumbled to a 2–4 start. After six games, James made a switch and benched me in favor of Rowland. It was difficult to sit back and watch. We won four of our last five games, ending the season with consecutive victories over USC and Washington State. Chris played only in the opening series in the Apple Cup against WSU due to illness, and I helped pull out a last-second, 28–27 victory.

We finished 6–5 overall and 5–2 in the Pac-8. It was the program's most league victories since the Athletic Association of Western Universities changed its name to the Pac-8 in 1969. We actually just missed playing our way into the Rose Bowl, and Coach James earned Pac-8 co-coach-of-the-year honors.

The season was definitely a learning experience for me. I threw for 587 yards but completed only 39 percent of my passes (48 of 122). I threw two touchdown passes on the year, including a seventy-eight-yarder to Spider Gaines. Besides beating out Rowland and dealing with the criticism, part of the problem that first year was that we really had a tough schedule, and we lost some close games. I guess the fans blamed me. It hurt, but I survived it. I was looking forward to a better season in 1976.

I figured it couldn't get any worse.

My junior season was described by the Seattle media as creditable. I completed 81 of 175 passes for 1,106 yards and six touchdowns, averaging better than thirteen yards a throw. I also threw only eight interceptions and set a UW record for most passes thrown without a pick. My two best games came against Stanford, when I completed fifteen of twenty-eight passes for 209 yards and two touchdowns, and Washington State in the season finale, when I threw two long touchdown passes of forty-five and forty yards.

It was in that game against Stanford, specifically my second-half performance, that left Coach James with the impression that I had arrived. Although we had lost 38–24, I rallied my team from a twenty-point deficit and played with poise and confidence in the pocket. I took a pounding on some plays, but I bounced right up and showed my line that I had complete confidence in it.

After completing just four of eleven passes for thirty-one yards in the first half, I went eleven of seventeen for 178 yards and two touchdowns, including one on a fourth-down throw to Spider Gaines that went for thirty-eight yards. At that point, the Stanford game was my best performance at UW. It improved my six-game totals that season to fifty-three completions out of 108 attempts for 675 yards. After my first six games in 1975 before being benched, I had completed only forty-four of ninety-nine passes for 461 yards.

The second half of our season didn't go as well, however.

We were still a young team with thirty underclassmen seeing playing time. Tailback Ronnie Rowland had a strong season, finishing with 1,002 yards, but we never found any consistency on offense. We dropped three of our last five games, including games to then-number-three-ranked UCLA (30–21) and number-three-ranked USC (20–3). But we did beat rival Washington State, 51–32, for the Apple Cup in our regular-season finale, which at least helped soothe the pain of a disappointing 5–6 season.

Of course, I still dealt with a far deeper pain that season.

I pretended my struggles, the cacophony of boos, and the racist taunts didn't bother me when I played at Washington. But Willie and Thelma Payne, as well as my best friend Clyde Walker, knew better.

I met the Paynes through one of my roommates, Leon Garrett. Willie, an airport skycap, became the father I never knew; Thelma, a Seattle social worker, was my mother away from home. Thelma had gone to school with the father of Leon Garrett, and one night she invited Leon to dinner. Leon asked if he could bring me along. It was the start of a great friendship that has flourished over the years and still remains strong today.

I could go to the Paynes's house and eat, laugh, and cry. When things were bad, there were nights that I would lay my head on Thelma's lap to try to relax and figure out what I had gotten myself into. Thelma would tell me to breathe and relax. She thought the pressure had built up so much inside of me that I might pop.

It was much worse on game day.

Clyde had to put up with the racist slurs hurled down from the stands. He listened to fans question my intelligence because of the color of my skin. And, yes, there were times when Clyde narrowly avoided fights in my defense. Felicia also attended my games with Clyde and heard all the nasty remarks, too. She couldn't believe what she saw and what she heard out of people's mouths. I told her not to wear a T-shirt with my name on it for games—I was worried she would get into trouble or, worse yet, hurt.

Those were some bittersweet days for me. I learned a lot about people, and I also learned about how tough I could be. I never expressed my bitterness or lashed out. My coaches and teammates credited my demeanor to my maturity. I think I earned a lot of guys' respect in just the way I handled the taunts and booing, because I never let it look like it bothered me. I never complained about it, never used it as an excuse.

I always thought of that deodorant commercial: "Never let them see you sweat." That was my mindset. I was nervous and worried on the inside, but that is where it stayed. But I never let my teammates see that side of me. I had to have my poker face. I had to be composed. I had to be in control.

While my friends and family had to endure the verbal onslaught in the stands, I really never heard the vitriol fans rained down on me, because I was on the sidelines. I just knew when the booing started.

After each play I ran to the coaches on the sidelines to get the next play, and then I ran back into the huddle. That was when the booing started, so I knew the fans' displeasure was with me and not the rest of the team. I knew the difference between "boo" and "Moon," and they weren't chanting "Moon." That was so tough for me, listening to that and then having to go into that huddle, look my teammates in the eyes, and prove to them I could move the chains.

As the quarterback, I was the team leader. I had to make the right call and make the right play. But that was one of the most difficult things I had to do, to show on my face in that huddle, play after play, that the booing didn't bother me. But inside it killed me.

I still believe it was my family issues, losing my father at such a young age, that forced me to mature more quickly than I might have otherwise. I just thought of this as another responsibility I had to take on. So even though this was a new situation, I had to act responsibly. I had to step up and be the guy with the big shoulders who was able to handle this burden. Still, I am really not sure what my teammates thought about it during my first season. A majority of players in the offensive huddle were seniors, and only two other blacks besides me started on offense. They were probably testing me to see how I was going to react, now that I think about it.

Although my mom wasn't into athletics, she had watched her share of football, and she knew trouble was in store for me after I had beaten out Rowland for the starting position. She understood why fans would be upset, especially since in most cases senior players usually have earned the privilege to start their senior season. Plus, Chris was a local hero. But Coach James had told the team that the slate was clean when preseason drills opened.

If anyone telephoned Mom and asked her about my situation, she answered politely that she was busy raising my younger sisters and that I had to live with any repercussions that my role as a starter caused. Coach James was also ridiculed for his decision to start me and was often called a certain racial slur. Mom used to write to Coach James thanking him for sticking with me. She told Coach that he and I were in her prayers.

That's not to say that Mom, deep down, wasn't upset with how I was treated by fans. She actually wanted to flood the NAACP

(National Association for the Advancement of Colored People) office in Washington, D.C., with postcards from people saying that what I had to endure wasn't right and it wasn't fair. Mom was upset, too, but she never got around to mailing those postcards.

Mom was relieved that I found comfort with the Paynes. They were my second family, and Mom stayed with them when she attended my games. When I moved into professional football, I still remained extremely close to the Paynes. That hasn't changed. I've always tried to visit them every Fourth of July; and the Paynes try to visit my family every Thanksgiving.

Thelma Payne has a great way with people. She is a program manager for the Seattle Public Schools system. For almost a decade she ran a clinic for what she called "children who need encouragement for achievement." I helped her run the clinic. It was an honor to be involved, and that's the least I could do for Thelma and Willie. It's helpful to me to do things for other people. Sometimes you can forget about football and remember it's a real world out there.

And it was the Paynes who helped me survive in that real world at the University of Washington.

I worked hard in preparation for my senior season at UW in 1977. I lifted weights daily and tried to develop a killer instinct in myself that I thought I had lacked my first two seasons. I also had come to better terms with the treatment I had received from hometown fans during the time, too.

I told the media that Seattle was a hungry sports town and people sometimes got upset and acted that way. I went to a lot of Seattle Sonics games, and when they didn't win, those players got a lot of abuse from fans. I knew it would be that way with the Seattle Seahawks, too, after they joined the NFL as an expansion team in 1976 along with the Tampa Bay Buccaneers. I grew up a fan of the Los Angeles Rams, and when they didn't play well, I got down on them. I understood what motivated fans, and athletes had to learn how take the good and the bad. I was excited about my senior season because I knew it was an important year for both the team and for me.

We had a strong running back in Joe Steele, a talented receiver in Spider Gaines, an accomplished center in Blair Bush, and a herfalded linebacker in Michael Jackson. The last thing we needed was a slow start, because newspapers had already started to speculate about what was wrong with the program. Coach James actually had us rip up our goal sheets for the year and write each day on paper what we could do to help the team.

Of course, what we didn't want to happen did.

We dropped our opener to sixteenth-ranked Mississippi State, 27–18. After we beat San Jose State 24–3 at home the following week in front of only 36,489 fans—the Seahawks were threatening to take away much of our attention—we lost tight road games to Syracuse (22–20) and Minnesota (19–17) to fall to 1–3. That was a long flight home from Minnesota. At that time probably nobody thought James's coaching career at UW was destined for greatness, and my legacy wasn't headed in the right direction, either.

But beginning with a 54–0 win at Oregon in the second week of October—we held the Ducks to ninety-seven yards—we found our rhythm. It was like we couldn't be stopped. We won six of our last seven games over Stanford, Oregon State, California, USC, and Washington State by a combined score of 172–83.

It was especially sweet to beat USC, 28–10, and coach John McKay for the second time in my career. I had never talked to Coach McKay, but it wasn't like the Trojans were hurting since I got away. Coach couldn't sign all the talent in Los Angeles. But I will never forget the headline in the newspaper the day after the game: CAL INVADED BY THE MOON MEN.

I didn't have big numbers in our offense. It was more about me managing the game and making big plays when needed. Against Southern Cal, we didn't want to let the game get away from us by doing anything stupid offensively. We had a great defense that knew how to play. We wanted to keep the chains moving and keep USC's great running back, Charles White, off the field, and that was my job. We were very methodical in everything we did, and we wanted to keep the clock running. Coach James trusted me with the football and wanted to keep it in my hands as the seconds ticked away late in the game. But a hole opened on a sprint out, and I scored easily.

Our lone defeat during that stretch was a 20–12 setback at UCLA. I had a solid season, completing 113 of 199 passes for 1,584 yards and eleven touchdowns. I also had 266 rushing yards and six touchdowns, accounting for 168.2 yards of total offense per game.

Although we finished 7–4 overall and 6–1 in the conference, we still needed help from USC to reach the Rose Bowl. That help came with two seconds remaining in the USC–UCLA game as USC's Frank Jordan kicked a thirty-eight-yard field goal to send the Bruins to defeat and us to Pasadena.

Sometimes teams need a break to advance, and we weren't about to complain. There already had been way too many complaints in my three seasons at UW as far as I was concerned. All I knew was that I was headed home, with my teammates, to Los Angeles. We were in the Rose Bowl. I couldn't think of a better way to script my last collegiate game.

It was a dream come true.

5

Rose Bowl

I grew up with the Rose Bowl.

It was in our backyard, ten miles northeast of downtown Los Angeles, in sunny Pasadena. It's nicknamed the Granddaddy of Them All because, well, it is the oldest college bowl game. It was first played in 1902 and it has been played continuously since 1916. The Rose Bowl, at least in my mind, is tradition at its finest.

The Rose Bowl was exclusively a Big Ten–Pac-10 affair for many years. I sat in my living room and watched on television as O. J. Simpson and USC, Jim Plunkett and Stanford, and Cornelius Green and Ohio State played in those games. I listened as sportscaster Curt Gowdy, in a slightly gravelly voice, described the action in his straightforward manner. I usually spent the entire New Year's Day in front of the television and watched a bowl lineup that began with the Cotton Bowl in Dallas and ended with the Orange Bowl in Miami.

While the Big Ten dominated the Rose Bowl in the late 1940s and 1950s, the Pac-10 dominated during my time as a young player in the 1970s. It also seemed to me as if USC was always in the Rose Bowl—then and now. Actually, it's true. At the start of the 2008 college season USC had played the most times in the Rose Bowl with thirty-two appearances, followed by Michigan (twenty), the University of Washington (fourteen), and Ohio State (thirteen).

The game's atmosphere at Rose Bowl Stadium, built in 1922 and home to the UCLA Bruins, also makes it special. The two teams in the nationally televised game usually are among the nation's best, and bragging rights, if not national-title hopes, are on the line. In

2002 and 2006, the Rose Bowl game was the Bowl Championship Series National Championship game.

The game traditionally starts in early afternoon and ends near dusk, and it's neat to see the flicker of the stadium lights against the light gray sky. While the stadium seating has been reconfigured several times over the years, the Rose Bowl Stadium had the largest football-stadium capacity in the country at 104,594 before eventually being surpassed by Michigan Stadium in 1998.

When I think of the Rose Bowl, I also think of its pageantry. The game is part of the Tournament of Roses, "America's New Year Celebration," and millions of spectators from around the world enjoy the Rose Parade the morning of the game. There were times as a child when I slipped away with friends and watched from a street corner as bright floral floats, spirited marching bands, and high-stepping equestrians passed by.

The parade has come a long way since the first Tournament of Roses was held in 1890 by members of Pasadena's Valley Hunt Club. History says that club members were former residents of the East and Midwest who wanted to showcase their new home's mild winter weather. "In New York, people are buried in snow," announced Professor Charles F. Holder at a club meeting. "Here our flowers are blooming and our oranges are about to bear. Let's hold a festival to tell the world about our paradise."

During the next few years, the festival expanded to include marching bands and motorized floats. The parade's elaborate floats now feature high-tech computerized animation and materials from around the world. While some of the floats are still built by volunteers from their sponsoring communities, most take professional float companies a year to build.

The parade also carries a new theme each year. The theme for the 120th Rose Parade in 2009, for example, was Hats Off to Entertainment. In 1978, when my Washington Huskies played the powerful Michigan Wolverines, the parade's theme was On the Road to Happiness.

I couldn't have said it any better.

When I had the chance to play in the sixty-fourth Rose Bowl with my University of Washington teammates against the Michigan Wolverines, the game, the pageantry, the atmosphere—combined with the storybook ending of being back home in front of family and friends for my final college game—all of it was everything I thought it would be. And more.

Our team didn't need any extra motivation for Michigan, mainly because nobody in the country gave us much of a chance against the third-ranked Wolverines. Count the Wolverines in that majority, too.

We rolled through our final seven games in 1977, including a 28–10 win over USC in Husky Stadium, and finished 7–4 to capture the Rose Bowl berth against the 10–1 Wolverines. It marked Washington's return to Pasadena for the first time in fourteen years.

Michigan, meanwhile, was the fourteen-point favorite. What made matters even worse was that the 10–1 Wolverines did little to hide their disdain for being matched against a four-loss team like the Huskies.

Michigan, coached by the fiery Bo Schembechler, made national news with several big victories, including a 41–3 victory over number-five Texas A&M and a 14–6 win over rival Ohio State to capture the program's second conference title and second Rose Bowl berth in as many years. Michigan's lone defeat in 1977 was an October stunner, 16–0, at Minnesota, when the Wolverines were the country's top-ranked team.

Michigan junior quarterback Rick Leach had a banner year, too. His 1,348 passing yards and fifteen touchdowns complemented the Wolverines' traditionally strong run game. Leach was a superb athlete, a two-sport star at Michigan who also was considered one of the nation's best baseball players. He later selected major-league baseball over the opportunity to play in the NFL and spent ten years in the show with four different teams. When Leach graduated from Michigan in 1978, he had shattered the program's career passing, total offense, and touchdown records and finished third in the balloting for the Heisman Trophy behind Billy Sims and Chuck Fusina.

Despite Michigan's well-deserved reputation and angry demeanor, my teammates and I believed we could play with any team in the country, especially after the way we handled USC in our regular-season finale.

Michigan thought differently.

When both teams were at Disneyland in a scheduled function days before the game, the Wolverines made it clear they wanted to have very little to do with us. Leach refused to pose with me along with Mickey and Minnie Mouse, as was the tradition for the quarterbacks. Instead, Michigan sent its all-American center, Walt Downing, to pose with me for the photograph.

I found out later that Leach had said the photo session from the previous year had distracted him from concentrating on the game—USC beat Michigan 14–6 and Leach completed only four of twelve passes for 76 yards. But at the time he declined to pose with me, it was almost like a slap in the face to me and my teammates. I didn't have any reason to think Leach's decision not to pose with me was a racial issue, but we were pissed. It was as if Michigan didn't believe we had earned the right to be on the same field with them.

On January 2, 1978, we showed Michigan and the country why we had earned that right.

When I came out of the Rose Bowl Stadium tunnel for pregame warm-ups, the stands were half full. When I came out of that same tunnel nearly an hour later for the coin toss with the captains, I was blown away.

The stands were filled beyond capacity at 105,312. To see fifty thousand fans dressed in University of Washington colors of purple and gold on one side of the stadium and fifty thousand fans dressed in University of Michigan colors of blue and gold on the opposite side—and to know that my family and friends were in those stands—I was nearly overcome by emotion. It was like a dream.

It had rained off and on the entire week before the game. The weather was so bad at times that we couldn't find a field that wasn't flooded and muddied by the rain. One afternoon we actually laced up our tennis shoes and practiced in a vacant parking lot to make sure we knew our assignments. But somehow on game day, all that rain had gone away. It was sunny, clear, calm, and sixty-two degrees, California perfect in January.

As I stood at midfield for the coin toss, I couldn't help but think of the California teams such as USC, Stanford, and UCLA that didn't recruit me and had played in the Rose Bowl all those previous years. And it was a dream of mine to lead an out-of-state team like my Washington Huskies into my hometown for the Rose Bowl. Well, it was no longer a dream.

Michigan won the coin toss and elected to receive. We elected to defend the north goal.

The Wolverines took the opening kickoff and drove to our thirty-eight-yard line, but our defense held and forced a punt. Michigan punter John Anderson received a low snap on one knee, which automatically downed the ball at the Michigan 49. With a balanced offensive game plan, we marched straight down the field, and I scored on a two-yard roll out to my left on second-and-goal. It was the perfect start.

We extended our lead to 10–0 early in the second quarter on a thirty-yard field goal after I connected with receiver Spider Gaines on a sixty-two-yard completion. We came right back on our next possession and marched sixty yards and scored when I went in from one yard out on a quarterback sneak that made it 17–0 at the half.

I thought we showed our resiliency on that drive, when we overcame a clipping penalty that erased a thirty-one-yard touchdown by Gaines on a reverse. I then connected with Gaines on a fourteen-yard completion on third-and-twelve from the Michigan 26. We also had a great opportunity to extend our margin with less than a minute remaining in the first half following a Wolverines fumble, but I threw a pick at the Michigan 10.

Even so, we had kept Michigan off balance with a few wrinkles that we really hadn't used much during the regular season. We had run a couple of reverses and a fake punt that I didn't even know had been called by our head coach Don James in that drive right before the half.

I came off the field and had a cup of water in my hand when I saw our punter Aaron Wilson take the snap, hesitate for a moment, and throw a perfect pass downfield to a wide-open Kyle Stevens for a forty-seven-yard gain to the Michigan 20. In his review of Michigan game film, Coach James had seen a weakness in the Wolverines' punt-return team that he wanted to exploit. We had practiced it many times and it worked perfectly.

We had outgained Michigan 246 total yards to 111 in the first half and, of course, felt great about our performance. But we also knew Michigan would be ready to play in the second half, and we couldn't afford any mistakes.

So what did I do? I threw an interception on our opening possession of the second half, but our defense bailed me out. Faced with fourth-and-one at our three-yard line, we stopped Michigan for no gain on a dive-over right tackle. Although pinned deep in our territory, I knew we couldn't panic. On third-and-three from our nine-yard line, Joe Steele busted up the middle for a thirteen-yard gain and first down.

That was the breathing room we needed. After we converted three more first downs on the drive, I connected with Gaines on a twenty-eight-yard corner route for another touchdown as we pushed our lead to a stunning 24–0 with five minutes, thirty-one seconds left in the third quarter. I had no idea what the national television audience must have thought—here was a Midwest giant being clobbered by an upstart team from the Pacific Northwest—but our fans inside the stadium were ecstatic. Still, we knew that Michigan had no intention of being embarrassed.

Following Gaines's touchdown catch, the Wolverines struck like lightning in two plays when Leach found a wide-open Curt Stephenson for a seventy-six-yard touchdown pass to make it 24–7. We answered with a twenty-seven-yard field goal from Robbins that pushed our advantage to 27–7 with fifty seconds remaining in the third quarter.

As I said, Michigan wasn't about to be embarrassed, and the Wolverines marched seventy-eight yards on eleven plays to open the fourth quarter. Russell Davis scored from two yards out, and Gregg Willner added the extra point to close the gap to 27–14. After we went three-and-out on two consecutive possessions, Michigan scored again when Leach, under pressure, threw a thirty-two-yard pass to Stanley Edwards. Willner, however, missed the conversion on a bad snap and we led 27–20 with three minutes and forty-four seconds remaining in the game.

Michigan held us again on downs and regained possession at its 42 with two minutes, forty-six seconds left. The Wolverines promptly marched fifty yards in six plays and had a first-down-and-goal at our eight-yard line. The scoreboard clock read 1:29. Leach took the snap and rolled to his right. He dumped a short pass into the flat to Stanley Edwards. The ball slipped through Edwards's hands, bounced off his helmet, and rested on his shoulder pads.

At the same time, our linebacker, Michael Jackson, came over the top of Edwards's shoulder pads and wrestled the ball free for the interception at the one-yard line. That play snuffed out what would have been the greatest comeback in both Michigan and Rose Bowl history.

Our sideline erupted, but there was still one minute, twenty-one seconds remaining in the game. We needed a first down to clinch the victory and my job was to keep everyone calm. I went three yards on a quarterback sneak and Ronnie Rowland gained six yards on a counter. But we were stopped for no gain on a dive up the middle and had to punt away our fourth consecutive possession in the fourth quarter. Forty-four seconds remained.

After Leach threw an incompletion on first down from our forty-eight-yard line, cornerback Nesby Glasgow made a spectacular leaping grab and intercepted Leach, who had thrown for a career-best 239 yards, at our seven-yard line with thirty-two seconds left. It was an unbelievable feeling as our players spilled out on the field to congratulate Glasgow.

After completing twelve of twenty-three passes for 188 yards, I went to my knee on consecutive snaps to end the game and my college career. When the scoreboard clock ticked down to zeros, it was bedlam on the field. I searched the stands for my mom and my family, and I finally found them. It was very special that they were part of this victory with me. They had been so supportive through everything that I had been through.

On the field I also looked for my teammates that I had been close to during my three years at Washington, players such as Michael Jackson, Nesby Glasgow, Antwoine Richardson, and Ronnie Rowland. It was such a tremendous moment. We had helped the University of Washington win its first bowl game in seventeen years. I was also named the game's most valuable player for my performance, which I appreciated. I had also been named the Pac-8 co–Player of the Year earlier, but our achievements weren't about me. It was about the team.

In the locker room after the game, Coach James, who was not prone to emotion, came to my locker, hugged me, smiled, and said, "Good job." Those two words meant the world to me.

A few days after our Rose Bowl victory, I received the community of Seattle's highest honor in sports achievement when I was named the *Seattle Post-Intelligencer* Sports Star of the Year for 1977. More than a thousand people jammed into the ballroom at the Olympic Hotel for the ceremony. I was one of nine candidates considered for the award. The list included Dick Erickson, coach of the University of Washington crew team that became the first American entry to win the Grand Challenge Cup of the Royal Henley Regatta in England; Carl Buchan, a young Seattle sailor who was named college sailor of the year in 1977; Seattle Slew, first undefeated Triple Crown winner in horse-racing history; Betty Stove, finalist in three events at the Wimbledon tennis championships and star of the Seattle Cascades; Jimmy McAlister, rookie of the year in the North American Soccer League and a standout in the Sounders' march to the NASL championship game; Lee Stanton, hard-hitting outfielder and emerging star of the Seattle Mariners in their first season in the major leagues; Sugar Ray Seales, number-two contender for the world middleweight boxing title and recently crowned U.S. Boxing Association champ after beating Doug Demmings in Chicago; and Norm Evans, veteran Seattle Seahawk offensive lineman and the leader of the winningest second-year team in NFL history.

The lights in the ballroom were darkened, and a spotlight danced across the faces of the candidates. When it stopped and shined on me, Royal Brougham, *P-I* associate editor, announced the verdict:

"The Star of the Year for 1977 is Warren Moon."

I was greeted by a prolonged standing ovation by the crowd. I thanked everyone and told them I couldn't think of a better way to end my college career and begin a new year. I also wanted to make sure I credited those people who were involved in my success, namely Coach James, my quarterback coach Ray Dorr, my teammates and, last but not least, my mother, Pat.

My selection proved to be a popular choice, quite a sweet turnaround from the two years of fan abuse that I endured in Husky Stadium.

That Rose Bowl game still ranks as one of the best games I have had the privilege to play in at any level. Some have said that it was probably one of the best Rose Bowl games ever because we were such huge underdogs and Michigan was favored big-time.

Nobody really gave us a chance at all. We jumped out to a huge lead, Michigan made a fierce comeback, and then we made some remarkable plays down the stretch to win the game for us. Those last six minutes or so were amazing.

What made it even better was our approach. We were thought of as a ball-control team, but Coach James turned 180 degrees. We passed when we should have run. We passed when we should have punted. We ran reverses. Coach James gave me a lot of freedom to audible to another play when I wanted to. We gambled and won.

And the roar of the capacity crowd that greeted us when we ran from the tunnel to start the game still rings in my ears. I think that probably helped our team more than Michigan, because the Wolverines were used to playing in front of that type of crowd. That was an electrifying moment that really juiced us up as a team.

The game kind of kicked off the whole Don James era and put the University of Washington on the map. People knew us all over the country. It was a start for me, too, as it got my name recognized. It's funny, but one of my fondest memories of that game actually happened a week prior to it, when we held our team Christmas party. It was a very touching moment because our team was so close that year. A lot of feelings came out. It showed the togetherness of our team, and it just carried over into that game.

To play that game and end my collegiate career in my hometown of Los Angeles, in front of family and friends, remains the highlight of my playing career. But it wasn't all roses, either. I honestly thought our victory and my performance in that game and during my career would catapult me to the NFL.

I was never so wrong.

6

Calling
Leigh Steinberg

I met Leigh Steinberg, who attended the same high school I did
in Los Angeles (though not at the same time), following the
Rose Bowl in 1978. Leigh had actually written me a letter first,
telling me how he had gone to Hamilton High before me and was
the student-body president. He wrote in his letter that he would
telephone me, which he eventually did.

We talked about forty times before I decided to hire Leigh as
my agent. Our relationship has grown stronger through the decades. We are now dear friends and business partners. Leigh jokes
that he could have been confirmed for secretary of state because I
checked him out so extensively, even calling an L.A. sportswriter
who knew Leigh well.

Leigh told me that I should have been a franchise quarterback
in the NFL, but there were doubts. I played primarily as a rollout
quarterback at Washington. To me, that sounded like code for
"We're not ready to start a black quarterback." Teams were asking
if I'd be willing to change positions. I got a lot of praise on the
banquet circuit and played in the Challenge Bowl, an all-star game
where NFL coaches and scouts had the opportunity to look at me.

But the attention stopped after that. I wasn't invited to the
NFL combine, though three or four of my Husky teammates
were. I wasn't asked to do any personal workouts for teams. I was
pissed. I was a Player of the Year in the Pac-8 and MVP of the

Rose Bowl. What more did they want? Leigh estimated that I could be drafted between the third and fifth rounds as a quarterback—but much higher at another position such as running back.

That was unacceptable.

Leigh likes to say he never planned on becoming a sports attorney, and that he essentially fell into the profession at age twenty-five. He was raised in Southern California in the 1950s and 1960s by socially conscious parents. He attended Hamilton High School and spent his undergraduate years at the University of California at Berkeley, where he was student-body president during the days of protest while Ronald Reagan was governor of California. He entered law school at Berkeley in 1970 with the intention of pursuing politics or possibly criminal or entertainment law.

During his first year in law school, Steinberg was a dorm counselor at Berkeley and he became good friends with Steve Bartkowski, a quarterback on the freshman football team. After Leigh graduated from law school and returned from his post–law school traveling to Europe in the spring of 1975, he got a call from Bartkowski. Steve enjoyed a great career at Berkeley and had become the NFL's first overall selection by the Atlanta Falcons.

When Steinberg began practicing, sports agency was in its infancy. There was no guaranteed right of representation. A general manager, like a Mike Brown with the Cincinnati Bengals, could simply proclaim "We don't deal with agents" and hang up the telephone. Athlete representation was pretty much a fledgling profession—fewer than half of the NFL's first-round picks were represented by agents.

Most players depended on family and friends for advice, or they simply conducted their own negotiations. When Bartkowski approached Steinberg, Leigh took it as his opportunity to apply his personal values and his love for sports to help change lives for the better. He did—and he has.

How Leigh handled Bartkowski's signing reflected the negotiating style that he has been known for through the years. He found out that the average salary in the NFL at that time was roughly $40,000. The previous standard bearers in terms of Bartkowski's position in the draft were O. J. Simpson, who received $350,000 for five years with the Buffalo Bills, and Joe Namath, who was paid $412,000 for four years with the New York Jets.

Leigh found out everything he could about the Falcons operation and factored Bartkowski's specific value to the Falcons as a quarterback and marquee player. And for good measure and bargaining power, he also opened discussions with the Chicago Winds and the Shreveport Steamers of the World Football League. To make a long story short, Atlanta's initial offer was $360,000 for five years. In the end, Steinberg forged a four-year $650,000 contract with the Falcons, establishing Bartkowski as the highest-paid player at the time in professional football.

From the beginning, when Leigh and I met, he believed that I was someone capable of great leadership and great impact on and off the field. As our relationship strengthened in those early years, he talked with me about how to walk into a room and visualize what everyone thought and who they were. He wanted me to introduce myself to twenty people I had never met, talk with them, shake their hands, get their business cards, network.

Leigh said that I was a unique personality and, because of my looks, speech patterns, and talent, he believed together we could make a real difference in the world. In a sense, that was the foundation of Leigh's recruiting pitch to me.

Since the industry did not offer any standards, he wanted to represent athletes who would serve as role models, athletes who honored their roots and gave back to their communities. He wanted to make sure he shared his life with people who shared his values, and that's the way I approached it, too, when I searched for a sports agent to represent me out of the University of Washington. We both wanted to make sure we used football as a springboard to the life I wanted to build.

It's easy to understand why Leigh is regarded as one of the country's leading sports attorneys. During his thirty-three-year career, he has represented over 150 professional athletes in football, baseball, basketball, volleyball, golf, boxing, and Olympic sports. He has represented the number-one pick overall in the NFL draft a record eight times, an achievement unrivaled within the sports industry. He is often credited as the real-life inspiration for the sports agent from the 1996 film *Jerry Maguire*, which starred Tom Cruise. Leigh served as a technical adviser on the set, and I had a cameo appearance in the movie. It was a great experience, and it gave me an opportunity to display my acting skills!

Leigh and I have had a great relationship and he's my dearest friend, but that's not to say I was in a rush to hire him after our initial meeting. No, sir.

Like everything I did, I was deliberate in my decision to hire Leigh. We talked so many times that years later we actually did a commercial for telephone provider Pac-Bell that spoofed our many conversations.

Leigh compared our discussions and my methodical nature to Chinese water torture. I also had sportswriter Bob Oates of the *Los Angeles Times* research Leigh in addition to some prominent Washington alums I knew personally. I wanted to make sure Leigh was the right person for me. Leigh normally met with a player, met with his family and a decision was made rather quickly. Not with me. I wanted to be absolutely positive, 100 percent, about Leigh.

Leigh said the most remarkable aspect of my preternatural maturity, which convinced him that I was unique, was the way in which I dealt with the Rose Bowl fame. After having been abused in my early seasons by the Washington Husky faithful, who didn't love the idea of a black Los Angeles outsider coming into their club to take the cherished mantle of quarterback, Leigh was impressed with how I didn't lash out at those same fans who now made me the toast of the Northwest. He felt that was a fairly monumental act of grace and class for a twenty-one-year-old.

Leigh also believed that was a defining moment in my relationship with the University of Washington, the city of Seattle, and professional football, because if I had expressed my true feelings at the time, the perception of me being a bitter, ungrateful militant, notwithstanding the unfairness of that characterization, would have defined me.

Leigh said that our conversations went on and on, that young men turned old, that winter turned to spring, and I still agonized over the decision to hire him or not by the time summer arrived. That may have been an exaggeration, but I did hire him after a few weeks—and those forty telephone calls.

Once we came to an agreement, it was time to get to work.

Leigh first visited me in my apartment in Seattle. That's when we had *that* discussion—I told him I was born to be a quarterback, and that wasn't going to change. Leigh said that was fine, but he also pointed out the reality of my decision.

The consensus was that I would be a third-to-fifth-round pick in the May NFL draft if I stayed at quarterback. However, others felt I might not get drafted at all, let alone if I stayed behind center or not. Most teams wanted me to play defensive back, receiver, or running back. Leigh said he thought there were two teams—the Los Angeles Rams and the Kansas City Chiefs—that were willing to give me a chance to play quarterback, but there were no guarantees.

It was true that many NFL personnel didn't believe I could play quarterback because I had "the wrong paint job," as some in the game said. Between 1945 and 1975, no less than a dozen African American quarterbacks were on the campuses of Middle America. Among them were Willie Thrower, Jimmy Raye, Tyrone Willingham, and Tony Dungy. To overcome the prejudice in the professional leagues, African Americans had to win the hearts of the coaches in the college ranks, which wasn't an easy task, either.

If African American quarterbacks wanted to play professionally at that time, they had to make difficult choices. They could switch positions, usually to wide receiver or defensive secondary, bolt to the Canadian Football League to play, or face the long odds of becoming a black quarterback in the NFL. All I wanted was an opportunity, but I also knew I would have gone insane holding a clipboard as a reserve quarterback on an NFL sideline. In my mind that would have been cruel and unusual punishment. I would have gone stir crazy. I was motivated to be a starter and a leader.

Another part of the equation was that I wasn't viewed as a pure drop-back passer. Washington coach Don James rotated the pocket and I was used primarily as a rollout quarterback to take advantage of my athleticism. Although I had been a starting quarterback since my junior season in high school and started three seasons at a major Division I school, the thinking in some circles was that I didn't face enough major college competition. Although I didn't agree with that opinion, the question for Leigh and I became, where would I have the fastest path to develop pro skills that would ultimately land me in the NFL?

If NFL coaches had questions about me, how were they going to find out what I could do or couldn't do unless they watched me? My game film was going to answer some of those questions. But whatever questions they had—only by working me out could they know or not. But nobody would do that. Nobody picked up the telephone and called. I also thought I played well in the one all-star game that I competed in, but nothing came of it. I never heard a peep.

The feedback that Steinberg came back to me with didn't look that great in terms of playing in the National Football League. It was just a forgone conclusion that quarterback was not in my future in the NFL.

As a young, stubborn person, I was not going to let anyone stop me.

The NFL might not have been interested in me, but the Canadian Football League across the border was.

Hugh Campbell played wide receiver at Washington State University from 1959 to 1962. Campbell was a solid player who eventually played in the Canadian Football League for six years before he went into coaching. In 1977, he was named the head football coach of the Edmonton Eskimos in the CFL.

It was at that time when Campbell first saw me play at the University of Washington. Campbell instantly liked me. He liked my poise, my demeanor, and my strong passing arm. When Campbell first visited me in Seattle for a workout—at least one professional team made that telephone call following my senior season—he said he was even more impressed by my skills in person.

Campbell liked my ability, but he was concerned because I was quiet. While most of the quarterbacks he had run into over the years were a little more outgoing than I was, he was still impressed by my ability. Campbell had a plan, too. The only reason he looked at me was that Edmonton had a nest egg of money put away, and he was determined to spend it and sign the best quarterback in the entire United States that he could.

Campbell researched the NFL's top-rated quarterbacks, and I wasn't even on that league's top-ten list. Even so, he told Edmonton management that he thought I was better than many of those players and better than the guys they had talked about spending money on. Campbell and his assistants reviewed my game film, and they decided to schedule a workout and visit with me in Seattle.

Campbell also felt like I had received exceptional coaching at Washington. That being said, however, he also wondered if I had reached my potential in college.

Sometimes you would find a quarterback at a small program—or even one at a major college, for that matter—who hadn't received the quality of coaching that I had received at Washington. The thought was this quarterback might have a greater upside in terms of his future development. Campbell was just being honest. He thought I was already close to my potential, and for a second, he wondered about my upside as a quarterback.

Campbell also heard the murmurs that many in the NFL wanted to make me either a defensive back or a receiver because I was so athletic. Campbell, a former receivers' coach during his time as an assistant, didn't see that in me. First of all, he thought I had the skills to be an outstanding quarterback. But he thought I would have failed as a receiver in the NFL because that wasn't my makeup.

He thought I didn't have the ability that a receiver has to have to quickly change directions when running routes. Campbell knew I could run with the ball, but he viewed me as more of a straight-ahead or angle-off-to-the-side-to-miss-a-tackler kind of runner.

In Campbell's mind, I was a quarterback, plain and simple.

When Campbell worked me out, he came to the conclusion that if I went into the NFL with the hope of being a quarterback, it had to be in the right situation. He believed I needed a year or two to develop and strengthen my skills behind a veteran quarterback. That turned out to be Campbell's sales pitch to me and Leigh.

He said that by signing with Edmonton I would be given that time to develop, that there wasn't a rush to throw me into the starting lineup, because he had veteran quarterbacks in starter Tom Wilkinson and backup Bruce Lemmerman. Campbell admitted I was more talented than either Wilkinson or Lemmerman, but he wanted to showcase my skills at a pace where I would always look good in the game. He stressed patience.

Campbell also discussed with Leigh and me a possibility that had already become obvious to me. If I signed with Edmonton before the NFL draft, there was probably a good chance that I would not be selected by an NFL team. That was actually the start of our master plan, one that, at least in theory, saw me develop, hone my skills, and succeed in the CFL. Better yet, I would also be a true free agent in the NFL if I went undrafted. That was part of Campbell's immediate strategy—to sign me before the NFL draft.

Of course, I still had hoped that somebody, anybody, from the NFL would telephone me and say, "Warren, we want you." Campbell and the CFL intentions were loud and clear. Leigh and I tried to hold off Campbell as long as possible, but he needed an answer with the upcoming start of the CFL season in June. The NFL's regular-season schedule started in September and ended in December.

I know my mother, Pat Moon, loved Coach Campbell. She quizzed Coach to make sure he would take care of me if I decided to sign with Edmonton, in the province of Alberta in western Canada. All Mom knew was that Canada was a long, long way from her home in Los Angeles. She told Campbell that my dad had been gone for many years and that he needed to be a father figure for me. Campbell promised my mother that he'd fill that role.

I decided to go ahead and take advantage of this opportunity and sign with Edmonton, even though it was six weeks before the NFL draft. I told myself that I wasn't going to pass up this chance, hoping somebody in the NFL was going to change his mind about me during the next six weeks. Leigh said I displayed extraordinary maturity in facing the world as it was, not as I'd have liked it to be.

But I still had my fingers crossed—although not for the reason you might think.

Texas running back Earl Campbell went to the Houston Oilers as the number-one overall selection in the 1978 draft. The first quarterback selected was Doug Williams out of Grambling, going to the Tampa Bay Buccaneers as the seventeenth selection in the first round. Williams actually went right after my teammate at Washington, center Blair Bush.

At six foot four, Doug was big, strong, and possessed a strong arm. He also played under the legendary Eddie Robinson, who churned out a number of professional players from Grambling— with the exception of quarterback, until James Harris went to the Buffalo Bills in the eighth round of the 1969 draft.

As hard to believe as it might be, though, Doug Williams, an African American quarterback, was still unsure of his draft status. Forget that in a three-year span with Doug as the starter, Grambling won thirty-five of forty games and three straight Southwestern Athletic Conference Championships. In his senior year, Doug was also named first-team All-American by the Associated Press and finished fourth in voting for the 1977 Heisman Trophy. Teams should have lined up to take him.

While it was obvious that Doug was an exceptional quarterback, I think it helped him that John McKay was the Buccaneers' head coach. McKay made his name at USC, which won four national championships (1962, 1967, 1972, and 1974) during McKay's tenure as head coach. His 1972 team is still regarded as one of the best teams in NCAA history, and two of his players, Mike Garrett (1965) and O. J. Simpson (1968), won the Heisman Trophy.

USC represented a diverse team that, under McKay, at times featured a nearly all-black starting backfield. The Trojans reflected the social changes that swept the nation in that era. While it was still difficult for an African American quarterback to make it in the NFL, McKay didn't let skin color influence his decisions.

The second quarterback selected was Pittsburgh's Matt Cavanaugh, who went to the New England Patriots in the second round. Stanford's Guy Benjamin, who was co–Player of the Year with me in the Pac-8, went right after Cavanaugh with the fifty-first overall selection, to the Miami Dolphins.

Steinberg actually represented two first-round selections in that draft—Stanford offensive tackle Gordon King, selected tenth by the New York Giants, and Michigan linebacker John Anderson, selected twenty-sixth by the Green Bay Packers—in addition to Benjamin. A second teammate of mine from the University of Washington, defensive end Dave Browning, was selected in the second round by the Raiders. Of course, my name was never called.

Other quarterbacks selected in that twelve-round draft included Bowling Green's Mark Miller (Cleveland Browns), Brigham Young's Gifford Nielsen (Houston Oilers), Missouri's Pete Woods (Kansas City), Maryland's Mark Manges (Los Angeles Rams), USC's Rob Hertel (Cincinnati Bengals), Lehigh's Mike Rieker, Arizona State's Dennis Sproul (Green Bay Packers), Utah State's Keith Myers (Green Bay Packers), Santa Clara's John Hurley (Washington Redskins), Tennessee's Pat Ryan (New York Jets), and Northern Colorado's Bill Kenny (Miami Dolphins), who was the next-to-last player selected in the draft with the 333rd selection.

It stunned me that I wasn't included in that group somewhere.

Not one of those fourteen quarterbacks—not even Doug Williams—was ever selected for a Pro Bowl during their NFL careers. Three players from that draft—first-round selections Earl Campbell, receiver James Lofton, who played in the same youth league that I did in Baldwin Hills, and tight end Ozzie Newsome—were elected to the Hall of Fame following their NFL careers.

Of course, I took a different route.

Although I kind of knew I wasn't going to get drafted, it was still a major shock when my name wasn't called. I hadn't gotten the interest that I thought I deserved. Once I got over the shock, it was like, "What are we going to do?"

I had sat down with Leigh prior to the draft, and we talked about the pros and cons of trying to play in the NFL and of going to Canada. The pros of going to Canada outweighed any other choice because I wanted to play quarterback. That was the bottom line. I just wasn't sure that would happen in the NFL.

I had signed with Edmonton six weeks prior to the NFL draft. It was a three-year deal worth $170,000 and also included a $35,000 signing bonus. Even though I had signed with the CFL, an NFL team still could have taken a flier on me, by drafting me with the intent of holding my exclusive rights if I ever decided to leave Canada. If that happened, I would only be able to negotiate with that particular team—and only that team—to get into the NFL.

Now you understand that while most guys had their fingers crossed in hope of being drafted, mine were crossed in hope of not being drafted.

Talk about reverse psychology, but it was the best thing that happened to me. I quickly packed for Canada.

7

Across the Border

Hugh Campbell, coach of the Edmonton Eskimos, brought me up to Edmonton—there was snow everywhere—but every day, deep down, I was still hoping the NFL would call. In the back of my mind, I would think to myself, *What else does the NFL want?*

My physical skills and character were tested daily at Washington. I was hopeful that somebody, anybody in the NFL would do an about-face and welcome me with open arms. I was wrong. It was the Edmonton brass and Edmonton's people who welcomed me with open arms. Plus, the team was offering me the money of a second-round NFL draft pick. They made it difficult for me to say no.

I received a $35,000 signing bonus and a three-year contract that paid an annual average of $55,000. It was also the first time in my football career when race wasn't an issue. It was funny that I had to go to another country, to an overwhelmingly white city, to feel that I was a player being judged simply on the merits of my performance.

Canada has been like a finishing school for black quarterbacks.

There were a number of us, and we all looked at the CFL as an opportunity to play and get better every week, figuring somebody in the NFL would see us and like us. Many viewed the CFL as the minor leagues, that it wasn't real football. Fans in America only heard about it when the Grey Cup—the CFL's Super Bowl—was being played. But playing in Edmonton was one of the most positive experiences in my life. I am sure there were racist people in Canada, but I never heard anything negative.

The first consensus all-American black starting quarterback at a major university was Sandy Stephens of Minnesota. He remains the only quarterback to take the Gophers to the Rose Bowl (1960 and 1961). In 1960, Stephens led Minnesota to an 8–2 record and the national championship, according to the Associated Press and United Press International polls, and finished fourth in the Heisman Trophy balloting.

Stephens was a second-round NFL draft choice of the Cleveland Browns and the fifth overall selection in the AFL draft by the New York Titans. Both teams, however, said that they wouldn't use him at quarterback, and he never played a down in either league. So Sandy headed to Canada for the opportunity to chase his dream, playing three seasons at quarterback for the Montreal Alouettes and the Toronto Argonauts.

The first black quarterback in the CFL was Bernie Custis from Syracuse. Custis was an all-star in his 1951 rookie season with the Hamilton Tiger-Cats, although he later shifted to running back. In the 1960s, a few more African American quarterbacks made their way to Canada and the CFL in order to play the position that was their specialty.

In 1972, no NFL team was willing to draft a black quarterback, not even one who had a perfect record in high school and university football. Chuck Ealey led his Ohio high school team to a 30–0 record and then won thirty-five consecutive games at the University of Toledo. Despite leading his conference in passing yards in 1970 and 1971, he was passed over in the 1972 NFL draft. Like Custis two decades earlier, Ealey found new opportunities with the CFL and the Hamilton Tiger-Cats. He led the Ti-Cats to a Grey Cup title in his first season and finished with 13,326 yards and eighty-two touchdowns during his seven-year career.

The trend continued, as NFL opportunities for black quarterbacks were next to nonexistent. A growing crop of black college quarterbacks chose to go to the CFL rather than be forced to change positions in the NFL. That group also included Jimmy Jones, Cornelius Greene, Jimmy Streater, J. C. Watts, and Condredge Holloway.

Tony Dungy, on the other hand, elected to change positions and play in the NFL, where he has enjoyed a remarkable career. Dungy, who became the first African American head coach to win the Super Bowl when his Indianapolis Colts defeated the Chicago Bears in 2007, was a successful quarterback at Minnesota the same time I was at the University of Washington. Tony was a four-year starter and finished as Minnesota's career leader in pass attempts (576), completions (274), touchdown passes (twenty-five), and passing yards (3,577). He also finished fourth in career-total offense in the Big Ten Conference. Dungy was a great athlete, too. He played college basketball as a freshman starter and was a teammate and roommate of former Detroit Pistons head coach Flip Saunders.

Tony was signed as a free agent by the Pittsburgh Steelers as a defensive back. He led the team in interceptions in 1978 and helped the Steelers win the Super Bowl that season. Tony finished his career in training camp with the New York Giants in 1980 before getting into coaching. Tony, of course, accomplished some amazing firsts in coaching, before he retired in January 2009.

On December 18, 2008, after securing his tenth straight playoff appearance with a win against the Jacksonville Jaguars, Dungy set a new NFL record for consecutive playoff appearances by a head coach. Tony and I took dramatically different paths out of college, but there's no question in my mind that Tony Dungy will be elected into the Hall of Fame one day.

There were a lot of guys like Tony, who played quarterback in college, changed positions in the NFL, and went on to become successful. I just didn't feel I was a great enough athlete to do that. I just really felt like I was good enough to play quarterback, and it was the position I had a passion for. I had played it since I was ten years old, and I was very good at it all through those years of playing in Pop Warner football. Once I got to high school, there was still nothing that told me I couldn't play at that level or move on to whatever level I wanted to play at. I kind of judged myself at every level. Once I was done with high school, I felt like, okay, my high school career was this way, and I think I can play at the next level.

The same thing in college. Once I got through with my college career, I knew I was good enough to play with these guys. I looked at the guys being drafted into the NFL, compared my ability to theirs and thought about what I did on the field, how much we won, and the honors I received. And I came to the conclusion that I should have been an NFL draft pick at quarterback.

Despite the push for racial equality in all areas by the NFL—in 2002, the NFL adopted the Rooney Rule, which requires any team engaged in hiring a head coach to assemble a diverse candidate slate—the push for black quarterbacks was sorely lacking, especially compared to the CFL. Andre Ware played for the University of Houston and was the first black quarterback to win the Heisman Trophy. A few months later, he was selected seventh overall by the Detroit Lions in the 1990 NFL draft. But he toiled in obscurity for five years in the NFL and then played in the CFL with the Ottawa Rough Riders, the British Columbia Lions, and the Toronto Argonauts, where he backed up fellow Heisman winner Doug Flutie.

In the late 1990s in the NFL, there were six black quarterbacks on rosters in the twenty-eight-team league. The CFL, meanwhile, had sixteen black quarterbacks on twelve teams and four had directed their teams into the playoffs.

Another historic moment was the 2007 CFL playoffs, when all six playoff teams were led by starting black quarterbacks: veteran Henry Burris of the Calgary Stampeders, Marcus Brady of the Montreal Alouettes, Kevin Glenn of the Winnipeg Blue Bombers, Michael Bishop of the Toronto Argonauts, Kerry Joseph of the Saskatchewan Roughriders, and Jarious Jackson of the defending Grey Cup champions, the British Columbia Lions. Joseph and the Roughriders ended up advancing and winning the Grey Cup, 23–19, over Glenn and the Blue Bombers. The game was viewed by approximately 3.3 million viewers on Canadian television.

And let's not forget Damon Allen, the younger brother of NFL Hall of Fame running back Marcus Allen. Damon retired in May

2008 after twenty-three seasons in the CFL, where he became the all-time passing leader in professional football with 72,381 yards to eclipse my combined mark in the CFL and NFL of 70,533 yards.

Landing in the CFL was a good thing for me. Actually, make that "a great thing." The league gave me my chance to be a professional football player. That's why I'll always be indebted to Canada and to the city of Edmonton. They gave me that opportunity when a lot of people wouldn't.

I felt at home in Edmonton.

Edmonton is a beautiful city, the capital of the Canadian province of Alberta. It rests on the North Saskatchewan River in the central region of the province and is the second-largest city in Alberta, with a population of just under a million. With more than two thousand restaurants in Edmonton, I never had to worry about finding a place to eat. Edmonton, of course, has a proud heritage in sports, also featuring the five-time NHL champion, the Edmonton Oilers, and an array of minor-league teams, successful university-level teams, and a circuit on the Indy Racing League.

The Edmonton Eskimos are one of the most successful teams in Canadian football history. Often compared to "America's Team," the Dallas Cowboys, in terms of popularity, they have won the Grey Cup thirteen times, more than any other team except the Toronto Argonauts, who have won fifteen times and are notable for being the oldest professional football team in North America (founded in 1873). The Eskimos hold many impressive records, including our five consecutive Grey Cup wins (1978 to 1982).

Since 1949, no other team in the CFL has even won *three* in row, let alone *five.* The Eskimos also made thirty-four consecutive appearances in the playoffs (1972 to 2005), a record no other North American professional team, regardless of sport, has equaled. The Dallas Cowboys, for example, have made an NFL-best nine consecutive playoff appearances.

There's no denying that the hometown fans support their team. In the 1978 season, my first in Edmonton, we played our last game at Clarke Stadium and moved to the newly constructed, 40,000-seat

Commonwealth Stadium. Commonwealth Stadium was built at a cost of $29.9 million to host the Commonwealth Games, a multinational event held every four years, just like the Olympic Games. The stadium was expanded by about 18,000 seats to a total capacity of 60,081 in 1983. In fact, the largest crowd in the stadium's history was for the 2002 Grey Cup, when Montreal beat Edmonton in front of 62,531 fans.

The CFL was officially founded in 1958 but can trace its origins to rugby in the 1860s. The league represents the highest level of play in Canadian football and is the most popular major sports league in Canada after the National Hockey League.

The league features eight teams and two divisions, East and West. The league's nineteen-week regular season runs from mid-June to early November, followed by the playoffs that culminate with the Grey Cup championship, the country's largest broadcast event in sports. While the league expanded into the United States for three years in the mid-1990s, teams such as Memphis and Birmingham ran into severe attendance problems because these markets couldn't compete with college football's popularity. By 1996, the CFL was once again based entirely in Canada.

When American football fans watch the CFL for the first time, they are usually intrigued by the rule differences between the CFL and NFL. The differences include a twenty-second play clock instead of a forty-second play clock, backfield forward motion instead of no forward motion, field width of 65 yards instead of 53⅓ yards, field length of 110 yards instead of 100 yards, a twenty-yard end zone instead of a ten-yard end zone, three downs instead of four downs, and twelve men instead of eleven men.

I think the differences in the CFL were a bonus for me and played to my strengths, especially my arm. The CFL field might only be ten yards wider, but ten yards is a lot. Plus, unlike the NFL, which places its hash marks on the field to match the width of the goal posts, the CFL places it hash marks twenty-four yards from the sideline, on each side. Those outside yards make the square footage almost twice as much. If a quarterback has an average arm, it might not make a difference. But when strong-armed quarterbacks like myself are able to pinpoint their passes on spots on the perimeter of the field, it puts so much more pressure on the defense.

The CFL game is exciting to watch because of its different rules. The offense, for example, has unlimited range of motion before the snap, excluding down linemen and the quarterback, as long as it is behind the line of scrimmage. Offensive players can all move at the same time, and can all move toward, away from, or parallel to the line of scrimmage. This can confuse a defense, so motion is used widely in the CFL. You won't see this in the NFL.

And you need to pick up yards in a hurry in the CFL. While the offense must move the ball downfield ten yards for a first down—this is the same as NCAA, NFL, high school, and other amateur American-football rules—CFL teams have only three downs to cover those ten yards.

Fumbles and special teams can be tricky, too. If there is a fumble on a play, and the ball continues to roll out of bounds, the last team to touch the ball will gain possession. This is unlike the NFL, where the last team to establish clear possession of the ball will gain possession after a fumbled ball rolls out of bounds. In the NFL, during a punt, if a punt returner believes he will not be able to advance the ball once he catches it, he will call a fair catch by waving his right arm in the air. The punt coverage team must give him space to field the ball cleanly. The ball will be dead upon reception. Under Canadian rules, there is no fair catch. The punt returner must field the ball, or else the punter or any coverage player who is behind him when the ball is kicked may field the ball and regain possession. No coverage player who began the play in front of the punter may approach within five yards of the ball until a return-team player touches it first. If the covering team moves within five yards, they will be called for a "no yards" penalty.

Just as in the NFL game, any field-goal try is a live ball, unless it hits the uprights or is successful. Where the NFL and CFL differ is on a play called a rouge. In the CFL, a rouge occurs when the kicking team, either punting or attempting a field goal, kicks the ball into the end zone. The return team must then move the ball out of the end zone and into the field of play. If the return team is tackled inside the end zone, lets the ball continue to roll out of the end zone, or kneels in the end zone, the return team concedes one point to the opposing team.

And let's not forget overtime. As far as overtime periods, in America, there is a difference between NCAA and NFL overtimes. The CFL overtime is different from both. In the NCAA, overtime consists of alternating possessions between the teams. There is no clock. The offense tries to score, and whether they are successful or not, at the end of their possession the teams will switch sides. Now the other team will have a chance to score. In the NFL, the first team to score in the fifteen-minute sudden-death overtime period wins, and games can end in ties. In the CFL, the highest-scoring team after two ten-minute overtime periods wins. If after the first round of two ten-minute periods the score is still tied, a second round of two ten-minute periods will begin. Overtime will continue in this fashion until a winner emerges, with more points at the end of the round than their opponent.

While I enjoyed the wide-open, rollout-pass-oriented league, the biggest change for me might have been off the field. For starters, it was cold. The average temperature in the summer in Edmonton is sixty-four degrees, and that number drops twenty degrees during the CFL season. It was so cold at times—the average temperature in January is two degrees—that people plugged their automobile batteries into battery chargers to make sure their cars cranked in the morning. I also had to get used to the long daylight hours. There were times when Leigh Steinberg and I walked out of a restaurant at eleven P.M.—and it was still light outside! Because many CFL players worked second jobs, we practiced in the mornings during the season.

When at Washington, I might have shied away from spending time with teammates because you are around them all the time, day in and day out, at workouts, at practice, and in games. In Edmonton, your teammates were your closest friends because you were in a different country and in unfamiliar surroundings. The team stuck together. People in Edmonton, including some of my teammates, liked to go out and have a good time. People in general, outside of football, were more into hockey. I liked basketball. I made friends easily, but I generally kept a small group of close friends. I was more withdrawn.

I definitely had a hard time adjusting to the different lifestyle in Canada. But football was still about producing and winning. I had also made a commitment off the field. In 1981, at the age of twenty-five, I married my childhood sweetheart, Felicia Fontenot Hendricks.

I could have reported to the Edmonton Eskimos for my first season in 1978 with a chip on my shoulder, angry about being bypassed by the NFL, but that wasn't my style. When it came time to play, I let my talent speak for me. I also had a great relationship with Coach Campbell, who was as straightforward as they come.

Campbell was a former CFL player who by 2006, when he retired as general manager of the Edmonton Eskimos organization, had coached in three different professional leagues—the CFL, the United States Football League (USFL), and the NFL.

As Campbell promised when he negotiated with Leigh Steinberg and me, following my senior season at the University of Washington, I wasn't thrown into the fire early in my career with Edmonton.

I platooned with veteran starter Tom Wilkinson and backup Bruce Lemmerman during my first two CFL seasons, which ended with consecutive Grey Cup wins over Montreal. In my rookie season, I actually replaced Lemmerman as the backup and completed 89 of 173 passes for 1,112 yards and five touchdowns and was our team's nominee for the Schenley Most Outstanding Rookie award. We beat Montreal 20–13 in the 1978 Grey Cup and 17–9 in 1979, when I threw my first playoff touchdown, thirty-three yards to Tom Scott.

While Lemmerman and Wilkinson were methodical in their approach, Campbell smiled because I ran the same plays but got us into the end zone more quickly. While they might throw a pass for eight yards, I threw it for eighteen. Campbell didn't hide the fact that I was our most talented quarterback, but he made sure I was put in the best possible position to succeed. He didn't put me in a position to be embarrassed at any time. I knew I could play, but my early success helped my development and confidence.

The new decade would start much the way the last one ended, and I emerged as our undisputed number-one quarterback in 1980. We piled up 505 points en route to a 13–3 regular-season record and a meeting with Hamilton for the 1980 Grey Cup in Toronto. Receiver Tom Scott had three touchdowns, running back Jim Germany added a pair, and I was named the game's MVP, as we hammered the Tiger-Cats 48–10.

It was during this time that Campbell became convinced I was more than good enough to play quarterback in the NFL. He actually told his assistant coaches that they wouldn't have me forever in the CFL. Again, it was my arm strength that was my strong suit. While most quarterbacks would put a lot of air under the ball on deep passes—forcing receivers to make adjustments—I'd throw that same pass on a line. I also could roll to either side and throw the ball to the right spot for my receivers.

Campbell also told anyone who would listen that I also won games with my head, not just my arm or my athletic ability. While quarterbacks of all backgrounds must combine degrees of intelligence, athleticism, and perseverance to succeed, it seemed as if every black quarterback at one time or another has faced his share of criticism about reading defenses poorly or not being prepared—the inference being that black quarterbacks are not mentally up to the task. But I knew my abilities, as did Campbell, and as time went on, all those elements made a difference in my career.

Winning had become a habit and was now expected of us in Edmonton. We set league records in 1981 with a 14–1–1 record and our fourth straight Grey Cup when we defeated the Ottawa

Rough Riders 26–23 on a last-second Dave Cutler field goal. Roughriders rookie J. C. Watts, another talented black quarterback who wasn't given an opportunity to play his position in the NFL out of college (Oklahoma), was named the Grey Cup's most valuable player on offense.

Many believed our 1981 team was the greatest in CFL history. Our defense showed no weakness, and I had a 108.3 passer rating, a CFL record that topped Russ Jackson's 1967 rating of 107.9. We also scored 576 points that season, the most in a single season in CFL history. My offense was anchored by linemen Bill Stevenson, Hector Pothier, Eric Upton, Leo Blanchard, and Ted Milian. We had talented running backs in Jim Germany, Neil Lumsden, and Angelo Santucci. We also featured great, athletic receivers in Brian Kelly, Tommy Scott, and Waddell Smith.

My big break came in 1982, when the NFL went on strike and the league showed three or four of our games on national television in the United States to make up for the loss of NFL games on television. Charlie Jones and Len Dawson were the announcers, and fans got to see our game across the border, the wider field, the passing game, all the action. Although we stumbled out of the gate with a 3–5 record and Coach Campbell announced it would be his last season, we rebounded and had a great season.

We won eight consecutive games, and I was named the MVP in our 32–16 Grey Cup win over the Toronto Argonauts. The game attracted close to 8 million television viewers, the largest television audience in the history of Canadian television. With the help of great talent around me, I threw for a career-high thirty-six touchdowns, had just sixteen interceptions, and finished with 5,000 passing yards, and we won our fifth consecutive Grey Cup. It was truly an amazing run, one that is still discussed today.

Pete Kettela had the unenviable task of following in Coach Campbell's footsteps in 1983, and he lasted only eight games before being replaced by Jackie Parker. We went 8–8 in 1983 and were eliminated by Winnipeg in the West Division semifinals. But I capped my final CFL season in style. I was named the league's outstanding player after passing for a then-league record 5,648 yards and thirty-one touchdowns. I got the nod ahead of Toronto's Terry Greer, who had become the first receiver in pro-football history to surpass the 2,000-yard plateau in a season (2,003 yards).

Our offense was unstoppable while I was with Edmonton. The key was our receivers, who were certainly good enough to play in the NFL. Brian Kelly and I were part of four Grey Cup titles. I completed 266 passes to Kelly from 1979 to 1983 for 5,046 yards and forty touchdowns. We added thirteen completions for 256 yards and three touchdowns in Grey Cup games and a few years ago were named by the CFL as Edmonton's top passing tandem. With Brian and our receivers, it seemed as though I could always get in the right position to throw and to place the ball where it gave them an opportunity to be creative and innovative.

We won five championships at Edmonton in six seasons, finishing 78–23–5 in the regular season and 9–1 in the postseason. In my CFL career, I passed for 21,228 yards and 144 touchdowns and rushed for 1,700 yards.

I can't say enough about my Edmonton teammates either. They were talented, wonderful, and zany goofballs, all rolled into one. Waddell Smith might be the funniest guy I have ever met. While we had a potent offense in Edmonton, our defense played a key role in our success. Nicknamed the Alberta Crude and named after the oil that accounted for much of the prosperity in the Alberta economy, the defense was anchored by our line—Dave Fennell, Ron Estay, David Boone, and York Hentschel.

Fennell, who had earned a law degree from the University of Alberta, was nicknamed Dr. Death. He was named CFL most outstanding defensive player in 1979, CFL Most Outstanding Canadian in 1979, and Defensive Star of the 1979 and 1982 Grey Cup games. We also had other great defensive players in Danny Kepley, Dale Potter, Tom Towns, Larry Highbaugh, and Joe Hollimon. Fennell, Estay, Kepley, and Highbaugh are all in the CFL Hall of Fame.

I also earned that honor and joined them in the CFL Hall of Fame in 2001.

Hugh Campbell has called me the Jackie Robinson of football. Robinson, of course, was the first African American major-league baseball player of the modern era in 1947.

That's a pretty strong statement from Coach Campbell, even though there were many other African American players who preceded me and accomplished their dreams of playing professional football. But Hugh felt that way because he believed I had the ability to be successful in different schemes and under different coaches.

Hugh felt I was the whole package. I passed, I ran, and I was smart. I made my teammates better, was respected by opponents on and off the field, and was active in the community. He didn't think there was another quarterback who had more positives than I did. Campbell believed I had every bit the ability and talent of Joe Montana. If I had had Bill Walsh as my NFL coach when I came out of the University of Washington, and Walsh displayed the same patience with me as he had with Montana, Campbell felt, I would have enjoyed the same success that Joe did with the same players around him. Campbell didn't say this to bring down Joe Montana, but to bring up Warren Moon.

Even so, Campbell doesn't believe we'd be talking about Warren Moon or would even know who I was if it weren't for the fact that I had gone to Canada first, that I had time to learn and time to play quarterback on a weekly basis at a high level with very good receivers. I had the chance to flourish and prove myself in the CFL.

Campbell described the NFL's reluctance at the time to sign black quarterbacks out of college as racial profiling, believing skin color impacted the league's vision when it came to African American quarterbacks. While he also believed every coach would do anything they could do, regardless of race, to win, times were different, people were different, and the thought process was different in my era. Still, Coach Campbell believed my success and the way I handled myself helped change people's mindsets.

I enjoyed a remarkable stretch of success in the CFL, winning five consecutive Grey Cups, and that was one of the reasons I thought of staying up there. I just loved playing up in Canada. I was successful. I was having fun. I wasn't being judged by my skin color or anything else. But then I reached the point where I had so much success that it was like I needed to do something else. I needed another challenge.

I had conquered this league, and I still watched NFL games on television and thought in the back of my mind that I should be out there playing with those guys or against those guys. Even though I became the best player in Canada, I wondered how I would fare against the best players who ever played the game. And I knew those players were in the NFL. The only way I'd find out if I was good enough was to play in the NFL.

That's when I decided to come back to the United States.

For good.

8

Shopping Spree

I signed the most lucrative contract in NFL history at $5.5 million over five years when I signed with the NFL's Houston Oilers as a twenty-eight-year-old "rookie" and unrestricted free agent in 1984. But it was that whirlwind "shopping spree" of teams in 1984, which my agent, Leigh Steinberg, helped stage, that continues to be discussed and debated even today.

The uniqueness of my situation led to a press frenzy where every step of the shopping spree was covered. Imagine ten to fifteen cities with NFL writers speculating whether their team and I had any interest in each other. Add every CFL team and every USFL team to that equation, and it generated plenty of excitement.

Another important part of that puzzle was Leigh's strategy. He created the definition of a franchise quarterback and stamped my face on it. Leigh understood it was vital to create a premium value on such an important position and describe how a team could build its future around a franchise quarterback like me.

The market was untested. Free agency didn't surface in football until 1993. A team only improved itself at that time via the draft or a trade. Available free agents were undesirable because they had been cut by their teams. There had never been a veteran quarterback, a multiple–Grey Cup winner, an MVP-type player on the market, like I was. The novelty created press and fan frenzy and enormous interest among teams. Everywhere I visited, Steinberg repeated that I deserved to be—and was going to be—the highest-paid player in professional-football history.

As the NFL's first legitimate, big-time free agent, I was treated like a rock star as we toured the league. Fans talked about our secret visit to Houston in the middle of the night, when we visited the Oilers' facility when no one was around and ate dinner at an obscure downtown restaurant. Houston owner Bud Adams, who made his money in oil, promised me some of the oil fields he owned as an incentive to sign. New Orleans owner John Meacham took us on a boat, pointed at the Big Easy skyline, and said, "All this can be yours."

I had never been to New York City and didn't know what to expect. Leigh and I arrived on a red-eye flight at five a.m., trash strewn in the streets, two cab drivers fighting on the curb. Leigh looked at me and said, "Welcome to New York." We picked up the *New York Post*, which featured the headline SPACED-OUT GIANTS SHOOT THE MOON on the back cover in bold, black letters.

While in New York, we also met with Donald Trump, owner of the New Jersey Generals in the fledgling United States Football League, which had started play a year earlier. Before we could meet with Donald, though, we watched a video of the Trump story and met a very pregnant Ivana Trump. We later had a reasonable discussion with the successful and interesting business magnate who would later become known for his extravagant lifestyle, outspoken manner, and hair.

Tampa Bay Buccaneers owner Hugh Culverhouse, who specialized in tax law and eventually made his millions in various real estate investments, showed me plans for a high-end retail and residential complex called the Tampasphere. Culverhouse told me if I played my cards right and signed with the Buccaneers, I could own a building like that in the Tampa Bay area.

Since I had a home outside of Seattle and was familiar with the Seahawks, I didn't have to make an "official" visit there. But I met with head coach Chuck Knox on the beach in Hawaii at the Pro Bowl, and I vividly remember everyone was in swim trunks and bikinis, but Knox, who was all business, had on a pair of red and black slacks.

I narrowed the list of seven teams to two: Houston and Seattle. Both teams offered $5.5 million for five years, the largest contract in NFL history at the time. The only difference was that Houston offered $4.5 million as a signing bonus, the Seahawks only $1.5 million.

Houston had also hired Hugh Campbell, my coach in Edmonton, at the last minute. That sealed the deal. With camera crews, newspaper reporters, and fans camping out in my front yard in Seattle, I had to walk out my front door and announce that I had selected the Oilers over my hometown Seahawks. My family was my first priority and, while football is a game, this was a business decision.

My goal was always to play in the NFL.

Even while in Canada, I was like a child with his nose pressed up against the store glass, wondering how I could ever buy a piece of candy beyond the window. I felt excluded. When Leigh and I attended the 1983 Super Bowl between Washington and Miami in Pasadena, I told Leigh I knew I could play in the NFL and match up against these guys. There was a yearning and a sadness that bubbled inside of me.

My window of opportunity to join the NFL was never better in 1984.

Honestly, I started to think about a switch from the CFL to the NFL following my third season with the Edmonton Eskimos in 1980. We had won three consecutive Grey Cup championships to tie the franchise and league record. We beat Hamilton 48–10 for the Grey Cup in 1980, and I was selected as the game's most valuable player. Overall, I had thrown for 6,624 yards and sixty touchdowns in forty-seven games since I had crossed the border from the University of Washington.

My thinking was simple: You reach a point where you can only do so much where you are. Although I had signed a new contract with Edmonton in 1980, I knew my future might be in the NFL. I always felt I could play in the States.

Steinberg had said a half-dozen NFL teams had expressed an interest in me on a consistent, ongoing basis while I played in Canada, but he emphasized my long-term contract with Edmonton. It was a binding contract. Although I did not have any automatic escape clauses, Steinberg always liked to say that a contract is one thing and market conditions are another. Translation: A deal could be worked out.

Both Leigh and I felt confident that I'd be able to make the move to the NFL at some point. I felt my skills had improved faster in the CFL than I had anticipated, mainly because I threw the football so much more than I did while I was at the University of Washington.

In interviews with the Canadian and American press following my 1980 season, I mentioned it might be time for me to set new goals and chase new challenges.

This Moon wanted to land in the states.

After the 1983 season, I had already accomplished almost every conceivable goal in Canada. That year alone, I passed for 5,648 yards, more than any quarterback in the league, and led the team in rushing. I also won the league's Most Outstanding Player of the Year award, though my last season there ended without us reaching the title game, after our string of consecutive Grey Cup titles.

I enjoyed Canada and had many fond memories. I made $240,000 per year at the end of my career, more than any CFL player, but I was ready to head back across the border to the United States. I had a great situation in Canada, and I knew I had to find something better to leave, but my heart was set on playing in the NFL.

Three years earlier in 1980, Leigh, with an eye to the future, had actually negotiated a new contract for me with Edmonton. The two-year deal expired in 1983, and that allowed me to chase my NFL dream. Steinberg wanted to time my exit to coincide with the perfect business climate in professional football. And this was it.

Our sales pitch was simple yet powerful: Teams would be getting a seasoned, six-year veteran at the most critical position on the field, a franchise quarterback who had proven himself, was healthy, and made for a good interview. I would also be a valuable asset to the community. What made me a novelty as a free agent was that teams wouldn't have to trade any draft picks to sign me. All they needed was money.

Plus, we had a choice of leagues—NFL, CFL, and the newly formed USFL—which gave us incredible leverage. I hit the pro-football trifecta in pursuit of my services. Leigh had made sure there were maximum bidders, and I was at my maximum value.

The USFL, which started play in 1983, was actually the brain-child of David Dixon, a New Orleans antiques dealer who had been instrumental in bringing an NFL franchise to New Orleans. Way back in 1965, Dixon had envisioned football as a possible spring and summer sport.

Nearly twenty years later, Dixon announced the USFL's formation and ESPN president Chet Simmons was named the league's first commissioner. The league was viewed as an innovative and serious challenger to the established NFL, thanks to its willingness to sign marquee talent, such as Herschel Walker, Marcus Dupree, Doug Flutie, Jim Kelly, and Archie Griffin—and in 1984, Mike Rozier and Steve Young. Young, under Leigh's direction, signed with the Los Angeles Express for a record ten-year, $42 million.

So Steinberg had planned this competition between the three leagues for me.

Steinberg knew he needed to establish a value for me in NFL eyes. John Elway, who was the overall number-one selection in the 1983 draft, had signed a six-year, $12.7 million contract with the Denver Broncos. Steinberg wanted more for me, so he made what he called his own reality in terms of my contract demands. Hypothetically, if Elway was worth a million, Steinberg smiled and said, then we wanted $1,100,000.

Steinberg kept repeating that figure over and over and over, which basically forced teams to adhere to the guidelines and standards that we had actually created in the marketplace. Steinberg's basic principle in shaping an offer for any negotiation was that you should always take an aggressive approach. And he certainly did.

While Steinberg felt my contract demand was unprecedented, he also called it reasonable. The media also turned out to be our greatest ally because it spread the word that Warren Moon was a $1,100,000 quarterback.

Steinberg and I planned our tour to visit different teams. The tour generated a ton of excitement because there had never been a football free agent like this before. Everywhere we went, there were stories in newspapers and magazines, fans and players alike talked about it on radio and television. Where would Warren go? Who would win the Moon derby? How much money will Warren get?

The press dubbed it a "shopping spree," which was only strengthened by Leigh's daily reminders that the most difficult position to fill in football was the franchise quarterback. He used *franchise quarterback* in every interview and in every breath he took, saying I was a player that a team could build around and win with now.

Race wasn't an issue for me this time around with the NFL, though I did confide in the Tampa Bay Buccaneers' Doug Williams and the Los Angeles Rams' James Harris, two of the league's three black quarterbacks. Both encouraged me, but they also told me to expect some difficult times. Doug warned me that there were going to be more people wanting me to fail than to succeed.

Steinberg believed that when it came to a franchise quarterback, team management made an evaluation that was different from any other player's. The owner ultimately had to have a high comfort level and make his evaluation on whether the player could be a great representative on and off the field. Leigh and I had researched every team and we prepped and studied the backgrounds of every person I was scheduled to meet. I knew exactly what to say and what questions to ask. I wanted to make sure I carried myself in a dignified manner, and that my clear strength of leadership was both felt and seen.

Plus, I was a good deal for teams. The team that signed me, a free agent, wouldn't lose any players or draft picks. Free agency had been part of baseball for years, thanks to Curt Flood, who in

1970 challenged a system that contractually bound a player to a team for life. But free agency hadn't yet come to football.

Steinberg wanted to create a constant in people's minds that would exult a player above the rest and make the quarterback position a huge premium, to make it the most lucrative position on the field. Steinberg told teams, "If you believe Warren can do it for you, all you have to do is pay him."

And to think the phrase *Show me the money!* wasn't coined until twelve years later in Hollywood.

Back to my finalists, Houston and Seattle.

The Oilers were owned by Bud Adams, who purchased the team in 1959 for an initial investment of $25,000. Adams, who made his early fortune in the petroleum business, was one of the original members of the "Foolish Club" (a self-imposed nickname), the eight men whose vision created the American Football League in 1959. The idea came from Lamar Hunt, who persuaded other men such as Adams, Ralph Wilson, and Barron Hilton to join his league.

Teams included Houston, Dallas, New York, Denver, Los Angeles, Boston, and Minneapolis-Saint Paul. Adams helped establish the league by winning the battle with the NFL for LSU's Heisman Trophy winner Billy Cannon.

The Oilers appeared in the first three AFL championship games, winning the first two in 1960 and 1961. While pressure mounted within the league to merge with the NFL, Adams believed the AFL could stand on its own two feet. With Hunt, Wilson, and Billy Sullivan, who purchased the Boston franchise, Adams was one of only four men who owned an AFL team for the entire ten years of the league's existence.

Adams and the other AFL owners received a tremendous boost in credibility and net worth when the AFL and the NFL merger was announced in 1966, effective with the 1970 season. The idea to start the AFL turned out to be a lucrative investment for Hunt, Adams, and Wilson. Their teams (Hunt, who died in 2006, had the Kansas City Chiefs, Adams has the Tennessee Titans, and Wilson has the Buffalo Bills) are now worth millions apiece.

The Oilers won only nine games from 1970 to 1973 before they started their rise back to football prominence in the late 1970s under head coach Bum Phillips, who dressed, spoke, and acted much like the popular image of a rancher, which he in fact was.

Houston won ten games in 1978 behind rookie running back Earl Campbell and Love Ya Blue signs were everywhere. The Oilers earned playoff berths three consecutive seasons from 1978 to 1980, losing to division rival and eventual Super Bowl champion Pittsburgh in two straight AFC championship games. Houston won eleven games in 1980 but lost to eventual Super Bowl champion Oakland in the wild-card game.

Dissatisfied, Adams fired Phillips after the season ended. Houston suffered through three consecutive losing seasons heading into 1984, and most of the Houston sporting public blamed Adams and his "micromanagement" style. Houston general manager Ladd Herzeg and coach Ed Biles were desperate to find a big-time quarterback. Over a five-year period, the Oilers had Dan Pastorini, Kenny Stabler, and Archie Manning as their quarterbacks, but all were in the twilight of their careers.

Adams also impressed me—he had a dozen roses waiting for Felicia when we arrived in Houston—and I liked the city of Houston. My in-laws lived in Houston. It was the largest city in Texas and one of the largest in the country. It had a multicultural population with a large and growing international community. There were a lot of economic opportunities as well. From an athletic standpoint, it had teams for nearly every professional sport.

Seattle, though, was home. I owned a home on the outskirts of Seattle in Redmond and many of my good friends lived in Washington. I also owned a chocolate-chip-cookie store in the area, too. Despite the boo-birds early in my career at the University of Washington, I had become sort of a folk hero after we beat Michigan in the Rose Bowl. My roots were in Seattle. The city was a newcomer to the NFL, too.

In 1972, Seattle Professional Football Inc., a group of Seattle business and community leaders, announced its intention to acquire an NFL franchise for the city. Almost two years later in 1974, the NFL awarded the group an expansion franchise. In December 1974, NFL commissioner Pete Rozelle announced the official signing of the franchise agreement by Lloyd W. Nordstrom, representing the Nordstrom family as majority partners for the consortium. Sadly, Nordstrom died of a heart attack in 1976, just months before the Seahawks played their first game.

The Seahawks, along with the Tampa Bay Buccaneers, joined the NFL in 1976 as expansion teams. Jack Patera, an assistant with the Minnesota Vikings, was named the team's first head coach.

The Seahawks lost their first five games before they beat the Buccaneers 13–10 in Tampa on October 17. A year later, in what has been called one of the dumbest moves in franchise history, Seattle traded its top pick in the draft to Dallas for three second-round selections. The Cowboys picked a player named Tony Dorsett, who, of course, ended up having a Hall of Fame career.

The Seahawks registered winning seasons in 1978 and 1979 behind quarterback Jim Zorn and receiver Steve Largent, but suffered losing seasons over the next three years. In 1983, under new head coach Chuck Knox, Seattle enjoyed a distinct home-field advantage that continues today—fans perfected the first "wave" cheer in 1983. Seattle finished 9–7 and earned its first playoff berth, losing to the Oakland Raiders in the AFC championship game.

Both Houston and Seattle had the inside track for me, and I felt I couldn't go wrong with either one. Joe Galat, a former Oiler assistant coach who was head coach of Montreal in the CFL, told the media that I would be successful in the NFL and "he'll make any team that gets him a winner."

Coach Campbell admitted he had great affection for me as a player and a person, but he had to be careful. He didn't want to oversell me and make me feel that I owed it to him to sign with the Oilers. Campbell simply told me that if I came to Houston I'd have a coach who believed in me and I would be given every opportunity to play. Technically, my contract offers from Houston and Seattle weren't no-cut deals, which meant I could be cut at any time for whatever reason. Campbell, of course, assured me that wouldn't happen in Houston. While he thought it would have been more logical for me to sign with Seattle because it was home, he felt Houston was the better choice because of him.

Needless to say, it was an agonizing decision.

Leigh and I told each team that we wanted to make a decision by February. We also kept the media informed of our intentions. Jill Lieber of *Sports Illustrated* had actually accompanied us on each stop of our tour. The night when I decided to announce my intention, television trucks were parked outside my Seattle home and lined up down the street, their metal antennae spiraling into the air. Reporters and fans dotted the neighborhood.

It was chaotic, to say the least, but I knew what I wanted to say. I knew what I had to do. In fact, I talked to Steinberg on the telephone that night and told him in a few minutes I would have to walk out my front door to face the local and national press, and I knew how much my decision was going to disappoint the Seattle fans. Seattle was my home, and everywhere I went people pleaded with me to sign with the Seahawks. I knew all the players. Coach Knox had been the coach with the Los Angeles Rams when I was a youngster, and he was very successful. But I wanted to explain what was important to me and what was important to my family, which was my number-one priority.

Seattle was the better team.

But Houston made better . . . cents.

In the end it came down to Houston's guaranteed money. It was an important and significant factor because you never knew when football was going to end. Even today, when injured in the NFL, players are only guaranteed their salary and a lump sum of $250,000 the following season, and that's it.

My decision also was based on Coach Campbell. I wanted to go with a team that I knew would eventually get the type of talent that would match my strengths. Coach Campbell knew my strengths as a player, and he knew what he needed around me. Going somewhere else like Houston, where people didn't know me, I wasn't sure about that.

Honestly, the entire episode was staggering. I had worked so hard to reach this point, and I had overcome so many obstacles. It was emotionally and financially rewarding for both Steinberg and me. Leigh had been with me every step of the way. It was big news, too.

CBS anchor Dan Rather led his nightly broadcast with the news of my signing. Since my chocolate-chip-cookie stores were a novelty, *Sports Illustrated* ran a picture of me with its signing story in a big white hat, holding a tray of my cookies, with the headline, THIS COOKIE IS IN THE CHIPS. On February 6, 1984, the Oilers announced in a press release, "Moon to Become an Oiler."

After the Oilers opened with the explanation that the hiring of Campbell was not part of a package deal that lured me to Houston, I told fans that coming to Houston reminded me of when I went to Washington. I had been through a rebuilding year and won. Washington was coming off a 2–9 season and people told me I shouldn't go there. But we won in Washington.

I thought the Oilers were better than people gave them credit for, and I knew what Coach Campbell could do. I promised to do whatever I could to help the Oilers win. On March 1, when my contract with the Edmonton Eskimos expired, I signed with Houston for $5.5 million over five years.

And, even before the ink dried, fans expected me to earn every penny. High expectations came with all those zeros at the end of my paycheck.

9

Houston,
We Have Liftoff

I never thought I would be the oldest quarterback in the National Football League at one point, not in a million years. I never thought I would play as long as I did, either, seventeen years from start to finish, with stops in Houston, Minnesota, Seattle, and Kansas City.

Want to know another secret?

I got rid of the ball—quickly. I learned early that it was not healthy to hold on to the football for very long. I was smart enough to throw the ball away when needed and I was athletic enough, even later in my career, to avoid a direct hit. Plus, I felt like I never lost any arm strength, which enabled me to either thread the needle or loft a long ball over a receiver's shoulder.

When I turned forty-one years old during the 1997 season with Seattle, I was one of only three men to play quarterback in the NFL at that age. George Blanda played into his midforties and Earl Morrall played at forty-two. But they were backups while I was still a starter. In 2008, my former Minnesota teammate and friend, Brad Johnson, made three starts with the Dallas Cowboys at age forty. At the time, Brad joked that forty was the new thirty!

There had come a point later in my career when it seemed I reached a milestone or set a record almost every time I stepped on the field. The numbers added up with the years.

I threw for 49,325 yards, the third most in NFL history, when I retired at age forty-four following the 2000 season with Kansas

City. I also threw 291 touchdowns, the fourth most at the time of my retirement. I also had 1,736 rushing yards and twenty-two rushing touchdowns. If you combine my NFL and CFL statistics, I had 5,357 completions for 70,533 yards and 435 touchdowns, all of which are significantly higher than the NFL records for each category.

I was football's career passing leader until September 2006, when quarterback Damon Allen, a twenty-two-year veteran of the CFL, threw for 207 yards in a Toronto Argonauts victory to push his career total to 70,596. Allen, the younger brother of NFL Hall of Famer Marcus Allen, retired in May 2008 at age forty-four, with 73,381 yards. But I do still hold the record for the most pass attempts in professional football history with 9,205.

Naturally, there were hardships, too.

I threw twice as many interceptions as touchdowns in my second season with the Oilers, in 1986. I was never able to reach the Super Bowl, a crowning achievement that defines many quarterbacks. I was benched one time in my career, in 1993, my final season with the Oilers. We opened the year 1–4 and Cody Carlson started against the New England Patriots. But Cody was injured on a touchdown run, and I came off the bench to lead us to a 28–14 victory, the first of eleven in a row for us in a season that ended with a playoff defeat to Joe Montana and the Kansas City Chiefs. After productive stops in Minnesota and Seattle, I played in only three games in my two seasons with the Chiefs before I announced my retirement.

Off the field was far more difficult at times.

Even though my mother had told me growing up that "if you win, nobody cares what color you are," that wasn't necessarily true in the NFL. I also had to deal with racism and death threats in the NFL.

When I arrived in Houston as a twenty-eight-year-old rookie with the highest salary in football, that meant I could be booed even louder and longer. The slurs that swirled around my family in the stands those first few years were so bad that I eventually moved them to a private stadium box. After games, I'd go home and explain to Josh, my oldest son, why it had happened. I told him there are ignorant people in the world who say ignorant things. Most people did not feel that way, but a few did. It was a sad fact of life. When we finally started winning, however, the animosity seemed to end, and Houston fans began to embrace me.

I probably heard more trash on the East Coast than I did down South. I honestly believe that even if I had won a Super Bowl, racial slurs still would have been directed my way. There was always somebody wondering if I was smart enough or savvy enough to play quarterback. People kept doubting me, but I kept putting up numbers.

I didn't play the game for records, numbers, or longevity, however. It was about being wanted, it was about winning, and it was about my passion for the game. I just loved it. I absolutely loved to compete and to step out onto that football field with my teammates. Looking back, I would have embraced the opportunity to play in a big-time market such as Los Angeles, my hometown, for either the Rams or the Raiders. It just never worked out. As an athlete, you always look for the right team, the right opportunity, the right mix.

To be honest, that chip I'd carried on my shoulder since I started playing football I carried into the NFL, too. I wanted to be Warren Moon the quarterback, not Warren Moon the black quarterback. I wanted to be professional about everything I did. I respected those around me, and I wanted to earn the respect of ownership, my teammates, and fans.

When I walked out onto that field, I always felt like I had something to prove.

I was excited about going to Houston because it reminded me of college—I was going to a rebuilding team. Though we didn't have all of our offensive weapons in place, that wouldn't stop us from trying to win a Super Bowl.

Houston general manager Ladd Herzeg did everything he could to put me in the best position to win after I signed with the Oilers in 1984. Houston used its third consecutive number-one pick in the

NFL draft on an offensive lineman when it selected guard Dean Steinkuhler out of the University of Nebraska.

Steinkuhler, the second overall pick in the draft behind teammate Irving Fryar, who went to the New England Patriots, won the Outland Trophy his senior season as the nation's top offensive lineman. He helped solidify our offensive line, which had added tackle Bruce Matthews and guard Mike Munchak in the previous two drafts. But winning never comes easy.

We finished 3–13 in my first season. It was ugly, even though I set a new club record with 3,338 passing yards, a mark I would break four more times. I was booed by our fans and criticized by the media. The situation got so bad in 1985 that Hugh Campbell was fired late in a 5–11 season and replaced by defensive coordinator Jerry Glanville. That was tough for me, because I watched how it happened, how Jerry manipulated the whole thing and poisoned everybody in the organization against Campbell. Plus, I didn't like the offense we were running; I just didn't feel like it took advantage of my abilities. Glanville just wanted to run the football and play hard-nosed defense. I felt as if I didn't fit into his plans.

The Oilers were 23–66 from 1981, three years before I arrived, through 1986. The team was a national laughingstock. Adding insult to injury, we also set an NFL record by losing twenty-three consecutive road games. After my second season, I wondered if I had made the wrong decision when I signed with the Oilers. It was also during this time that the racial slurs being directed at me were almost unbearable. My teammates couldn't believe what I had to put up with, both at home and on the road.

My sister, Renee, who often sat in the stands with my family, had an unsettling experience at her doctor's office when she overheard two people talking about me. They said that no decent white man would follow a black quarterback, among other racially charged opinions. The receptionist also overheard the conversation and apologized to Renee. It took every bit of Renee's strength not to give those people a piece of her mind. But she knew it wouldn't accomplish a thing and would only add fuel to the fire.

But it wasn't only white people who were sharp with their tongues. Many black people weren't happy about my performance either and were just as loud and obnoxious with their criticism.

It was a miserable time. I played one of my worst games as a professional when, in the freezing rain at Buffalo in 1985, I completed three of fourteen passes for only twenty-two yards with three interceptions. After winning our season opener in 1986, we lost eight straight. Following that eighth defeat against a Miami team that had the league's second-worst defense—and eighteen of our first twenty plays were runs—I knew things had to change. And that moment came when we played Cincinnati in the Astrodome. Only 32,130 fans bothered to show up.

Before that game, owner Bud Adams and Herzeg ordered Glanville to open up the offense. They told Glanville that they didn't sign me to the richest contract in league history to hand off the football. That Cincinnati game proved to be a defining moment for the franchise. We beat the Bengals 32–28 as I completed twenty-five of forty-four passes for 310 yards. We won five of our last eight games and from that time on Glanville began to show he believed in what I was doing. We made the playoffs for the next seven seasons.

We started to run a version of the run-and-shoot in 1987. We had started adding needed playmakers when receiver Ernest Givins came along a season earlier. Haywood Jefferies, Alonzo Highsmith, Lorenzo White, and Webster Slaughter followed. It was a learning experience for everyone, but with time we became a very potent offense, one that could win games every Sunday. Our wide-open offense showcased my strong arm, running skills, and big-play ability. I felt comfortable and wanted.

The 1987 season had great moments and bad moments for everyone associated with the NFL.

In a season shortened by a player's strike that eliminated the third week, known as the scab season—I was our player representative—we went 9–6 to post our first winning season since 1980, when Bum

Phillips was head coach and Ken "the Snake" Stabler was the quarterback. I passed for 237 yards and a touchdown while leading the Oilers to a 23–20 overtime win over the Seattle Seahawks in the wild-card round of the playoffs in my first NFL postseason game. I was proud of what we accomplished. But the season had its share of trouble, too.

The twenty-four-day strike by NFL players in 1987 was actually a product of the past. The 1982 strike, which lasted fifty-seven days, produced unexpected player solidarity. Although average player salaries in the NFL rose from $90,000 in 1982 to $230,000 in 1987, most of this increase was due to opportunities players had to jump to USFL clubs for higher salaries or to be paid more by their NFL clubs to stay. But a number of issues remained, ranging from free agency to pensions to severance pay. Plus, in 1987, the new television agreement paid each owner $17 million annually, and that triggered a new struggle between players and owners over revenues.

The players' union tried to get more quarterbacks like myself involved because it gave us more power. Team management was not going to touch or criticize a Dan Marino for being a player representative. The chief negotiator for the union was executive director Gene Upshaw, while Tampa Bay Bucs owner Hugh Culverhouse was the chairman of the NFL Management Council.

It got really nasty. About two-thirds of the teams signed replacement players who promised to continue the season in the event of a strike. Just two weeks prior to the start of the season, there had been a hundred players on each NFL team's training-camp roster. The guys gladly took the thousand dollars proffered by the owners for standing by as potential replacements. On September 22, the players' association announced its intention to strike.

As our player rep and quarterback, I made sure guys stayed in shape, I organized picket lines, I updated everyone on the negotiations. It was difficult on the players, and during that first week several veterans in the league crossed picket lines. I tried my best to keep the peace. We had some egg-throwing incidents at the buses that carried the Oilers' replacement players to practice. Naturally, we also had guys who almost got in fights with some of the replacement guys, but it really never got out of hand. It was reported that about 84 percent of the 1,585 regular players stayed out for the duration of the strike.

The league played on Sunday, October 4, 1987, without its players. Wannabes suddenly became NFL players for three Sundays overall. I honored our picket line, and I wanted my teammates to honor it as well. Our coaching staff understood our position, even though they were company guys. I think Mr. Adams, when it was all said and done, respected me a little bit more because of the way I handled it all. It was a difficult time, but I got to show my leadership abilities off the field during the strike.

We ended up going to the playoffs, so the strike didn't ruin our football season. Houston's replacement players went 2–1. A couple of the replacement players made our team, including a quarterback named Brett Pease. I was a little indifferent toward him at the beginning, which was kind of uncharacteristic of me. But I totally warmed up to him and understood his plight. He was just doing whatever he could to get a job. He ended up earning my respect and we became pretty good friends.

Our good roll continued in 1988. Our offense ranked second in the AFC, and I was rated the conference's third-best passer even though I had to sit out the first five games with a fractured shoulder, my first major injury. But I came back and helped the Oilers finish the season at 10–6 and earn a second consecutive playoff berth. I was also named as the starter in the Pro Bowl and threw nine straight completions in that game.

In April 1989, I signed a five-year, $10 million contract with the Oilers that made me the NFL's highest paid player ever until quarterbacks Bernie Kosar of the Browns, Troy Aikman of the Cowboys, and Joe Montana of the Chiefs signed similar deals a few weeks later. After an inconsistent start, we won five of six games and earned a spot in the playoffs as a wild card. But we lost to the Pittsburgh Steelers in overtime and Glanville was fired and replaced by Jack Pardee.

Glanville was really the only head coach that I didn't see eye-to-eye with during my career. I know he didn't like me a lot, because I got a lot of attention, and that was one of the things that he craved as head coach. He demanded and wanted everything for himself.

He wrote a book after he was done coaching in the NFL, and he never mentioned me in the book by name. It was always "the quarterback." I never got into it with him, because I am not a confrontational person. But I didn't agree with a lot of his coaching philosophy or the extra things that he brought to the table. He was a good football coach as far as Xs and Os. But all the other things he did, like his antics leaving tickets for Elvis Presley, I could do without. Every city we played in, he left tickets at will call for a famous dead person from that city. It was a big distraction. That was just part of playing for Jerry, however.

The things he did throughout the week to motivate the other teams, the things that he would say to the different coaches that would get the other team and its fans fired up were aggravating. When we walked into their stadiums, we were the most hated guys in the league. It was tough enough to win on the road as it was, but when you have that extra adrenaline going because of things that your head coach has said throughout the week in his press conferences . . . it was just unnecessary. It just made it that much tougher for us to win. But that was his personality. Our team colors were Columbia blue and red and white, but Glanville wore all black. He wore this huge belt buckle; he wore a cowboy hat. Our colors weren't black. What are you wearing black accessories for? He'd ride up to the games on a Harley motorcycle, just anything he could do to get attention. I didn't agree with those things at all. It made it tough on us.

The 1990 season had a humiliating start when we lost to the Glanville-coached Atlanta Falcons, 41–27. We hovered around the .500 mark the entire year, even though I turned in one of my best seasons as a professional, earning Offensive Player of the Year honors.

I led the league with 4,689 passing yards, owned a quarterback rating of 96.8 percent and completed 62 percent of my passes. Statistically, it was my best year as an NFL quarterback. I also led the league in attempts (584), completions (362), and touchdowns (33), and tied Marino's record with nine three-hundred-yard games in a season. That included throwing for 527 yards against Kansas City on December 16, 1990, the second most passing yards ever in a single game. We won three of our last four games and squeezed into the playoffs as the sixth seed. But our postseason ended quickly with a loss at Cincinnati.

My game against Kansas City in 1990 was definitely a high-water mark in my career. Legendary quarterback Sid Gillman, who often reviewed film for the Oilers, called it the best performance he ever saw from a quarterback. The Chiefs had the best secondary in the league when we lined up against them at Arrowhead Stadium. It was rainy, cold, misty, perfect conditions for a stout Chiefs' defense to shut down our passing attack.

The Chiefs liked to play man-to-man on opposing teams' receivers, and we felt this would play to our advantage. And we were right. We led 10–7 at the end of the first half. Every play was competitive. Each pass I threw became a contest between my receivers and their corners. As the game wore on, we stepped up and won those individual battles. As much as we were rained on, we poured it on the Chiefs secondary. I finished the game with 527 yards passing, twenty-one yards short of the NFL single-game record.

With about three minutes left in the game, I hit my thumb on someone's helmet. The coaches asked me if I wanted to stay in the game and try to throw for another twenty-two yards, or come out. I elected to come out. There wasn't any reason for me to stay in the game just to throw the football around. We ran the clock out and left Kansas City relatively healthy and with a win for us.

The statistics will say I threw for 527 yards that day, but it may be more accurate to say my receivers caught for 527 yards. Haywood Jeffires had an outstanding game, catching nine passes for 245 yards. He and I hooked up for an eighty-seven-yard touchdown.

Ernest Givins had the other two touchdowns. Tony Jones also had a great game.

When we returned to Houston, everyone was talking about our performance in Kansas City, especially my performance. I was surprised to find some newspapers in the city critical of the decision to sit out the remaining three minutes and forgo a chance at the record. I was being called an "Uncle Tom" by some fans because I didn't break the record, losing a shot at what would have been a great achievement for black people. Some believed it was the decision of the Oilers—just another racist move by an NFL team. What they didn't understand is that I was given the choice—it was my decision to make. All I wanted was the win. I play football to win, not to break records. That was something some people did not understand.

I had another solid season personally in 1991, passing for a league-best 4,690 yards. I joined Dan Marino and Dan Fouts as the only quarterbacks in NFL history to post back-to-back 4,000-yard seasons. I also established new NFL records that season with 655 pass attempts and 404 completions. But the best part of the season was that we got off to a 7–1 start. Although we ended twenty-four years of frustration for the franchise when we finally won a division title, John Elway turned in one of his magical comebacks in the fourth quarter as the Denver Broncos beat us 26–24 in the division round.

I continued to deal with racism off the field in 1991. I had thrown five interceptions on the road against the Pittsburgh Steelers and we followed that game with a tough 13–6 home loss to the Philadelphia Eagles in early December. I was on the verge of signing a five-year contract extension, and the news had become public. We struggled against the Eagles, and my son Joshua was in the stands. He heard all kinds of nasty words that day, and he was pretty upset when he came into our locker room after the game. There were reporters and cameras in the locker room, but I am the type of person who confronts things when they arise. And this was something to confront, so I patiently explained to Joshua what these people said.

John McClain of the *Houston Chronicle* watched my emotional conversation with Joshua, and he said it made him want to cry. I was a solid member of the Houston community at this time. I lived in Houston year-round with my family. I had established my own charitable foundation—Crescent Moon Foundation, which provides college scholarships. Was I a "quarterback" when we won but a "black quarterback" when we lost? My foundation logged more than two hundred calls immediately following the game that echoed the racist words in the stands. I heard rumors that I had AIDS, because I was a friend of basketball player Magic Johnson. McClain said he talked to one man who was convinced I had thrown the Eagles game, though I was about to sign a new contract. It didn't make any sense.

Although the rumors persisted, I apologized to the Houston fans on my weekly radio show. I told them I was sorry that I played so lousily against the Eagles and that the loss was my fault. I promised that I would try to play better. Many of my teammates were shocked when they heard what I did. Sure, I could have talked about the passes that were dropped or the routes that were run incorrectly or the missed blocks. But I am not wired that way. I knew I could handle the burden, and I figured that was the best way to diffuse a difficult situation. Yes, I was to blame, end of story.

The phones started to ring again following my radio show, but the tone of fans had turned 180 degrees. People called to apologize for what they had said. They talked about what we had accomplished and not what we had failed to do. We beat the Steelers in a rematch the following week, 31–6, and I threw for 258 yards and a touchdown.

I only played in eleven games in 1992 due to injuries, but we were once again one of the top teams in the AFC. We finished 10–6 and qualified for the playoffs. It was a different year but with the same result in the postseason. After we beat Buffalo in the final game of the regular season, we faced the Bills again in the playoffs in Buffalo. It's a game that will always haunt me, a definite low point of my career, as we blew a 35–3 third-quarter lead, the largest in history, and lost 41–38 in overtime to the Bills. Needless to say, I was shell-shocked after the game. My teammates were shocked. The entire community was shocked. It was like a bad dream that we could never wake up from.

Following the disaster in Buffalo, Mr. Adams gave the team one more season to reach the Super Bowl before he started to trade players and rebuild with the league's new salary cap on the horizon. While everyone thought we'd fall flat on our faces because of what happened in Buffalo, the 1993 season proved to be our best with me under center—but it was also my last season with the team. We went 12–4 and won the AFC central-division crown, but lost to Joe Montana and the Kansas City Chiefs 28–20 in the divisional round of the playoffs. It was frustrating to play well in the regular season only to struggle in the postseason.

I really thought our 1992 and 1993 teams were good enough to win the Super Bowl. The Dallas Cowboys, a team that we had defeated during the regular season, beat the Buffalo Bills for the second consecutive year in the Super Bowl to end the '93 season. We felt like Dallas was the team to beat and we knew there was a good chance we would face the Cowboys in that Super Bowl. We just had to get there, but we didn't.

Due to the suddenly changing landscape in the NFL, I also knew there was a good chance the Oilers would trade me following the 1993 season. I was thirty-eight years old and had spent ten seasons in Houston. When the 49ers traded Joe Montana to the Kansas City Chiefs a year earlier, I knew I was not safe. I think every starting quarterback in the league felt the same way when they saw Montana get traded away after all he had done in San Francisco.

That's the harsh reality of professional sports. It's a business, and management is going to do what's best for the organization. That's not to say management won't keep you for a year longer than it wants out of loyalty, but it's not going to be much longer than that.

I enjoyed my time in Houston, and I enjoyed my teammates. We had a lot of success together. While I had to endure the racial outbursts by fans, I was embraced by my teammates. But, yes, that was something I'd worried about when I arrived in Houston, especially coming from Canada and not really having a background or relationship with any of the guys on the team. Then all of a sudden the organization pays you all this money, and there are immense expectations. But as soon as you go out and you show what you can do around your teammates, you earn their respect.

One of the great things about team sports is that it brings races together. If you have the ability, and you have a chance to help your team win, and if everybody is in it for the same reasons—then they are going to accept you if they think you're good enough.

Every guy that I think can help us, I don't care what he believes in or what he does in his off time. When he's in the locker room and we're on this field together, as long as he does his job and helps us win, that's all that really matters. You don't like all of your teammates all the time, because you don't get a chance to get to know each other that well, but you definitely respect them if you think they can play.

And I still wanted to play in Houston, but the writing was on the wall. The Oilers wanted to go with the younger quarterback, Cody Carlson, who actually came at a pretty penny, too, at $3 million per year. I was set to make $3.25 million, and you just didn't see too many teams in the league with the backup quarterback making almost as much money as the starter.

I told Floyd Reese, Houston's assistant general manager at the time and a former linebackers coach with the Oilers, to mark my words that I would play in the league longer than Cody. It wasn't anything against Carlson, but I wanted Floyd to understand that I was the better player for the team at that time. Floyd smiled that smile and told me I had my opinion and he had his opinion. And his opinion counted more than mine.

Although a few years later he apologized to me and said he made a mistake trading me, he also said if he had to do it all over again, he would probably do the same thing based on everything they did in the evaluation process. I told him I would have probably done the same thing, too, if I were him. But I knew how I felt physically and emotionally. Reese said my age was a concern and that he had to base his judgment on my skills and the future of the football team.

As a Houston Oiler, I set a franchise record for wins, with seventy, which stood until Steve McNair broke it in 2004, long after the Oilers had become the Tennessee Titans. In 1994, the NFL's new salary cap caused Mr. Adams, as he promised, to take drastic measures. The Oilers allowed defensive ends Sean Jones and William Fuller to leave as free agents. Overall, we had twenty-eight players whose contracts were about to expire. Decisions had to be made.

A decision was made in my case, too. I was no longer a member of the Houston Oilers.

Hello, Minnesota.

10

On the Move

Minnesota was a different experience for me, primarily because Vikings head coach Dennis Green expected me to make an immediate impact when I arrived. I was wanted in Minnesota, and I didn't want to let down Coach Green.

Minnesota was a good fit for me from the very beginning. I was determined to excel in a pro-style offense, where teams can run and pass equally well, without the four-receiver set we employed in Houston. Cris Carter and Jake Reed were already established as go-to receivers I could rely on to make plays. Terry Allen, a thousand-yard rusher in 1992, provided welcome balance after missing the 1993 season following knee surgery. These guys were really the keys to my success in Minnesota.

Another benefit that came with the Vikings was playing under Coach Green.

Denny had a similar approach to football as I did. We had many similar characteristics, and I think that's what allowed me to make an immediate impact with the Vikings in my first season in 1994. He was really level headed and analytical. Sometimes he could be a little quiet, but you knew he had that fire inside him, and if he felt like we needed it, he would let it out. He was an intense motivator if the situation warranted it.

As a coach, he was very organized. Practices were very up-tempo and crisp. He didn't believe in doing a lot of hitting during the week or driving players into the ground and wearing them out. He wanted his players as well rested by game time as possible. At this point in my career, I didn't need to add any extra wear and tear to my body.

Instead of long, physical practices on the field, we spent more time meeting as players and coaches, breaking down game film, analyzing opposing teams, building strategies. We were expected to know both ourselves and our opponents inside and out by game time. Coach Green was a real believer in efficiency. Every meeting had a beginning time and an end time, and you had better be there five minutes early, not five minutes late.

We had a real need for facilities in which to schedule these meetings, continue with our workouts, and hold team practice. The Vikings' organization, in a testament to their commitment to success, filled most every one of these team needs. We had a huge indoor practice facility that allowed us to keep up with our schedule demands.

We also had a first-class cafeteria with a couple of chefs there to cook for the team. Denny believed that in order to get the best workouts from his players, they needed to be fed well and fueled. He wanted to make sure you got at least two good meals every day. A good breakfast, a good lunch, and hopefully you would do the right thing for dinner.

All the ingredients were in place for us to win.

It felt strange to be in a new uniform and in a new city in Minneapolis, but I was excited to be part of the Vikings organization when I signed the richest deal in team history at $15 million for three years.

I helped lead Minnesota to the playoffs in my first season, putting me in rare company. I joined Terry Bradshaw and Joe Montana as the only quarterbacks in history to lead teams to the playoffs eight consecutive years.

We finished 12–6 to win the NFL Central, and I threw for 4,264 yards, my third-highest total in eleven seasons, and I was elected to the Pro Bowl. Carter, one of the most talented receivers I played with, caught an NFL-record 122 receptions for 1,256 yards, while Reed finished with eighty-five receptions for 1,175 yards. Receiver Qadry Ismail and running back Amp Lee combined on ninety catches, and Allen rushed for more than a thousand yards. Unfortunately, the playoffs were the same story for me. We stumbled and lost to the Chicago Bears in a wild-card game. It was Minnesota's third consecutive playoff defeat in the opening round.

I would be lying if I said I didn't keep an eye on the Houston Oilers. It felt strange not to be in Houston. My family still lived in Texas. Plus, my final season with the Oilers was such an emotional roller coaster. I went from star to footnote, from tragic hero to inspiration. I thought I was going to have my best season, and everything came apart. I was benched. I was slowed down late in the season by a cracked rib. And, of course, there were the constant attacks on my personal life. It was said that if you listened to some fans, Felicia and I were divorced and remarried more times than Elizabeth Taylor and Richard Burton. Not even an eleven-game win streak and an AFC Central title could accurately explain the most bizarre season in my career. But somehow I was still able to keep it all together.

I wanted to stay in Houston, but the Oilers wanted me to go. The Oilers knew I could still play; they just didn't know for how long. I played hard, I played hurt, and I did everything I could to help the Houston organization. For the most part, I think Houstonians appreciated me. I received so many more positive comments than negative ones. There were a lot of people who supported me, and I had a lot of good friends in Houston.

Any animosity I felt was toward the organization and not the players. I always felt for those guys on the field. All those guys were good friends of mine, guys I had played with for a long time, so I didn't want to see them struggle. But the Oilers certainly struggled in 1994—they finished last in the AFC Central at 2–14. They lost nine of their first ten games and head coach Jack Pardee was fired and replaced by Jeff Fisher.

Three different players were used at quarterback at Houston: Cody Carlson, Billy Joe Tollivar, and Bucky Richardson. The trio combined to throw for 3,716 yards and thirteen touchdowns, numbers that ranked below my season totals. I was pleased I showed the Houston organization that I could still play at a high level, but I was disappointed for those guys.

The following season in 1995 was certainly a disappointment for the Vikings. Although I passed for 4,228 yards and was elected to the Pro Bowl for the second consecutive season, we finished 8–8 and missed the playoffs. We averaged 25.8 points per game to rank fourth in the NFL, but our defense allowed 27.1 points per game, twenty-seventh in league rankings. We dropped our final two regular season games to fall out of playoff contention.

One highlight, however, came in the season's sixth week, when we beat the visiting Houston Oilers 23–17 in overtime. Needless to say, that was one of the toughest games for me to prepare for, to get ready and compete against the guys that I had played, sweated, and worked with for ten years. But, at the same time, being the competitor I was, I really wanted to beat the snot out of them! I finally got the satisfaction of saying, "I told you so," about all those things that bothered me about my situation with Houston when I left.

I threw for 289 yards and two touchdowns in the game, which we won on Robert Smith's six-yard run in overtime. While the Oilers had cast an eye to the future when it drafted quarterback Steve McNair with the third overall selection, he opened the season on the bench behind free agent signee Chris Chandler, a Washington alum. Chris threw for 156 yards without a touchdown against us. It was a nice feeling to beat the Oilers, but it was also tough for me to watch the organization, especially later, in November of that season, when owner Bud Adams announced plans to move his team to Nashville as soon as the lease at the Astrodome expired in 1998.

Houston fans expressed their displeasure with the Oilers by staying away in droves in 1996. Most of the home games were played in front of crowds of less than 20,000, a far cry from the capacity crowds of 62,000 we played in front of. Houston was also able to break its lease with the city a year early, which meant the '96 season was the Oilers' last in Houston. Since I left the quarterback reins in Houston, no quarterback, for the Oilers or the Texans, has led his team to a record over .500. The 2008 Texans finished 8–8.

I enjoyed two really good seasons in Minnesota under Coach Green, but the 1996 season started off poorly for me. I suffered severe sprains to both ankles in the first half of the season opener against Detroit. I stayed in the game, but my mobility was limited to almost zero. The coaches were worried that I wouldn't even be able to protect myself in the pocket, so they took me out for Brad Johnson, a young, talented guy from Florida State. Brad played an excellent game and threw the game-winning touchdown pass in the final minutes. It was a great start to a successful career for Brad, who later won the Super Bowl when he was with the Tampa Bay Buccaneers.

Although I ended up behind center again when Brad was injured later in the year, we lost to the Dallas Cowboys 40–15 in the wild-card game, after we had won three of our final four games to finish 9–7 and advance into the playoffs.

My career, however, was at a crossroads. Again.

Unfortunately for me, Brad was in the last year of his contract with the Vikings and was scheduled to become a free agent after the season. The question for the Vikings was obvious: Do you keep me, at age forty-one, with a gimpy ankle, at $3.5 million, or do you keep Brad, who is playing pretty well, and who you have groomed to be your guy? When Brad signed a $15.5 million, four-year contract extension during the final week of the regular season, it was clear that my time as the starter in Minnesota was over.

They chose Brad, and I can't blame the Vikings. It didn't affect my friendship with Brad at all, because we both realized football was a business. But, once again, I knew I could still play professional football at a high level and be successful at quarterback. All I wanted to do was find somewhere else to play.

When the telephone buzzed, it was Seattle, of all places, on the line.

I was pretty much left for dead when my season ended in Minnesota. I was slowed by ankle injuries and was the backup for Brad. To be honest, I initially thought I'd retire after the 1996 season if I had finished the season the way I wanted to—healthy and productive. But the way it ended, I was determined to prove to myself and to the NFL that I could still play.

And the Seattle Seahawks offered me the best opportunity.

My return to the city of Seattle with the Seattle Seahawks organization came as a welcome relief to me. While I also talked with the San Diego Chargers new coach, Kevin Gilbride, a good friend who had built and directed our offense in Houston, Seattle made more sense.

Seattle was where I wanted to live when my career ended. I was also impressed by the Seahawks. They had that tough defense teams hated to play against, and coach Dennis Erickson spread the offense wide across the field, just the way I liked it. San Diego offered wonderful potential, but I wanted to be part of Seattle's future. I felt Seattle could win, so I agreed to a two-year, $1.65 million contract.

The fans in Seattle knew me as a person, and they knew what I was capable of accomplishing on the field. In thirteen NFL seasons with Houston and Minnesota, I had thrown for 43,787 yards, 254 touchdowns, and 208 interceptions and was voted to eight consecutive Pro Bowls, the all-time record for quarterbacks. Seattle felt like a fresh start again.

Seattle and I had a relationship that dated back to my college days at the University of Washington. Fans had witnessed how I played my position during my three seasons as their starting quarterback. They had followed me twenty years earlier to the 1978 Rose Bowl in Los Angeles, where we upset the favored Michigan Wolverines. They were there when the Tournament of Roses named me the player of the game. They followed me in Canada, Houston, and Minnesota.

With my fan base from college still around in Seattle, I had high expectations for myself. They remembered me for my success in college, but I wanted them to know me now for my success in the NFL. The Seahawks signed me as the backup to John Friesz, who was recovering from a broken leg that cut his season short in 1996.

All I know was that I was used to playing and my mindset had not changed: I planned to work and prepare like a starter.

The season got off to a slow start, for my standards. Losing two games at home is not how any football team wants to start the season, plus Friesz, who opened as our starter, was out with a broken thumb he'd suffered during the opener.

Finally, in week three, against Indianapolis, we were able to establish our team identity and left Indiana with our first win of the season. In that game, I also became the oldest player in NFL history to score a touchdown, when I scored on a one-yard run. Getting that first win took some pressure off my (aging) shoulders! Seriously, my age did not matter. I wanted to perform for the Seattle fans, and I felt like I had let them down with those first two losses. Getting my first win as a Seahawk allowed me to shrug off some of the demands I had placed on myself.

I enjoyed a hot streak in the middle of the year. I threw for 295 yards and two touchdowns in a 37–31 victory over San Diego. In a big victory over the Oakland Raiders, I became the first forty-year-old quarterback to throw for 400 yards and the first to throw five touchdown passes. In a three-game span that included a tough loss to the Denver Broncos, I threw for 960 yards and ten touchdowns.

We had hoped to post our first winning record since 1990, but it didn't happen. A four-game losing streak toward the end of the year hurt, and we finished 8–8 and a disappointing third in our division. I threw for a franchise-record 3,678 yards, completed a team-record 313 passes, and was named MVP of the Pro Bowl. I appreciated the honor, and felt the fans were happy to see me chosen. But I didn't come to Seattle just to give fans and the city a Pro Bowl quarterback. I wanted to win a Super Bowl.

The business side of football slowed my start to the 1998 season. I stayed away from camp for three-and-a-half weeks as my agent, Leigh Steinberg, renegotiated my contract. I wanted to be paid fairly, and I got two years for $5 million. There was added pressure, too. The team had a new owner in Microsoft co-owner Paul Allen, and Erickson was given a playoff-or-else ultimatum.

We got off to a solid start, winning our first three games. But we then dropped our next three. We lost by a field goal at Pittsburgh. I went down with broken ribs in the second half of our game at Kansas City, our worst game performance that season, and was replaced by Jon Kitna. We lost by five at home to John Elway and the Denver Broncos, the defending Super Bowl champions. That string of losses, coupled with my injury, tested our team's resolve and shook the confidence of the Seattle fans.

We stood at 6–6 following my return, but we lost a tough game in New York against the Jets. It seemed like we could never string enough wins together. We ended the season 8–8, missing the playoffs by just one game. Coach Erickson was fired following the season and Mike Holmgren was hired away from the Green Bay Packers to fill the dual role of general manager and head coach.

When Holmgren crunched the numbers following the season, he really had no choice—it was going to cost the Seahawks too much to keep me on the roster as they worked to get under the salary cap. I was now left in the same position I was in after being cut by Minnesota two years earlier.

I had to look around for a team that wanted to take a chance on me. This time at age forty-three.

Playing at such a high level every Sunday takes its toll on your body. It takes a lot of preparation, care, and recovery time to maintain physical abilities in such a demanding contact sport. While I played, I dealt with my body almost like it was some piece of fine china.

Toward the end of my career, I lifted and ran more than when I was younger. It was not unusual for me to spend three hours a day working out. I was a workout perfectionist and probably one of the strongest weightlifters, pound for pound, on my teams. But I also focused on massages, chiropractic therapy, acupuncture, and maintaining a healthy diet. At six feet three and 218 pounds, my weight rarely fluctuated during my career. All of these techniques helped me enjoy a much longer career than was normal for my era.

I also think my throwing mechanics helped, too. Somebody mentioned that if you photographed me, I had the perfect bio-mechanics for throwing the football—high right elbow and arched back. Many of my peers thought I threw a pretty football, meaning it was a tight spiral and didn't wobble. In fact, the nail on my index finger clicked off the football on my release. You could actually hear it click, and I always needed to ask for a file during the game to keep that nail smooth.

I was extremely fortunate not to be hurt seriously on the field. Football is a physical, violent sport. I was injured only three times in all of the football that I played. I had a broken thumb, a fractured shoulder, which kept me out half the season in 1992, and broken ribs. I also had minor surgery on my knee one off-season, but I didn't miss any games. I was so conscious of staying healthy that there were times, when I went back to Los Angeles on business or to visit during the off-season, I wore a plastic cast on my right arm because everyone wanted to shake my hand. This way I could simply reach out with my left hand.

Honestly, I never took extended breaks from the time the season ended until I reported back to the team. I might take two weeks off, and then I would start back slowly. I'd sit down with Steve Waterson, our strength and conditioning coach at Houston, and we'd formulate a plan on how we wanted to attack that off-season workout. I carried that approach throughout my entire career.

I might focus one off-season on strengthening my shoulders; one year it might be the core section of my body, making sure my abs and back were strong—that became a big thing later in my career, that everything is related to your core. It was just something different all the time.

Or it might just be that I wanted to increase my overall strength, so I'd go on a crusade to strengthen myself. If I wanted to go from completing a 325-pound bench press fifteen times to a 350-pound bench press as many times, how do we do that? I always gave myself something to shoot for.

Goals also made the off-season go by quickly. They made the off-season worthwhile and, better yet, you were still competing. I never felt like I just showed up each day and went through the motions.

Teams didn't have detailed off-season programs early in my career. Those arrived on the scene ten or so years ago. In the off-season, we had two mini camps and the rest of the time you were on your own. Teams mailed a workout program that they'd hope you'd follow. Most players then lived all over the country and not in the cities where they played. Many of my teammates in Houston lived in Houston, but the numbers don't compare to what it's like now. Eighty or 90 percent of the players live in the city of their teams because management wants their players in the facility working every day.

Due to free agency, you have an influx of players every year go to different teams, anywhere from fifteen to twenty new players. You have to get all these players in one place working together so you get that cohesion and camaraderie back together as quickly as possible. Plus, you're learning a new system.

Every year some rosters change by nearly one-third. We didn't have that in the earlier days when I played. One of the things that led to my retirement was the off-season program in Kansas City. Team management wanted us at team headquarters three times a week for off-season workouts. I wanted to be with my family in Seattle because I was gone for six months during the season. I wanted to go home.

I was forty-three years old, and the coaches had me doing three-step drops and other drills that they had the young quarterbacks doing as well. I didn't need that. But because I was the quarterback, they wanted me to set an example. I understood it, but that was one of the things that swayed me away from wanting to keep playing.

I usually stuck to my own program along with the team's regimen. I made sure to do all the little things right, too, like take all the supplements and different things, eat right, and avoid alcohol. Like I mentioned before, I received a massage twice a week, saw a chiropractor twice a week, and had acupuncture treatments whenever I needed them.

I did all these things during my playing days. Current players are using that same approach, that's why you see these guys who are playing so much longer. A lot of these guys have personal trainers and assistants that travel with them.

When other guys played golf or fished or vacationed, I worked on my body. The combination of these health programs has a lot to do with why I was able to last so long and make an impact on the NFL's view of the quarterback position.

I put myself in the best situation possible to avoid any major injuries, and let dumb luck handle the rest. My arm stayed strong my entire career, and if you don't have any major knee injuries or shoulder injuries as a quarterback—I had neither—you are going to be able to play successfully for a long time if you keep your body in shape.

I always kept my body in shape, and my NFL career was a body of work that I was proud of.

As I looked at teams following my release from Seattle, I honestly liked what I saw in the Kansas City Chiefs. They needed an experienced quarterback. Their other serious roster candidates were Elvis Grbac and Todd Collins, both of whom hadn't reached thirty yet. They had forty-two career starts between them; I had 202.

My playing career ended in 2000 in Kansas City after two seasons. I didn't go out as planned—I only played in three games in two years—but I don't have any complaints.

The head coach of the Chiefs, Marty Schottenheimer, retired before the 1999 season, my first with the team. Defensive coordinator Gunther Cunningham was promoted to head coach. I arrived during this transition, and that first season ended up being tougher than I expected.

I was the backup behind Grbac, not exactly my ideal role, but I was still involved. Elvis had a good year, and we finished 9–7, a field goal short of ending 10–6 with a playoff berth. We needed to beat Oakland in our regular-season finale at Arrowhead Stadium, where we won eleven consecutive games over the Raiders. We jumped out to a 17–0 lead, but that only started the fireworks. The game featured six lead changes by the fourth quarter, and Oakland tied the game at 38–38 in the closing minute of regulation on Joe Nedney's thirty-eight-yard field goal. Nedney followed that kick with a thirty-five-yarder in overtime for the victory.

My final season in the NFL was punctuated by a 54–34 win over the defending Super Bowl champions St. Louis Rams in October, and, of course, my last career start on November, 26, 2000. Unfortunately, it wasn't a fairytale ending.

We lost 17–16 at San Diego on John Carney's fifty-two-yard field goal early in the fourth quarter. I completed twelve of thirty-one passes for 130 yards and an interception. I wasn't able to get our team in the end zone, which was frustrating. We scored on three field goals and an interception return. We dropped five straight games late in the season to fall out of playoff contention and finish 7–9.

I knew the time had come to call it a career in 2000 after seventeen seasons in the NFL. I didn't like my role. I didn't feel like I was that involved, and I started to lose that intensity in my heart. Once you start to lose it there, in your heart, then you know it's time to go. I think I played that one final year because I needed football. Felicia and I had decided to divorce after nineteen years, and I think I needed football more than it needed me at the time.

I needed something to focus on. I felt like with my divorce being final and my football career ending, all at the same time, I could start the second phase of my life with a clean slate. I called a news conference in January 2001 and made my announcement. It was emotional, but I made the right decision. I wanted to time it all together, which really fit my personality because I like how everything panned out.

Of course, there are some things that can never be planned for. I had found that out earlier in my career in a game at Cleveland.

11

Death Threat

N FL players are good targets of bad guys because of their celebrity status and wealth. Those are two reasons why team
security is such a big deal nowadays.

Each NFL team is required to contract with a security specialist—
often an ex-FBI agent—to look out for the players' physical well-
being. This person also might perform background checks on
players' personal associates and head off potential off-the-field indis-
cretions and mischief by maintaining close ties with law-enforcement
officials. They also try to make sure players aren't fleeced by scam
artists or identity thieves, and they regularly brief the team on people
and places to avoid on road trips. It was that way when I was in the
league, too.

NFL Security, which serves as the league's internal police force,
was created by league commissioner Pete Rozelle as a result of the
1963 players' betting scandal. NFL Security directors over the years
have included Jim Hamilton, the former chief of intelligence with
the Los Angeles Police Department, William Hundley, the chief of
Robert F. Kennedy's organized-crime division in the Justice Department, and Jack Danahy, a New York FBI agent. Milt Ahlerich, the
league's security director in the early 2000s, was an ex-FBI agent
himself.

In July 2008, Colonel Jeffrey Miller, the Pennsylvania police
chief who oversaw that state's investigation after a gunman two
years earlier killed five girls at an Amish schoolhouse before taking

his own life, was hired to direct the NFL's strategic-security program. It's Miller's job to work on issues involving the integrity of the game, from fan conduct to security planning.

Officially, the directors of NFL Security have attempted to protect the league against the corruption of its more than 1,500 coaches, players, trainers, owners, and referees, all of whom are potential targets for blackmail and payoffs in exchange for inside information and other favors. NFL Security is supported by a network of private investigators, mostly former officials with the Justice Department and other law enforcement agencies, who are stationed in the cities where NFL teams are based.

Teams have even gone high-tech in recent years to keep operations locked down, from protecting their sophisticated game plans and the medical status of players from leaks to outsiders, to defending ticket-holder data from potential exposure. From a player's standpoint, it's not a surprise that the league's effort to maintain a favorable public image has intensified as salaries have skyrocketed over the years.

As early as 1980, however, the Cleveland Browns were the first team to hire their own security person to complement the NFL security specialist, when they employed a retired New York City police officer to travel with the team.

The Houston Oilers and owner Bud Adams followed suit in 1982 when Adams hired Grady Sessums, a former Texas Ranger and Texas Highway Patrol officer, as the team's security director.

I never thought in a million years I would need Grady's protection. But I did.

Sessums, seventy-one years old in 2008 and retired in Abilene, Texas, with his wife, Sandra, worked for Bud Adams for fifteen years. He answered directly to Adams and actually served as security director for Adams's entire business corporation, which also included KSA Industries and Adams Resources. Sessums handled every investigation that involved Adams's farms, ranches, truck lines, automobile dealerships, coal mines, and personal properties, not to mention the Oilers. Sessums even made sure that Adams's suite in the Houston Astrodome had food and booze in it when he watched our Oiler games.

With the Oilers, Sessums primarily dealt with player behavior, which is as old as the game itself.

One of the stories most oft-repeated over the years by NFL media centered on the very first Super Bowl in 1967, when Green Bay receiver Max McGee, who thought he'd never play a down behind starter Boyd Dowler, sneaked out after curfew and partied all night, barely making the Packers' team breakfast the morning of the game. But Dowler was injured on the game's second play and McGee ended up with seven catches for 138 yards in the 35–10 victory over the Kansas City Chiefs.

Innocent fun has certainly advanced since those days.

The Super Bowl, for example, has since been designated a National Special Security Event, with none other than the Secret Service overseeing the operation. The number of police and security personnel that surround Super Bowl venues is nearly double that of a normal game. Around 2,000 were scheduled to work the 2002 Super Bowl between the St. Louis Rams and the New England Patriots, as a shaken country dealt with the aftermath of the terrorist attacks of 9/11.

At the other end of the spectrum, in May of 2008, a convicted steroids dealer met with NFL security officials in the Dallas area in May of 2008 and gave them the names of players he said bought steroids from him, according to his lawyer.

Player temptation probably won't ever stop.

Sessums dealt with many minor problems in Houston, like having to bail players out of jail. Or he'd help soothe the feelings of locals to keep others from being arrested and spending time behind bars. If Sessums thought a player needed an attitude adjustment off the field or had simply forgotten how to act, he'd advise that player to calm himself and be careful, for the good of the team and for the good of community relations.

Like the time a visiting player from Florida, who thought he might sign with Houston, was pulled over for speeding four times during the 385-mile drive from Houston to our training camp in

San Angelo. When the player jumped back into his Corvette for the drive back to Houston, Sessums alerted local police en route to keep their eyes open and suggested it might be a good idea to get the needed paperwork in order to ensure that this player paid his fines before he left Texas for good.

Sessums had a good rapport with me and other players. He initially thought I was aloof, but he later attributed that to my calm demeanor and professional approach. I liked to dot my *i*'s and cross my *t*'s in everything I did. But I also always had a quick smile for Grady, too.

During our home and away games, Sessums, with that ten-gallon cowboy hat atop his head, usually stood behind the bench or off to the side, out of the way but close enough if needed. He was always cautious when at Buffalo's Rich Stadium because the fans were so close to our bench, fifteen to twenty feet, max. Sessums enjoyed his visits to Denver's old Mile High Stadium because it literally swayed when cheering fans cranked it up a notch. Sessums believed the vibrations from that stadium were enough to start an avalanche on the nearby ski slopes, and he was probably right.

Grady also attended all of our news conferences. He worked closely with the Houston police department for our home games and with the local police department in the city of our away games. Sessums was also aware of the verbal abuse my family endured during games from crude and crass fans and was confident that posted law enforcement officers were poised and prepared to handle any situations. Grady also advised players that they needed a "business" and a "memorabilia" signature to guard against fraud.

Bottom line, Grady was a nice, friendly guy. Very professional, too; a man I trusted and counted on.

After he retired in 1997, Sessums built and sold a recreational-vehicle-storage center outside of Houston. Grady and wife, Sandra, purchased a new truck and thirty-six-foot trailer and traveled the country before they settled in Abilene. In 2008, he served as the president of the former Texas Ranger Association and the Texas Ranger Foundation, where he helped solicit funds to build an education center to preserve the true history of the Texas Rangers. Grady was a self-described good old boy who had five sisters, four of whom were older and, as he described it, owned "ass-kicking rights."

Of course, when Sessums was with the Oilers and he wanted to talk, it usually involved an issue or a concern, and it was time to be serious. When he ran toward me on the field following our Oilers game at Cleveland in 1990, I was caught off guard by what he had to say.

And I was scared as hell, too.

The weather was absolutely miserable. I was frozen, head to toe, as frigid, winter winds and snow flurries whipped across Cleveland Stadium. But I was feeling warm inside. As the final seconds ticked off the scoreboard clock at Cleveland Stadium, I couldn't wait to celebrate. My Houston Oilers teammates were all smiles as we were beating our archrivals, the Cleveland Browns, and climbing back into the NFC Central Division race.

Winning in the National Football League is difficult enough, but winning on the road and proving your critics wrong makes it extraspecial. Plus, that day—November 18, 1990—was my birthday. Yes, Warren Moon was thirty-four years old, a relic by professional-football standards. I was one of the oldest starting quarterbacks in the NFL, but I didn't feel old—childhood nicknames Pops and Daddy Warren aside, of course. I was still having fun competing and proving I could lead my team to victory.

It was a huge victory for both me and my team. By winning in these conditions, we showed the country that our run-and-shoot offense was one to be reckoned with. And I showed I had plenty of zip left in my throwing arm. Cleveland Stadium was considered among the toughest places to play in the NFL. The center-field bleachers at the east end of the Stadium held many of the home team's most avid fans and became known during the 1980s as the Dawg Pound after the barking noise that fans made to disrupt the opposing teams' offensive plays. Some of the fans even wore dog masks and threw frozen dog biscuits at us.

But today, we made sure their bark was worse than their bite.

Cleveland's defense actually gave me the best birthday gift possible: man-to-man coverage on my speedy receivers. The Browns couldn't keep pace, as I completed twenty-four of thirty-two passes for 322 yards and a career-high five touchdowns. We scored 21 fourth-quarter points to blow the game open and were just a few seconds away from evening our record to 5–5 and rejuvenating our sagging spirits. Everyone couldn't wait to get into the locker room and onto our flight back to Houston. The win set the stage for our all-important next game—before a national television audience on *Monday Night Football*, at home, against the Buffalo Bills.

I had a great game, statistically, against the Browns, though winning—not stats—was my motivation. It was the twenty-third time in my seven-year NFL career that I had thrown for more than 300 yards in a game. It was also my seventh 300-yard outing, and third consecutive, during the 1990 season. My scoring passes went to five different players and covered three, forty-six, thirty-seven, twenty-three, and seven yards. That was the balance and big-play ability I wanted to show as a quarterback.

"I've had some pretty good days on my birthday, but none like this in terms of production," I told the media following the game. "You get this old and people start talking about your age and how you can't do things. I think I showed them I have a few games left in me. We came into this game knowing we wanted to throw deeper than we had been. We wanted to throw it deep and get big plays. I was tickled pink when they went with man-to-man coverage. It's hard to cover our receivers man to man."

Catching the touchdown passes were running back Lorenzo White and receivers Haywood Jeffires, Curtis Duncan, Tony Jones, and Ernest Givins. Duncan had a game-high seven receptions for 130 yards. Givins caught five for forty-one yards, and running back Allen Pinkett snagged four for forty-six yards. Duncan praised me following the game for spreading the ball around. "Warren is a great quarterback, and I just hope he continues doing that (spreading the ball around)," Duncan said. "He is a great one. He's a Hall of Famer."

The Hall of Fame, of course, was a faraway dream of mine. This was the moment's reality.

As I grabbed my helmet off the bench and the scoreboard clock finally read zeroes, I noticed Sessums rushing toward me. Grady, who was flanked by a contingent of local police officers, didn't look like he was in the mood to help celebrate our victory. As Sessums came closer, I could see the concern in his eyes. Much like the offensive line that protects me when I drop back into the pocket to pass, I was suddenly surrounded by armed security personnel on my own sideline.

"Grady, what's wrong?" I asked.

Grady's no-nonsense tone was sharp and pointed as he pulled me close. My body went numb—not from the freezing conditions but from the message—as I tried to comprehend what Grady was telling me. I heard the words but I didn't want to believe.

"There's been a threat on your life," Grady mumbled quietly so as not to tip off the surrounding media. "And there are reasons we are taking this one seriously. This one sounds credible."

My eyes darted from side to side. One of the Cleveland police officers who had worked the game approached Grady after halftime and told him he had heard from another officer at the game that somebody had earlier said, "Warren Moon ought to be killed." After Grady and the police huddled and talked, they alerted the chain of command within the Oilers' team structure.

I scanned the stands, looked closely at everyone walking my way. Grady assured me that they had taken all appropriate measures and didn't want to alarm me, but they wanted to make sure I realized this wasn't a game, either.

But this is a game, I thought. It's the Houston Oilers versus the Cleveland Browns on a Sunday afternoon, for Christ's sake.

One moment I was ready to celebrate an important victory, and the next I was in fear for my life. It just didn't make sense. My mind was racing. I was thinking, "Somebody is threatening to kill me over a football game. You have to be joking."

My thoughts immediately reverted to my high-school career, when a member of the notorious Los Angeles gang the Crips threatened to kill me if my team at Hamilton beat archrival Crenshaw one Friday night. My coach, Jack Epstein, had the stadium circled by police. We won the game and the threat proved to be just that—a threat.

I wondered what my mom or Coach Epstein would think now, as Sessums and his armed guards surrounded me. Sessums quietly, but sternly, instructed me to stay close to him and the guards as we walked off the field. My smiling teammates, meanwhile, were jogging toward the locker room. They were oblivious to the threat on my life. The incident wasn't reported in national news wire stories on the game the following day, and hardly anyone beyond the gun-toting circle understood the ramifications.

I didn't want to believe it, either, as I stared toward the 76,000 fans in Cleveland Stadium. Was somebody out there staring back at me, with hatred in their heart, crazy thoughts in their head, and a loaded gun in their hand? The short walk to the locker room lasted what seemed like a lifetime. But it was my life, one that I wanted to live without fear.

I knew better.

The specifics of this death threat may not have been known, but I knew firsthand there were ignorant people in the world who say ignorant things. It's a sad fact of life. There was a person, possibly in the stands above me, who not only hated me as an African American quarterback but hated a race of people.

When the locker room doors closed behind me, and I felt a little more secure, I took a deep breath and began to relax. Then I asked Grady about his first words to me. "What did you mean when you said you had reason to believe 'this one' was credible?" I asked. To my complete shock, Grady told me this wasn't the first threat made on my life. However, those previous threats weren't considered serious enough to merit the tremendous protection like I had at the moment. Grady and the Cleveland police officers who worked the game believed this threat was credible.

I've always been able to push any bad things that happen to me toward the back of my mind, tucking them in an isolated corner for another day. When it came to doubters and detractors, what I did on the field and in life was always my answer. This was different though. How do you deal with a shadow? Or a smiling face in the stands that actually is a facade for an angry demon who wants to kill you?

Over a football game?

When Grady told me about the previous threats—and there had been several—he'd asked if I would rather know about them before the game or afterwards. I told him I would rather know later. I didn't want to go into a game being worried the whole time, looking in the stands and wondering. A few years after the 1990 death threat, I had another one in Cleveland. In fact, every time I played in Cleveland from then on—and even though nothing ever happened, thankfully—the threats were in the back of my mind.

And though I tried not to seem rattled, honestly, it scared the living hell out of me.

I understood that hatred can extend beyond the playing field and into daily life. I have faced it for many years. The taunts and threats were hurdles that I opted to deal with quietly. I never wanted to talk about them or share them, because I didn't want to bring any more attention to my situation. I also knew the ugly things that my family had already endured throughout my career. Like the time a Houston fan had stripped off his Oilers jersey in front of my daughter Blair, and then motioned as if he had wiped his butt with it before he threw it on the ground.

But to hear from Grady that somebody had said, "Warren Moon ought to be killed."

Well, believe me, it wasn't the Cleveland weather that sent chills up and down my spine.

12

One Regret

While my list of accomplishments can fill a news reporter's notepad, my lone regret on the field takes up one line. But it's a line that some say speaks volumes: I departed the NFL without a Super Bowl ring.

It's the goal of every player in the NFL to play for that ring. It's the Holy Grail of the NFL.

Yes, I won five consecutive Grey Cup titles in six seasons in the Canadian Football League, and I am extremely proud of each one. I had great teammates and coaches, and I wouldn't trade any of those memories or championships.

But there's only one Super Bowl. It's a huge deal for players and fans.

The Super Bowl is considered a national holiday in many living rooms around the country. Over the years the Super Bowl has become the most-watched television broadcast of the year. Ratings have indicated that on an average, 80 to 90 million fans tune in to the Super Bowl. NFL press releases have indicated that recent Super Bowls have been available to potential audiences of approximately 1 billion worldwide.

I would have loved the opportunity to play in a Super Bowl, but it didn't happen. What can I say? There's always part of you that thinks you haven't done enough. As a team, we just didn't get over that hurdle.

I played in ten playoff games—nine with Houston and one with Minnesota—and won three, all wild-card games that advanced us into the divisional round. But we never advanced past the divisional round, which sends four teams into the conference championships. The two conference champions advance to the Super Bowl.

Overall, I played in six wild-card games and four divisional games, throwing for 2,834 yards and seventeen touchdowns with fourteen interceptions. My 84.9 career playoff passer rating is eighth all-time. I lost two of four divisional games with Houston by seven points or less—Buffalo beat us 17–10 in 1989, and Denver won 26–24 in 1992. Both Buffalo and Denver were beaten in their respective AFC championship games, one win away from the Super Bowl.

Players such as Don Beebe and Mike Lodish were fortunate enough to play in six Super Bowls each during their careers, while hundreds and hundreds and hundreds of other players like me over the last four decades can only wonder what the experience felt and tasted like.

I understand that quarterbacks are measured by Super Bowl rings. It helps define greatness. There are no Super Bowls on my résumé, only championships, but that's okay, because I have learned to accept it. It wasn't meant to be. And I am truly happy for players and my fellow quarterbacks who have appeared in the Super Bowl. That's why we play the game, to reach the Super Bowl.

As of the 2008 season, Terry Bradshaw and Joe Montana, with four wins each, were tied for the most Super Bowl rings at quarterback. Next were Troy Aikman and Tom Brady with three each.

In terms of impact and historical significance, Doug Williams needs to be at the top of that list, too. Williams is best known for his MVP performance with the Washington Redskins against the Denver Broncos in Super Bowl XXII in 1988, when he became the first starting African American quarterback to reach and win the Super Bowl.

There probably isn't an African American sports fan in America who doesn't remember where he was on that day.

I was envious of Doug because I wanted to reach the Super Bowl, too. But I also felt immense pride for Doug and what he had accomplished for all African American quarterbacks, past and present. Some believe it was the greatest performance by a quarterback in the history of the Super Bowl, because no other quarterback had to carry that burden of responsibility and anxiety and perform at that level.

Other African American quarterbacks who have won Super Bowl rings are Joe Gilliam of the Pittsburgh Steelers (1974–1975), Tony Banks of the Baltimore Ravens (2000), Shaun King of the Tampa Bay Bucs (2002), Rohan Davey of the New England Patriots (2003–2004), and Charlie Batch of the Steelers (2005).

Doug was the first and only African American quarterback to win a ring as a starter. I tried my best to get there, too.

When it comes to playoff games and opportunities to reach the Super Bowl, who can forget the 1993 playoff game between the Buffalo Bills and my Houston Oilers?

I can't.

I want to, but I can't.

It's known simply as the Comeback.

I still have a difficult time talking about that game, and I refuse to watch it when it is aired on ESPN Classics. I flip the channel or turn off the television.

We finished in second place in the AFC Central Division with a 10–6 record. Our run-and-shoot offense led the league in passing with 4,231 yards, and our defense ranked third in the league, allowing only 4,532 total yards. We had nine Pro Bowl selections that season—me; receivers Curtis Duncan, Ernest Givins, and Haywood Jefferies; tailback Lorenzo White; guard Mike Munchak; center Bruce Matthews; defensive tackle Ray Childress; and linebacker Al Smith.

The Bills were the American Football Conference (AFC) champions the previous two seasons. Buffalo's no-huddle offense led the league in rushing yards (2,436) and ranked second in the league in total yards (6,114).

We beat the Bills in the final game of the regular season, 27–3. During that game, Buffalo starting quarterback Jim Kelly suffered strained ligaments in his knee, which left backup Frank Reich to finish the game in his place. With Kelly out, Reich was named the starter against us in the wild-card game at Rich Stadium in Buffalo on January 3, 1993.

We dominated the game early. I completed nineteen of twenty-two passes for 220 yards and four touchdowns in the first half. We had possession for twenty-one minutes and twelve seconds, which kept the Bills' high-powered offense off of the field for most of the game's opening thirty minutes.

Buffalo also lost starting running back Thurman Thomas early in the game to a hip injury. Thomas was replaced by Kenneth Davis, which meant the Bills had to use a second-string backfield of Reich and Davis against our third-ranked defense.

In the first quarter, I completed six of seven passes on an eighty-yard scoring drive that ended with a three-yard touchdown pass to Jefferies for a 7–0 lead. After Buffalo kicker Steve Christie made a thirty-six-yard field goal to make it 7–3, I led us on a second-quarter scoring drive that was nearly identical to the first one.

I completed six of seven passes on the eighty-yard march and finished it with a seven-yard touchdown pass to Webster Slaughter to make it 14–3. After our defense forced a three-and-out, I threw a twenty-six-yard touchdown pass to Duncan. With one minute fifteen seconds left in the first half, we drove for another touchdown, aided by an encroachment call against Buffalo on fourth-and-one. I threw a twenty-seven-yard touchdown pass to Jefferies, and we led 28–3 at the half.

I obviously felt pretty good about our chances at the half. We were aggressive on both sides of the football, but I also knew we had to continue to be aggressive. I went around and told the guys, "It's not over, it's not over." According to newspaper reports in the days following the game, the Bills' locker room at the half was pretty emotional.

Defensive coordinator Walt Corey had angrily chided his unit, saying later, "I was hollering the same things the fans were hollering at me when we left the field. I can't repeat the words, but the more I talked, the louder I got. The thing that bothered me was their approach. To me, they looked timid. They looked like they were going to get in the right spots, but they weren't going to make anything happen afterward. This is an attitude game. Sometimes you can start playing, and you're afraid to make things happen or afraid to make a mistake."

Buffalo head coach Marv Levy told his team, "You've got thirty more minutes. Maybe it's the last thirty minutes of your season. When your season's over, you're going to have to live with yourselves and look yourselves in the eyes. You'd damn well better have reason to feel good about yourselves, regardless of how this game turns out."

It appeared as if it was going to turn out in our favor.

Barely two minutes into the third quarter, defensive back Bubba McDowell intercepted Reich's first pass of the second half and returned it fifty-eight yards for a touchdown to increase our lead to 35–3. A Houston radio announcer was immortalized on NFL Films with this statement: "The lights are on here at Rich Stadium, they've been on since this morning, you could pretty much turn them out on the Bills right now."

Unfortunately, the lights did not go out on the Bills. They started to dim on us.

On our ensuing kickoff, the wind altered the ball moments before it was kicked by Al Del Greco. As a result, it became an unintentional squib kick that the Bills recovered near midfield. Buffalo then drove fifty yards in ten plays and scored on a one-yard touchdown run by Davis to cut the deficit to 35–10. Buffalo kicker Steve Christie then recovered his own onside kick, and the Bills scored on the fourth play of their drive when Reich connected with receiver Don Beebe on a thirty-eight-yard touchdown to make it 35–17 with seven minutes forty-six seconds left in the third quarter.

While Corey, the Bills' defensive coordinator, had switched from a 4–3 to a 3–4 defense in the second half, I still thought we could move the football. But we were forced to punt for the first time in the game on our next possession, and Buffalo once again had great field position at its forty-one-yard line. Reich completed an eighteen-yard pass to James Lofton, Davis gained twenty yards on a screen pass, and then Reich threw a twenty-six-yard touchdown pass to Reed that trimmed our lead to 35–24. In a span of ten minutes in the third quarter, the Bills had run eighteen plays, gained 176 yards and scored twenty-one points, while we had run three plays for three yards.

It didn't get any better for us. Henry Jones intercepted my pass and returned it fifteen yards to our twenty-three-yard line. Faced with fourth-down-and-five on the 18, Reich connected with Reed for the touchdown to make it 35–31. With the score, the Bills had cut their deficit from thirty-two points to four. Buffalo had outscored us 28–7 in the third quarter and held me to two of seven completions for nineteen yards.

We started to move the football effectively in the fourth quarter and reached the Buffalo 14. But we botched a thirty-one-yard field-goal attempt on a fumbled snap, and Buffalo recovered the ball on its 26. Faced with third-down-and-four, Davis ran for thirty-five yards and a first down. Reich then completed a nice pass to Reed for another first down. With three minutes and eight seconds left in the fourth quarter, Reich threw a seventeen-yard touchdown pass to Reed to give Buffalo its first lead of the game at 38–35.

We couldn't believe what was happening to us, but I knew we had to keep our composure and make plays. And that's what we did. We marched downfield on a sixty-three-yard drive to score the tying twenty-six-yard field goal from Del Greco to send the game into overtime.

We won the coin toss and had possession at the Buffalo 20. I opened the drive with two completions for seven yards. On third-and-three, I threw a pass intended for Givins five yards downfield. In a struggle for separation with Talley, Givins could not raise his arms to make the catch. The ball went over Givins's head and into the arms of Buffalo cornerback Nate Odomes for an interception. It was my fiftieth pass attempt—and my last—of the game. With possession at the Houston 20, Buffalo rushed twice to set up

Christie's thirty-two-yard field goal that gave the Bills the win, 41–38.

Reich finished with twenty-one of thirty-four pass completions for 289 yards, four touchdowns, and one interception. Reed had eight catches for 136 yards and three touchdowns. Davis, in place of Thomas, rushed for sixty-eight yards and a score. On our side, I completed thirty-six of fifty passes for 371 yards, four scores, and two interceptions. Givins caught nine passes for 177 yards while Jefferies had eight receptions for ninety-eight yards and two scores.

But our statistics were meaningless. We had lost the game with a team that I thought was good enough to advance in the playoffs. As I told my teammates in the locker room, we didn't finish, time ran out on us.

The game remains the largest comeback in NFL history. Ironically, in 1984, Reich also had been responsible for what was then the biggest comeback in the history of college football. As the backup for the Maryland Terrapins, Reich replaced injured starter Stan Gelbaugh and led the Terrapins back from a first-half deficit of 31–0 to a 42–40 victory over the previously unbeaten Miami Hurricanes and quarterback Bernie Kosar.

Our locker room was dead quiet after the Bills game. John McClain, the columnist for the *Houston Chronicle*, said I had a blank stare on my face. I answered everyone's questions, and then found a telephone. I called Felicia in Houston and discussed whether or not the kids should be sent to school the next day because things might be said. We decided to keep them out for one day, but it really wasn't bad for them. The entire city of Houston was in such trauma for about a week. Nobody said much of anything other than asking, "What happened?"

What happened?

I am still trying to explain it to this day.

I think to a certain point we shut it down as far as our aggressiveness on offense and in our play calling. I think our defense shut it down as far as its aggressiveness, because the things we did in the first half, really attacking and blitzing, playing a lot more man coverage, really getting in their face, that stopped. We just stopped doing that in the second half because when we got the lead, all of a sudden human nature made us say, "Okay, let's play it safe, let's play some zone and make them catch everything in front of us, let's make the tackle and keep the clock running."

Buffalo did more than just make catches. The Bills made runs after the catch, they made big chunks of yards, and the momentum just changed. Plus, it's Buffalo's Rich Stadium. I've always said it was one of the toughest places to play in the league. Plus, we played a really good football team. They had played in four Super Bowls during that era. We had just played the Bills in the regular-season finale and beat them. That's always tough, to try to come back and again beat a team that you just beat, especially going back to their place.

Our style of offense, the run-and-shoot, probably played a role in that game, too. It was predominantly a passing offense that didn't allow you to run the ball at the end of the game, to line up two tight ends and just pound the ball and eat time off the clock. Even if you didn't score, you'd try to get a couple of first downs moving the football.

Because we always looked to throw the football, our opponents were allowed to stay in close games. If you throw an incomplete pass, the clock stops. So I think the offense that we played, even though it was exciting, and I was able to do a lot of good things, it was also limiting, especially in closing out games.

The weather had a lot to do with it, too. We had to keep throwing the football, and it got windier, and the Bills were much more used to the elements. We were an indoor team. But honestly I don't think any of that hurt us that much. It was more our mentality, how we attacked the Bills in the second half as opposed to the first half.

When the momentum changed, they rode it. A lot of plays in that game could have put it away. I threw two interceptions after halftime. We had a field goal that we missed, an easy one. We had another one where our holder dropped the ball, and we got nothing out of that one. We had an interception that we could have made on defense that would have put the game away, which went right through our linebacker's hands, right into one of their receiver's hands. Little stuff like that. So I think that was a big part of it. You have to be able to play defense down the stretch, too. You can't let a team come back on you when you're up twenty-eight points.

Bottom line, it just wasn't meant to happen for us. That's how I tried to sum it up at the end of the game. Even though we got beat, when you look at all those different plays where the game could have been put away, it wasn't meant for us to win.

That game was easily the toughest defeat in my professional career.

Some of the best and most exciting games I was involved in during my NFL career were playoff games.

In a divisional game in 1992 with Houston at Denver's Mile High Stadium, we led from the opening whistle. Trailing 24–23 with two minutes, seven seconds remaining, John Elway marched the Broncos from their own two-yard line to the winning twenty-eight-yard field goal, scoring with sixteen seconds remaining. On the drive, he converted on two fourth downs. On fourth-and-six from the Denver 28, he rushed for seven yards. Then on fourth-and-ten, he completed a forty-four-yard pass to receiver Vance Johnson.

Elway's comeback in this game is known solely as the Drive II, so I am part of two game monikers—the Comeback and the Drive II. (The Drive, of course, refers to Elway's comeback against the Cleveland Browns in the 1987 playoffs, when he led Denver ninety-eight yards to tie the game with thirty-seven seconds remaining. The Broncos won in overtime, 23–20.)

I think one of the most exciting moments I experienced in Houston was our first playoff win, when we beat Seattle at home in a 1988 wild-card game. We had gone through three years of rebuilding and survived some tough times, and we finally got to the point where we made it to the playoffs, and we beat Seattle 23–20 in the Astrodome in overtime on Tony Zendejas's forty-two-yard field goal. Although we outgained Seattle 427 total yards to 250, it was a close game until the very end.

That game was a validation game for me, because it lifted a lot off my shoulders. I had carried that burden of expectation. We had struggled for three consecutive years and fans in Houston wondered if management made the right decision to sign me and give me the league's highest contract. But I felt like I had finally helped get the team to the point where we were a competitive football team.

I've always been a fan of the Super Bowl, the games and the heroes who have emerged from them.

The Super Bowl was first played on January 15, 1967, as part of an agreement between the NFL and its younger rival, the American Football League. After the league merged in 1970, the Super Bowl became the NFL's championship game, played between the champions of the league's two conferences: the American Football Conference (AFC) and the National Football Conference (NFC).

The Green Bay Packers won the first two Super Bowls and were led by quarterback Bart Starr. Super Bowl III, of course, featured one of the biggest upsets in Super Bowl history as the New York Jets, behind the guarantee of Joe Namath, defeated the eighteen-point favorite Baltimore Colts.

The 1970s, when I grew up, were dominated by the Miami Dolphins and the Pittsburgh Steelers, winning a combined six championships in the decade. The most successful franchise in the 1980s was the San Francisco 49ers, which won four titles in that decade. Led by coach Bill Walsh and quarterback Joe Montana, they were known for using the fast-paced West Coast offense.

The Dallas Cowboys were the dominant team in the early 1990s. They won three of four Super Bowls during one span and were led by quarterback Troy Aikman, tailback Emmitt Smith, and receiver Michael Irvin—all three Hall of Famers. The early

I loved chocolate cake, even as a baby in a high chair.
(COURTESY OF WARREN MOON)

Looking sporty and ready to play at ten years old in Pop Warner.
(COURTESY OF WARREN MOON)

Check out my passing form and the high-top football shoes.
(COURTESY OF WARREN MOON)

I never enjoyed taking pictures as a young guy. (COURTESY OF WARREN MOON)

High school action in Los Angeles; Hamilton against league rival Westchester. (COURTESY OF WARREN MOON)

Escaping the rush in 1974 during my one season at West Los Angeles College. (COURTESY OF WARREN MOON)

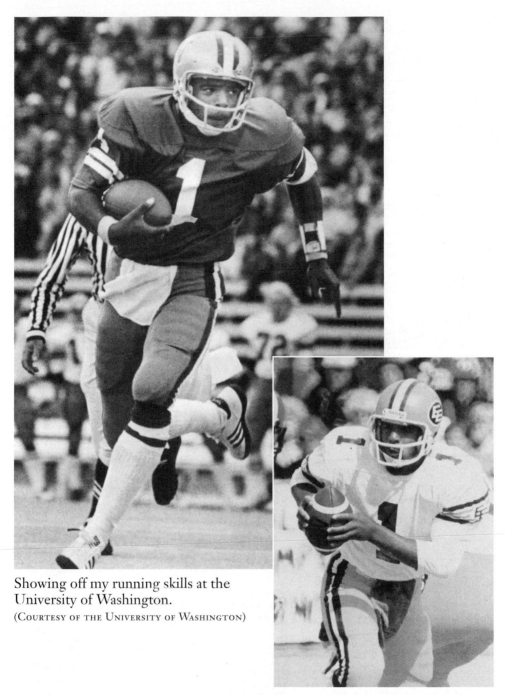

Showing off my running skills at the
University of Washington.
(COURTESY OF THE UNIVERSITY OF WASHINGTON)

Having been told by NFL teams that I would not be
drafted as a quarterback, I chose to play in Canada where
I threw for more than 21,000 yards over six seasons. Our
Edmonton Eskimo team also won an unprecedented five
straight Grey Cups, the CFL's Super Bowl.
(COURTESY OF THE EDMONTON ESKIMOS)

Oilers owner Bud Adams and I are all smiles as we shake hands after agreeing to a contract extension. (COURTESY OF AND THANKS TO THE HOUSTON OILERS/TENNESSEE TITANS)

Firing a pass into the flat with the Houston Oilers.
(COURTESY OF AND THANKS TO THE HOUSTON OILERS/TENNESSEE TITANS)

Check out my cowboy hat and belt buckle as I pose in front of the Alamo.
(Courtesy of the *Houston Chronicle*)

After the Oilers decided I was too old, they traded me to Minnesota, where I passed for more than 4,200 yards in each of my first two seasons with the Vikings. (COURTESY OF MINNESOTA VIKINGS FOOTBALL, LLC)

Marlin Briscoe, the first African American quarterback to start an NFL game in the modern era, joins me at the L.A. proclamation ceremony.
(COURTESY OF COUNCILMAN BERNARD PARKS)

The 2006 NFL Hall of Fame class (L–R): Harry Carson; Rayfield Wright; Warren Moon; Reggie White's widow, Sara; John Madden; and Troy Aikman.

Posing with my good friend Leigh Steinberg, who presented me at the Hall of Fame in Canton, Ohio.

Bernard Parks, L.A. City Councilman and my youth football coach, awarding me city proclamation in 2008.
(COURTESY OF COUNCILMAN BERNARD PARKS)

Mandy and I celebrating Ryken's christening.
(COURTESY OF WARREN MOON)

Joshua, Blair, Warren, Jeffrey, Chelsea, and my grandson, Trey (front).
(COURTESY OF WARREN MOON)

1990s also featured the Buffalo Bills, who beat my Houston Oilers in that 1993 wild-card game and appeared in four consecutive Super Bowls but lost all of them. Quarterback John Elway and the Denver Broncos upset the Packers in Super Bowl XXXII in 1998 to snap the NFC's thirteen-game winning streak. In turn, the Broncos' victory started a streak in which the AFC won eight of the next ten Super Bowls.

The New England Patriots were the dominant team of the early 2000s, winning the title in three of the first five years of the decade behind quarterback Tom Brady.

In another proud moment, Indianapolis's Tony Dungy became the first African American head coach to win the Super Bowl when his Colts defeated the Chicago Bears on February 4, 2007. The Patriots accomplished an NFL first during the 2007 season when they finished the sixteen-game regular season undefeated, which included a road win over the defending Super Bowl champion Colts. But the New York Giants and quarterback Eli Manning upset the Patriots in Super Bowl XLII.

It's an instant-access world, and when fans Google the greatest players to have never won a Super Bowl, my name appears on that list. And fans often asked if it bothers me.

Honestly, it bothers me, and it doesn't bother me, but it was something that disappointed me because it was one goal that I wasn't able to accomplish. I exceeded a lot of other things that I never dreamt that I would do, but I thought that I would win at least one championship. But a lot of great players—and great quarterbacks, even Hall of Fame quarterbacks—haven't won a Super Bowl.

You look at Dan Marino, you look at Dan Fouts, Hall of Famers like me, and you look at some other guys who never won a Super Bowl. There are pretty good quarterbacks on that list. Fouts, in fact, set a precedent in 1993 when he became the first Hall of Fame quarterback never to have played on a Super Bowl or an NFL/AFL championship team. Fouts went on record and said, "The Super Bowl is a year; the Hall of Fame is a career."

A lot of great players haven't won a Super Bowl, but I didn't want to be on that list.

So many things have to happen within the team concept for you to win a championship. It just didn't happen during my NFL career with Houston, Minnesota, Seattle, and Kansas City. When you look at a guy like Trent Dilfer, who was maligned his whole career, and then he got in the right situation and won a Super Bowl with the Baltimore Ravens in 2001. It just shows it can happen to anyone if the right combination of offense and defense clicks on game day. Every player on the field plays for that championship.

I had some championship years at other levels, but I would have loved to have gotten one during my NFL career.

13

Wearing Number One

I wore number one on the front and back of my football jersey for two reasons. That number represented my goals to be the best and to be a leader. I took both seriously.

I first wore number one in my junior season at the University of Washington. I actually wanted that jersey number in high school at Hamilton, but we just didn't have it. You selected a numbered jersey that hung in the equipment room. If the numbered jersey wasn't there, it wasn't available.

I first got the idea to wear number one when I watched Ohio State quarterback Cornelius Green on television. The number looked like it fit Green perfectly. Green led Ohio State to a 42–21 Rose Bowl victory over Southern Cal during my senior year in high school in 1974, and he was named the most valuable player in the game.

The number one seemed perfect to me, too.

It symbolized my desire to be the number-one quarterback on my team. I also wanted the responsibility that came with that position. Plus, the number one reminded my teammates where I wanted us to be as a team: Number One. It was a symbol that my teammates always looked to. They knew how I felt about them and where I believed they belonged, too—at the top as one of the best.

Wearing number one also meant that I had to do the right things, the right way, at the right time, to set the right example. Then, when my teammates saw that number one displayed, they followed me and tried to perform to the best of their abilities and make the right plays, too.

When I was at the University of Washington, my teammates gave me the nickname One Dog. That eventually became Top Dog. When my teammates recognized me by my jersey number and by names like One Dog and Top Dog, I knew my message had gotten through to my team. When that happened, it also enabled me to become a better leader.

I also reminded my teammates that the hardest part of being number one was staying there. Number one meant you had a bull's-eye on your back.

When I joined the Edmonton Eskimos in the Canadian Football League and we won five consecutive Grey Cup championships, we had a bull's-eye on our back every game. We had to bring our A game every week because every opponent wanted to knock our heads off. That didn't change when I signed the richest contract in league history and joined the NFL in 1984. I had to prove I was worth every cent. We made seven consecutive playoff appearances (1987–1993) when I was with Houston, and I was proud of what we accomplished.

Honestly, that's the way I wanted to be looked at by the competition. When you are at the top of your profession or at the top of the league standings, you are a measuring stick for other players and other teams. By wearing the number one, it was my job as the team's leader to make sure we were not complacent and that we remembered our goals to be the best.

I've always believed I needed to be held accountable for my performances—good or bad. And that meant dealing with the media following games. As a leader, one thing you never want to do is duck out on those guys. The media can make or break you. I quickly learned that, if anything, it made more sense to take the blame even when it wasn't my fault.

There were many times after games when I stood up on that podium and told the media, "We lost, and I didn't play well enough for us to win, and I have to play better next week." I might have thrown for 300 yards in that game, but I took all the blame because I knew I could shoulder it.

There were just many times when my teammates approached me and asked, "Why did you say all of that? It wasn't your fault." My then wife Felicia got mad. "Why did you say that? It wasn't your fault." It made it so much easier for me and so much easier for everyone else. If I blamed myself, what else could the media ask me? What else could the media poke me about? I already said that I wasn't good enough today. That was as cut and dried as you could get. That's why I wore number one. I wanted to be that leader. I handled it.

I've been asked many times where and how I learned to be politically correct, for the lack of a better description. I don't think it was one particular person. Maybe it came from my interest in politics. I really followed politics as a kid because my mom was so into it. When you have only one or two televisions in the house, you watch what your mom watches. She loved politics. That's another reason why I got hooked on soap operas. My mom watched them, and I had to watch them. I was hooked. You may laugh, but I watched *All My Children* and *General Hospital* until I was an adult.

My agent and dear friend Leigh Steinberg also provided a lot of wisdom and talked to me about different things. Leigh told me, "You never are going to be wrong taking the blame." He was right. I never was wrong when I shouldered the blame.

I made it simple when I met with the media after games. I didn't get into Xs and Os. I always made sure I was the last player who talked, too. That was another lesson that Leigh taught me. I wanted to make sure I composed myself and got my thoughts together after a game. I always wanted to look proper and professional when I met the media, too, so I dressed beforehand. I never did interviews with a towel wrapped around my waist in front of my locker.

I always met the media in a group setting, so I didn't have to answer a million of the same questions over and over in a one-on-one interview. As I mentioned, I always waited until my teammates had talked. I then met with a member of the team's media-relations department to get a feel for what everyone had said. I wanted to make sure I followed with the same theme. I also repeated what our head coach had told us because I wanted my interview to be an extension of his thoughts. Whatever his comments were to us about why we lost or why we won, that's what I repeated to the media so it all sounded like one voice.

Even in games, I knew I had to be a calming influence. But there was one time, in 1989 with the Houston Oilers, when I lost my composure. We were playing Kansas City, and Chiefs linebacker Derrick Thomas, a talented rookie who died tragically in 2000 following a single-vehicle accident, shoved me out of bounds. I was frustrated because we hadn't played well, and when Derrick gave me that extra shove, it added insult to injury. I ended up near the Kansas City bench, which is not the best spot to lose your temper—on the opponent's sideline—but I retaliated and threw the football at Derrick. We tussled underneath the bench, but I really didn't care at the moment. I told Derrick that I wasn't a rookie and I didn't appreciate what he had done.

But that's football. There was so much chaos around you. Guys lost their tempers. It's an extremely physical game, and somebody had to be a voice of reason, and I always felt I had to be that voice in the huddle. There had to be one person who my teammates could look to and know that everything was okay, that everything was under control, and that person was me. Once I stepped into the huddle, it was my huddle. Everything else that was being said at that moment stopped. The only voice in the huddle was mine. That's why I wore number one.

With so many different personalities on a team, I had to make sure I was on the same page with my teammates, especially with my receivers. They all wanted the football. All of them thought they were open on every play, some of them more than others. That was the nature of the beast with the receivers on every team I had played on.

If a receiver was upset about not getting the football, he usually mentioned it to me in a one-on-one conversation during the week, or even during the game. They never used a tone like, "I am open, so why don't you throw it to me?" It was more, "You may want to look at me on that route because I am getting open." Nobody ever challenged me in a group setting or a team meeting because they didn't get enough passes thrown their way.

One of the most talented receivers I played with was Cris Carter in Minnesota. Cris was always in my ear, chirping that he wanted the football. If Cris wasn't open, he'd always try to figure out a way to beat the coverage. He might make up a play or script some variation of a play that got him open. And Cris knew how to get open—when he left the Vikings after the 2001 season, he held most of the team's career receiving records.

Cris and I had a great rapport. I helped Cris set the NFL single-season record for receptions with 122 in 1994. A year later, however, that record was broken by Detroit's Herman Moore. Toward the end of the 1995 season, Cris wanted me to get him more receptions to keep pace with Herman, but we weren't able to get him the ball as much as he liked. So he got a little upset about it and complained to the media. We quickly met one on one, and I straightened him out.

Tough love. That also came with wearing number one.

There are some famous number ones in other sports. Oscar Robertson, Ozzie Smith, Pee Wee Reese, and Billy Martin, just to name a few, all wore jersey number one in their respective sports.

There are seven players in the football Hall of Fame, including myself, who wore number one as their primary number—Earl "Curly" Lambeau (class of 1962), Jimmy Conzelman (1964), John "Paddy" Driscoll (1965), Ray Flaherty (1976), Benny Friedman (2005), and Fritz Pollard (2005).

Many sports organizations, such as the NFL, follow strict guidelines when it comes to jersey numbers. The NFL began to assign jersey numbers in 1952. The league updated its system in 1973 and made it even more rigid. For example, numbers one to nineteen are worn by quarterbacks, kickers, and punters. But there's a loophole that says wide receivers also are permitted to wear numbers ten to nineteen as well.

Jersey numbers can be a big deal for athletes, too. Following the career of Michael Jordan, for example, his basketball jersey number, twenty-three, took on a special significance. Basketball players, not to mention athletes in a vast array of sports, want to wear this number in honor of the iconic Jordan.

Bottom line, I liked the number one because I felt like I could lead teams. My good friend Lorenzo Romar, the head basketball coach at the University of Washington, said I wore number one as well as anyone because of my leadership ability. He laughed and said when I emerged from the womb, I probably told doctors who in the room should hold me. Romar felt I was born to lead. It's also a quality that I strengthened over time through my experiences on and off the field.

Throughout my career, from high school to college to the pros, I watched other quarterbacks compete and lead teams. And on every level, I compared myself to them—from natural skill, to passing ability, to leadership qualities—and I always felt I was as good as anybody that played the game. I never told anybody that at the time, but in my mind, that's what I deeply believed. I had an inner confidence that I could evaluate myself against other competition, and just kind of put myself up against other people and realize that I was as good, or better, than the players I competed against.

I never showed that in my personality or anything like that, but I never lost confidence in myself. I wanted people to acknowledge my potential without my having to toot my own horn. I wasn't comfortable with that particular personality trait. I was confident, but I wasn't going to promote myself. I always hoped that somebody saw the light, or saw my ability and wanted to take a chance. And fortunately, some people did along the way.

People never questioned my arm strength or my footwork. Instead they questioned the intangibles that came along with the position, such as decision-making and leadership abilities.

Even as a kid in Baldwin Hills, I studied all the plays and knew the assignments of my teammates. I thought that made me a better leader. I never just winged it in a game. If our coach Bernard Parks gave me ten plays to study, or the entire playbook, I studied the plays, and I studied the playbook. I wanted to be there for my teammates. I wanted them to believe in me.

As I grew older, I played with a sense of payback for my doubters. Not only did I feel that way for myself, but I also felt this other obligation, this other responsibility as a black man, that I had to do well in order to help others. It appeared that for every one of us that got the opportunity, which wasn't many during that time, the better we performed, the more doors would be opened for the other young guys along the way. Especially once I reached the NFL.

In the NFL you are placed on a pedestal, especially by young kids looking up at you and wondering if they might have an opportunity to play that position. I was providing that same motivation that James Harris, Roman Gabriel, and other guys gave me when I was a young up-and-coming player. The payback feeling was always there—always kind of inside of me—thinking, *I'm going to show you. I'm going to show you either that you made a mistake or I'm going to show you that I belong.*

You can only go by what your agent tells you, as far as which teams are interested in you as a quarterback and which teams aren't. You don't know which teams or representatives are really for you and which ones are really against you in terms of race.

There was an overall stereotype at the time I played about what African American quarterbacks could do. Somehow, some way, somebody had to change that, and it wouldn't happen all at once, but it would be a cumulative effect of a bunch of guys doing very well.

During my era, there were quarterbacks like Doug Williams, winning the Super Bowl, or Randall Cunningham, with his exciting play, who were able to change the minds of a lot of people in the NFL that African Americans could play that position at a very high level. I thought the consistency I displayed during my career also helped change minds. Our group of players managed to open a lot of doors for a lot of younger guys.

I always understood that the most effective way to lead others well is to lead yourself well first. People notice how you lead yourself—how you manage your energies, your time, your activities—and follow suit based on what they like about your style. I always tried to incorporate things that were successful for me off the field to my teammates on the field.

Playing quarterback involves a combination of many things, most notably a short memory. Despite what happened the previous play, good or bad, you still have to come up with the next play. Did something bad happen? Did something good happen? Was it the play itself, or was it one of your offensive linemen? Do you have to deal with that before you even get into the next play? Was it one of your receivers that you have to deal with before you call the next play? Do you wait on it until the next play, or until the next time you go to the bench because you don't have time to deal with it on the field? All these different things go through your mind in just a few seconds.

When you get older, even though some of your physical abilities start to fade a little bit, the game becomes so much slower for you, and so much more relaxed. I wouldn't say it became more fun for me, but it definitely got easier to play.

During my career and in retirement, I always felt that if I was in the same system my whole career as some of those other guys, like a Dan Marino or like a Joe Montana or a John Elway or even like a Brett Favre, who spent the majority of his career with the Green Bay Packers before he signed with the New York Jets in 2008, I thought things may even have been easier for me.

But, like many players at this stage of the game, I had to learn different offenses everywhere I went, so I never got to the point where I perfected them like I wanted to. There's no telling what I would have done if I had.

Given a choice, I would probably take the run-and-shoot offense that we ran in Houston, because that system is much more complex. You are delegating the whole time on how to do everything, based on what the next play is going to be. What can you deal with within that time frame to get yourself ready for the next play and execute successfully? You're almost anticipating the call, because you've gone through all the situations in practice that week.

It is third-and-seven, and I have a list of the top five plays that I like on third-and-seven that I go into the game with. I'm just anticipating that hopefully our offensive coordinator is going to come with this one. If that comes, it's great, and if it doesn't, I go ahead and execute whatever play is called. But then I've got to get up to the line, and that could change based on what the defense is going to do.

All these things rest directly on the quarterback and team leader's shoulders. I've felt them there before. I knew that kind of pressure would be there during my career, and I knew what I could do, but I wanted to make sure my teammates also had confidence in me. During these pressure situations, it was good to have that number one on my chest and back—it gave me a visual to use to refocus myself and to draw my teammates onto the same page.

When the game was on the line, I wanted the ball to be in my hands rather than to pass the responsibility on. It all stems from an ultracompetitive quality I'd developed over the years of playing junior college and college ball. During those two-minute drills, the outcome of the game is pretty much in your control. You had to take it over with your skills, make things happen.

I loved playing in this environment because it was a challenge, something I am used to overcoming. When the game was in my hands, I wanted that win—that extra something to be successful. I deserved to wear the number one and wanted you to know why.

After the years and seasons wear on you, you begin to notice you're one step slower, or a few yards shorter when you throw the ball downfield. All these things are expected for a player—some happen sooner rather than later for some players.

I was fortunate enough to maintain my skill set for seventeen years in the NFL. I had an opportunity to compete every Sunday. I got to show people what I could do on a football field. I led a group of guys weekly and helped push them for success. When I retired, I lost some of those chances to lead and show what I could do. But I understood my responsibility as a role model more clearly at the end of my career than I did at the beginning. And even today, I take that responsibility seriously.

Understanding my impact as a role model, I've tried to help people who can't help themselves by establishing scholarship funds at Hamilton High in Los Angeles, at the University of Washington, and through the Crescent Moon Foundation. Leigh Steinberg said that at a banquet a few years ago, the emcee asked every college graduate whose scholarship I had paid for to stand. One by one they stood, until an entire room was filled with college grads whose scholarships I had funded, representing thousands and thousands of dollars and dreams. Leigh also remembers walking into the home of a young African American quarterback; two photographs were on the wall above his trophy case—one was of Martin Luther King; the other was of Warren Moon.

I may have counted my pennies, but Leigh, of course, made me millions of dollars through his negotiating style. He also instilled in me his philosophy about giving back and using your status as a professional athlete to make a difference in communities where you live.

Whether I wore the number one on my jersey on a football field or in my mind at a fund-raising dinner, the principles are still the same. I want to remind those I work with what our goal is and how to achieve that success. And I want to be reminded what my role is in that success. As the leader, the majority of that responsibility to be successful is on my shoulders.

I've traded in my football jersey for a suit and tie, now. But I never traded my principles on leadership—the definition of number one for me. I still want my Crescent Moon Foundation—my new team—to be number one. The only real difference between putting the bull's-eye on my team's backs and my foundation's back is that with my foundation, no one wants to see you fail and fall from grace.

I've been fortunate enough to have many great teammates throughout my career, on the field and off the field, especially while growing up. Much of my success can be attributed to qualities my mother, Pat Moon, instilled in me while I was growing up. She had a great sense of pride. She didn't come from a lot, and we didn't have a lot. But you would never know it because of the pride that she had, and she always showed that face to us. She always kept me motivated—just seeing what she did to help me reach the level that I did—whether it was providing equipment for me, or the money that it took to register for some of these programs I was involved in, or driving me to practice or to games.

Here she was trying to raise six other kids and working a job through the night and providing for all of us as well. It was a tremendous sacrifice on her part to try and not only make my life full, but all the rest of the kids' lives full. I owe a tremendous amount of gratitude to her for that.

I wanted Mom to know, and to see, what she meant to me, and that all her sacrifices had made both of us special.

I wore number one for Mom.

14

Forty Seconds, Whistle to Whistle

One reason many NFL owners and general managers were able to say that a black man couldn't be a quarterback was because of the extraordinary amount of information that you had to process during the forty seconds between plays. For many years, this was the excuse: There is simply too much to process, and blacks are not mentally up to the task.

It was the subtle racism in questioning a black quarterback's Wonderlic score, which has become best known for its use in the NFL predraft assessments of prospective players. Defenses are mind-bogglingly complex, and liberal personnel substitutions are the norm. Learning to recognize them week-to-week can be a staggering task, especially since the game is played in fast-forward.

Team management wondered if a black quarterback could really do all this. Forty seconds is not much time. Television commercials are longer.

In order to better understand what all this means let me take you through a single play.

My favorite was Trips Right or Trips Left. Right or Left depended on the formation, called Scat, and the play was run with three receivers to one side. It was a play I ran often with the Minnesota Vikings, and the reason I liked it so much was that it gave me so many different options after the ball was snapped. But I had to be able to process and communicate a lot of information in a quick period of time to be successful.

That's an important component of being a quarterback, much like being a leader in the business world.

This particular play speaks volumes when you are talking about leadership, decision making, knowing your personnel, understanding the strengths and weaknesses of each player, and understanding the opponent and playing off their weaknesses.

A quarterback has to cram a lot of information and be able to communicate it during the forty-second window from the time the referee whistles the previous play dead to the time the play clock ticks to zero. Your brain must work quickly, and you must make good, smart decisions.

One of my best games with the Vikings was at home against the New Orleans Saints on November 19, 1995. I completed twenty-five of thirty-two for 338 yards and four touchdowns without an interception in the 43–24 victory. As the second quarter wound down, we wanted to put some more points on the board to extend our 27–7 advantage heading into halftime.

We had first-and-ten at the New Orleans 24 with nineteen seconds left in the quarter. I looked toward our sidelines and offensive coordinator Brian Billick signaled in what he wanted called. We were on the same page. I leaned into my huddle and called my favorite play:

"Trips Right, Scat Right, DigYseamX8, on two."

There's a lot to accomplish in the forty seconds between plays. Call it organized chaos.

Both teams need to call offensive and defensive plays, substitute appropriate personnel groups, possibly change offensive and defensive plays, and let's not forget, snap the ball on time. Across the line of scrimmage, the defense doesn't sit still and twiddle its thumbs. It shuffles players on and off the field, depending on its scheme, which is usually dictated by down, distance, and field position. Both units try to keep an eye on each other, but there's not much time for cat-and-mouse maneuvers.

Coach Billick and I had a good rapport. During the practice week that led up to the New Orleans game, I was able to incorporate my top five plays wanted in the game plan in certain situations, just like in this moment against the Saints. A lot of quarterbacks in the league are not given that opportunity. But it's a great example of communication between me as a leader on the field and Billick as the offensive coordinator and architect of the offense. The chain of command needs to work together and have an open line of communication. We exchanged ideas and discussed what we felt worked best.

As a quarterback, I hoped Coach Billick understood what plays made me the most comfortable and that was based on what we practiced during the week, how practice had gone, how those plays looked and how I felt about them. They were all part of the game plan and our strategy.

Since we were in our two-minute offense against the Saints, we had our best three receivers on the field—Cris Carter, Jake Reed, and Qadry Ismail—and that usually meant we wanted to throw the football. I also wanted Amp Lee in the backfield in this situation because of his pass-catching abilities. Amp was our two-minute back. He had a special skill set that made him valuable in certain situations, and I wanted to make sure we incorporated him into our scheme. Our tight end, Andrew Jordan, also was on the field and gave me a fifth pair of hands, the most eligible pass receivers allowed on a given play in the NFL.

I had just hit Carter on a short pass completion for a first down, and he stepped out of bounds at the New Orleans 24. At that moment, I had already started to anticipate the next play from Coach Billick based on the situation—we were near the red zone (the twenty-yard line)—and based on the five plays I had given him earlier in the week.

I had scripted my top five plays for every situation—first-and-ten passes, second-and-medium, second-and-long, third-and-medium, and third-and-long. I wasn't sure what play was coming next from the sideline, but I hoped. I counted on it being one of the plays that I had given to Coach Billick during the week.

It was.

Helmet radios were invented in 1956 and used by the Cleveland Browns but were then banned until 1994. At one time only one player, the quarterback, was allowed to get instruction radioed in from the sidelines. But now defensive players also have been given the same advantage. By design, this new communication window is supposed to supplant hand signals. But bottom line, the players still have to execute the play that has been called.

In 1993, the NFL changed its play-clock rule between plays and reduced it from forty-five seconds to forty seconds. According to statistics compiled by the league through the first fifteen weeks of the 1992 season, an average of 14.35 seconds remained on the forty-five-second clock when the center bent over the ball and 9.42 seconds were left when he snapped it.

After Carter stepped out of bounds against the Saints, we were on the clock. And we had to snap the ball in forty seconds.

The first thing I heard in my helmet from Coach Billick was the name of the personnel group. At Minnesota for this particular play (Trips—three receivers) the personnel group was called Eagle. I didn't have to hear the call, I could see it, too. Any player coming in the game from the sidelines quickly flapped his arms in the motion of two wings.

Everywhere I went, Trip receivers might have had a different name, such as Tiger. Tiger at Minnesota, however, was two tight ends and two receivers. That's why they say that when players change teams, learning the new terminology is the biggest obstacle. There is so much overlap in the league. Say a Two Route for the New York Jets is a Curl and the Two Route for another team is the Slant. You have to rethink everything. That is a problem because you want it to be automatic.

When a receiver breaks the huddle and he hears the number two being called, he might think *Slant*—but the number two was a Slant on his old team and the number two is a Curl on this team. Honestly, players want to take the thinking out of the game as much as possible so it becomes automatic. A player doesn't want to break the huddle and, in the heat of battle, revert back to a play or technique he learned somewhere else. That happened to me, too, but usually it was during practice.

When Eagle formation was signaled in, I knew what group of players were expected on the field, and I knew I'd like whatever play was relayed in. There were always plays that I liked a little bit better than others, but I was confident in our game plan and in Coach Billick. We had done a great job moving the football against the Saints' defense to that point.

If I had a free moment, this was the time I normally tried to sneak a peek at the Saints sidelines. But I knew in this situation, first-and-ten and their twenty-four-yard line with just nineteen seconds remaining in the first half, they weren't about to run too many different players in, unless they needed fresh linemen. They had their best personnel to match our personnel, and I expected them to stay in their nickel package (five defensive backs). What I looked for was how they wanted to play us. By film study during the week, I had a pretty good idea how they liked to defend a two-minute offense, whether they implemented zone coverage, man-to-man, or mixed it up.

When the team was huddled, nobody talked but me. Everyone did their talking before I entered the huddle. There was never any chaos or confusion in my huddle. A player may have been pissed about something, but I came up with whatever I needed to say and calmed him down. The play clock was ticking.

There were other factors involved, aside from down and distance. The hash marks were important, too. When I ran the Trips formation I wanted to be on the wide side of the field. Even if you were in the middle of the field, most teams called Trips Right because most quarterbacks, like me, are right-handed.

The next call from Billick was formation—Scat, which meant strong-side hot. That simply meant the side where the tight end lined up, which gave me a six-man protection: center, two guards, two tackles, and the tight end. The tight end was also my strong hot side read on a pass pattern if the defense blitzed a linebacker or a cornerback. Adjustments had to be made quickly.

Depending on where the safeties lined up as I got to the line of scrimmage, I could change Scat to Scram, which alerted the offensive line and my running back, Amp Lee, to slide the protection to their right. When I dropped back into the pocket, I knew I was protected to the right side because I knew that's where the strength of the defense was coming from.

Our play—DigYseamX8—represented pass routes. Reed was lined up to my left at receiver. Jordan was strong-side right. Carter was in the slot to my right, and Ismail was on the outside right at receiver. What I liked about this particular play was that it had so many layers to it.

For instance, the safeties were my fixed compass point. They helped me plot my course of action. If I looked across the line of scrimmage and I had two high safeties in the defensive backfield, Jordan, our tight end, would go down the middle and try to bring one of the safeties inside with him. I could throw the ball to Jordan if the safeties separated too much. If one of the safeties shadowed Jordan, Carter ran a corner route and Ismail sat down in the flat. If the cornerback stayed down with Ismail, I looked over the top to Carter. But if that same cornerback drifted back with Carter, I'd hit Ismail for an easy chunk of yardage.

Again, I loved this play because it had so much variety.

I loved to throw the backside route to Reed if it was open. Jake was a big, physical receiver. If Jake was lined up against single coverage, he'd automatically be my first option because I always wanted to take a shot at the backside route. If I didn't get single coverage, Ismail sat down on the outside in the flat. If the corner bit on Ismail, I knew Carter could beat the safety over the top. I think every receiver has his favorite route, and Carter loved the corner route. We tried to get that corner route for him any way we could. Cris was so good at how he sold the post pattern (spring downfield and then cut toward middle of the field) and he was explosive on his break to the outside. I'd throw the pass high on his outside shoulder on the corner, and he'd let his athleticism take over.

When Carter stepped out of bounds, I quickly looked at the scoreboard clock. Nineteen seconds remained. I would have loved nothing more than to put up another seven points on the board.

My helmet receiver, under the rules, was disabled with fifteen seconds left on the play clock, and most of the time I received information until the last possible second. But Coach Billick was great about giving me the play as fast as he possibly could so I had enough time to decipher it, get everyone on the field and get to the line of scrimmage so if I had to change the play based on the defense I had time to do that.

If Coach Billick was slow to select a play and slow to call it in, that meant I was slow to the line, which gave me less time to review my options. The faster the play was called in, the faster I called it and the faster the offense got to the line of scrimmage. If the defense showed a scheme and I knew our play wouldn't work, that gave me time to audible (call another play) out of it. I wanted to break the huddle with fifteen seconds left on the play clock. We'd get to the line and in position with twelve seconds remaining and usually get the play off at the seven-second mark.

That gave me enough time to get out of a play if I didn't think it would work. We had a check system to accomplish this—they were called must checks and advantage checks. Must checks meant the play wouldn't work if I don't get out of it. Advantage checks meant it was a good play, but it could be a really big play if I audibled to another call. If it's an advantage check, and I don't have enough time to get out of the play, I might as well run it. If it's a must check and it's going to be a disaster, and I don't have enough time to change it since the clock is running down, well, just chalk it up to the defense or call a time-out. But you really don't want to burn your time-outs. You can call time-outs in the first half and get away with it, but you really want to save your time-outs in the second half of a game.

As I approached the line against the Saints on first-and-ten from their twenty-four-yard line, I made my pre-snap read. I looked at their defensive configuration and it was pretty basic—four down linemen, two linebackers, and five defensive backs. It was the Saints' nickel package.

I looked at their two safeties in the middle of the field, because they were going to tell me what they were going to do. Since they stayed two high, I stayed with Trips Right. I knew if one of the safeties gave ground and the corner on Ismail's side dropped back, my read was to go to Ismail. If not, I wanted to give Carter a hard look over the top. I also had a chance at my tight end in the middle of the field, but I wasn't as confident in Jordan's pass-catching abilities. I also thought I wanted a sideline pass in order to stop the clock and not use one of my timeouts.

As we broke the huddle and got to the line, this was an opportunity for me to talk to or signal my receivers. I might want one of them to run a variation of their route. I might tell Carter, for example, instead of running the corner route, stay inside, and I can throw it on your inside shoulder. I might tell Reed, "If you get pressed at the line, I will throw you the fade."

When I played with Houston, we had a lot of hand signals. I might grab my facemask or tap the inside of my leg to change a route. But it wasn't anything extravagant like what you may see with the Colts' Peyton Manning, whose arm flaps, leg stomps, shouts, and wild gesturing are being mimicked in Pop Warner football. But that's also in part because the Colts don't huddle on offense, and Peyton calls his plays at the line of scrimmage.

Still, huddle or no huddle, every quarterback has to be quick. Once I got to the line of scrimmage, I reacted to the defense. If, all of a sudden, a safety drops back or a cornerback steps inside toward the line, I need to change our protection. I have to be able to communicate to ten other guys during that short time frame. That alerts everyone to what they are supposed to do. That alerts receivers who now might run a hot route if a linebacker or corner blitzes.

That's why a pre-snap read is so important—that eliminates a certain defense, unless they do something at the snap of the ball. So right there, I eliminated one side or another. I knew where I wanted to go with the ball against the Saints because of the defensive look that I saw across the line. All these things helped simplify the game. The more I simplified the game, the easier it was. You hear about players talking about how the game slows down. That happens because you've made it so simple, and you don't have to think about it. It becomes automatic. It's quick process. It's repetition. It's confidence in your ability to make the play.

Take a young quarterback, for example. If he's coming out of the huddle and he's still not sure where all of his guys are going to be, it's hard for him to pay attention to the defense. Veteran quarterbacks reach a point where they know where guys are going to be against every possible defensive look, so they're able to pay extra attention to the defense as they approach the line.

Of course, Coach Billick was also in my helmet, giving me some extra things to look for that he anticipated. But the coaches have more information on their charts than I have in my mind.

Once I put my hands under center, it was go time.

The ball was on the left hash mark, and we were in our Trips formation Right. I didn't see any surprises from the Saints' defense.

The ball was snapped, and I took my five-step drop in the pocket. New Orleans rushed four down linemen and everyone else dropped back into zone coverage (every player was responsible for an area). The cornerback on Reed's route to my outside left held with help over the top from one of the safeties. Jordan raced down the middle of the field and split the safeties. Carter took his man downfield on a corner route near the ten-yard line. The cornerback who had played soft on the outside against Ismail—he was lined up seven yards deep—drifted back and helped cover Carter.

That left Ismail wide open in the flat. I had an easy choice.

I flicked the pass to Ismail around the twenty-yard line. He turned and veered towards the sideline, running eight yards before diving out of bounds at the Saints' twelve-yard line for a twelve-yard gain. We moved the chains, first down. The play took five seconds, and fourteen seconds remained on the game clock. The play worked perfectly, just like it was drawn up and run in practice.

Anytime I got to the line of scrimmage, I always wanted to think we could score a touchdown. If I got the right defensive look, I'd take a shot. While I also realized that being successful as a leader is being a risk taker—ask any businessman—I knew the last thing I wanted to do was put my team in a bad position, or force a pass that was tipped or intercepted. We weren't in a desperate situation against the Saints. We were also in field-goal range and I wanted to make sure we put points, any points, on the board.

This time, safer was better.

Against the Saints on this particular play, I decided to take what the defense gave me—a twelve-yard completion to Ismail for a first down. Again, I knew by watching film and how they had played us on that drive that they defended our receivers loosely and didn't want to give up the big play. Three plays later we settled for a Faud Reveiz nineteen-yard field goal that pushed our advantage to 30–7 heading into the second half. It was a successful drive and a successful first half.

Our play from the twenty-four-yard line was a good example of how quarterbacks must manage a play, both in a forty-second window and in the context of managing an entire game. That plays right into what everybody said that a black quarterback couldn't do. I had to be methodical. I had to be precise. I had to make the right decision. All this worked and came together because I knew everything about my personnel. We practiced it repeatedly, and I knew what every one of my players was capable of, who I could rely on and who I couldn't.

NFL owners and businessmen, for that matter, can all relate to how a great leader, no matter their skin color, in moments like that, can be inspiring and successful.

15

Hall of Fame Weekend

I admit it. I wanted to make the Hall of Fame. It was a goal of mine, probably like any other player who is fortunate enough to reach the NFL. But it wasn't something I ever thought of as a player.

The Hall of Fame is another zone to a player. It represents the cream of the crop, the best of the best, and I honestly didn't feel like I could talk to those guys. When I played in the NFL and I saw Hall of Famers, such as Joe Namath (class of 1985) and Roger Staubach (class of 1985), they were royalty to me.

I never envisioned being able to rub elbows with Namath and Staubach, and I still feel that way today. The respect factor is so great. I shake my head because I get treated that way now by current players. When Seattle receiver Bobby Engram introduced me to his parents at the team hotel in Tampa in 2008, he smiled and told his mother and father they were looking at history. I nearly turned around to see who had walked in behind me!

I had been to the Hall of Fame at least four times on business prior to my induction. Each February, the Hall of Fame offers its annual African American Pioneers in Pro Football seminar in observance of Black History Month. The program is designed for area high school students, and it's so important and so neat to be involved with pro football's pioneers and historians, such as Marlin Briscoe, Bobby Mitchell, and Willie Lanier.

I twice played in the Pro Football Hall of Fame Game, once with the Houston Oilers in 1985 and once with the Seattle Seahawks in 1997. The game is the annual NFL preseason exhibition game, held the weekend of the Hall of Fame induction ceremonies. The game is played at Fawcett Stadium, which is located next door to the Hall of Fame building in Canton, Ohio. The stadium has an NFL flavor with artificial turf, a pro-style press box, and lighting system. The Ohio state high school playoffs use this site, along with nearby Paul Brown Stadium in Massillon, for its six championship games.

I also appeared with Mike Webster (class of 1997) at an autograph-signing event at the Hall of Fame in early 2000. "Iron Mike" was widely considered one of the best centers in NFL history, and he anchored the Pittsburgh Steelers' offensive line during their dynasty era, when they won four Super Bowls.

One of the Hall of Fame's events during the year is to pair a Hall of Famer with a current NFL player for an autograph session for fans. It was late in my career, but as a player, your free time is so valuable that one of the last things I wanted to do was catch an airplane to Ohio to sign autographs for an afternoon. But, honestly, it was one of the best decisions I made, because it was so neat to share the experience with Mike, who tragically died a short time later, in 2002.

After Mike and I signed autographs, I walked into the Hall and looked around and saw the busts of all the great players. It was also around this time when friends and fans began to mention to me that I might make it into the Hall of Fame one day. As I studied the busts, I wondered what mine might look like and where it would sit. It was such a weird feeling because you don't look at yourself as a Hall of Famer when you play the game.

But it was fun to dream.

It was Thursday, August 3, 2006, and the red-eye flight from Los Angeles to Cleveland arrived on time. When Mandy and I got our rental car and headed south on I-77 for the hour drive to Canton,

I promised myself that I would enjoy every minute of this Hall of Fame weekend and let it all soak in. Of course, that was easier said than done, especially since I am so hands-on with everything I do.

I had more than three hundred family, relatives, and friends flying in from all parts of the country and Canada for my induction. My college roommate, Clyde Walker, left Seattle on the red-eye Thursday night. My mom, Pat Moon, arrived from Los Angeles on Thursday. My mother-in-law, Bonnie Ritter, made the fourteen-hour drive from Minneapolis. My aunt, Mary Kilpatrick, was scheduled to leave Atlanta on Friday. One of my cousins, Christopher Fomby, didn't have far to travel because he lived in Cleveland. He had a big cookout on Thursday and put his roll-away couch to good use to host family members.

Getting ready for the weekend was like putting together a family reunion, a wedding, and an induction ceremony all at the same time. Because I have always tried to please everyone, I wanted to make sure my group had its tickets for the weekend's events. I wanted to make sure that everyone's accommodations were okay—Canton, a two-hundred-year-old town with 80,000 residents, isn't very large—and that they all had plenty to do. Most important, I wanted to make sure everyone arrived safe and sound and had a good time.

I worried about every little detail, so I didn't really have time to be nervous about the induction ceremony that Saturday. I guess that's my nature. If I had had nothing to do, I might have been nervous. But not even all my worrying helped when my daughter Blair and other family members arrived and discovered they didn't have a room reservation. Of course, the mistake was quickly corrected, and everyone had a good laugh. It was great to see everyone, and I just went with it and enjoyed every moment. I wanted to have all these people around me on this special weekend because all these people had passed through my life and had something to do with my career.

There are so many events tied into the induction ceremony, but the weekend's ceremonial kickoff is held each Thursday and is called First Play. That's when 2,000 youngsters form a three-mile link and pass an official NFL football from downtown Canton, where the NFL was founded in 1920, to the front steps of the Pro Football Hall of Fame.

On Friday afternoon, there was a news conference for the six people—Troy Aikman; Harry Carson; Rayfield Wright; John Madden; the late Reggie White, who was represented by his widow Sara; and me—to be enshrined in the Hall of Fame. I was the last of the six to arrive because I was worried about making arrangements for everyone and trying to get everyone where they needed to be.

Our induction class was first "officially" introduced at the enshrinees' cocktail party and dinner at the Memorial Civic Center and Cultural Center on Friday evening. More than 4,000 guests watched a program that featured returning Hall of Famers; NFL team owners, including Houston's Bud Adams; and sports celebrities. Naturally, our induction class was the guest of honor. That's when we received our Hall of Fame–NFL Alumni gold jackets.

Mine fit perfectly.

When I had time to slow down and relax, it hit me. I felt so fortunate to be part of the class of 2006, one that was described as a "glamorous class" by the media. No wonder. Aikman, Carson, Wright, Madden, and White represented some of the game's best. While I never had an opportunity to play for an NFL title, each of these other guys won at least one Super Bowl. Aikman, White, and I were inducted in our first year of eligibility.

Aikman, of course, was an outstanding quarterback. He enjoyed a great career in Texas, too, with the Dallas Cowboys. At age thirty-nine, he was one of just seventeen inductees who were under the age of forty at the time of their enshrinement into the Hall of Fame. Gale Sayers, at age thirty-four, was the youngest to be inducted (1977). Aikman won ninety games as a starting quarterback during the 1990s—no quarterback in history won more games in a single decade than Aikman—and was named the MVP of Super Bowl XXVII, when he completed twenty-two of thirty passes for 273 yards and four touchdowns in the Cowboys' 52–17 win over the Buffalo Bills. Aikman and I also shared the same agent in Leigh Steinberg.

White, who died in December 2004, was an ordained minister as well as an NFL superstar. He was a two-time defensive player of the year who made thirteen consecutive Pro Bowls. White, a defensive end, was the career-sacks leader with 198 when he retired, and won a Super Bowl with Green Bay in 1997. White's widow, Sara, and his son, Jeremy, who presented his father on Saturday, cried and shared a long hug after Reggie's bust was unveiled. I was really moved when Sara said, "It's not how we die; it's how we live. I encourage you to live like Reggie lived."

Carson's enshrinement was a long-awaited honor for the inside linebacker. He retired in 1988 after thirteen seasons, nine Pro Bowls, and a Super Bowl title with the New York Giants. In 2004, after he made the final fifteen candidates for the sixth straight year but was not elected by a panel of sports writers, Carson asked to have his name withdrawn. Thankfully it wasn't, and Harry finally made it.

Wright also played thirteen seasons with one team, the Dallas Cowboys. Wright played tight end, defensive end, and offensive tackle during his first three seasons. But he really excelled at tackle, where he went on and helped the Cowboys to ten division titles, six conference championships, and five Super Bowls, winning two.

Madden might be known as a football-video-game magnate and one of the top broadcast analysts for NFL games, but he also was a great coach, too. Madden, who was just thirty-two years old when he was named head coach of the Oakland Raiders in 1969, was the thirteenth Raider elected into the Hall of Fame. Madden led the Raiders to a 12–1–1 record and division title during his first season as coach. He also led the Silver & Black to seventeen consecutive wins over a two-season period (1976–1977), and the Raiders never suffered a losing season under Madden. Madden led the Raiders to eight playoff appearances and a victory in Super Bowl XI.

Over my career in the NFL, I passed for more than 49,000 yards, threw for 291 touchdowns, and was selected to nine Pro Bowls.

Our induction class was the largest since 2001, and I was so proud to share the stage with these guys.

Although the weekend sped by at one hundred miles per hour, I also stepped back and concentrated on what I wanted to say to everyone. I like to think everything out before I do it. It is God's honest truth, but I wrote down the bullet points for my twenty-minute acceptance speech on paper Friday night, the eve of my induction.

I wanted to speak from my heart, and I didn't want to forget anything. I normally don't write anything down when I speak to groups. I just speak from my heart. But because of the volume of information that I wanted to remember, I had to write it down. So I wrote out eight different bullet points. And that's what I did—I spoke off every topic. Some guys read page after page, but I didn't want my induction speech to come off that way. I wanted the audience to feel that my speech was directed to them personally.

I had also decided that I wanted my dear friend and business associate, Leigh Steinberg, to be my presenter. I had contemplated asking Felicia, my ex-wife, because she also was such an important part of my journey. My wife, Mandy, understood and didn't have a problem with it. In fact, Mandy and Felicia, who was accompanied by her husband, got along great. It was a special weekend in more ways than one for Mandy and I. I also announced to everyone that Mandy was pregnant with our first child. And Felicia was one of the first people to playfully rub Mandy's stomach and congratulate her, telling Mandy I'd make a great father.

Saturday morning, induction day, was met by warm, brilliant sunshine, a far cry from the February snow flurries of Detroit when I was told that I had gained entry into the Hall of Fame. The first event we attended was the Timken Grand Parade, which was televised and showcased our induction class and the large contingent of returning Hall of Famers. The parade had giant helium balloons, floats, marching bands, antique vehicles, and more than two hundred thousand people lined the 2.2-mile route. It was a great experience.

And then finally, a few hours later on the field at Fawcett Stadium, our enshrinement presentation started at one P.M. My family, dressed in white shirts, khakis, and sporting straw hats, was in the front row as I sat in a chair on the stage with my induction class and other Hall of Famers. ESPN announcer Chris Berman served as the master of ceremonies. I was the fourth inductee and followed, in alphabetical order, Troy Aikman, Harry Carson, and John Madden.

Following Leigh's six-minute intro, we both lifted the garment that covered my Hall of Fame bronze bust that was positioned on a stand near the podium. I kind of had an idea of what it might look like, because I had met with my sculptor months earlier in Utah. Receding hairline aside, I wanted to make sure the bust reflected my smile.

It did.

I smiled back and gave the bust a quick kiss on the cheek and a thumbs-up with my left hand. I took a few steps to the podium and glanced quickly at my family. My football journey was complete, and just as I promised myself, I spoke from my heart as I addressed the crowd in excess of 40,000. But I have to admit that while I talked about my mother I lost control of my emotions. "Mom, you're the most important person in my life, and I don't think you always believed that because of the busyness of my career. You are that."

Mom responded by blowing me a kiss.

I also didn't mention race during the opening twelve minutes of my acceptance speech, but that was by design. I didn't mention race when I talked about my lack of major-college opportunities coming out of high school. I didn't say it was discrimination when I went to the Canadian Football League for six years before I joined the NFL. I didn't say anything about that subject until I was more than halfway through an induction speech that was supposed to last eight minutes but ended up going for more than twenty.

It's a subject that I am very uncomfortable about sometimes, because I've always wanted to be judged by my play on the field.

My friend Marlin Briscoe, the first African American to start an NFL game at quarterback, was seated in the section allotted for my 330 guests. I was proud Marlin was able to share this important moment with me—it was Marlin's first trip to Canton and the Hall of Fame. Also in attendance were former quarterbacks James Harris and Doug Williams, who with Briscoe are partners with me in the Field Generals, a nonprofit foundation that offers college scholarships and seeks to educate and preserve the history of African American quarterbacks.

Marlin knew that while race certainly had an effect on my career, I never let it affect my success. But he also didn't see my induction as a starting point for minority quarterbacks; he saw it as a punctuation mark. The NFL became integrated permanently in 1946 when Bill Willis and three other African American players entered the league. That was one year before Jackie Robinson signed with the Dodgers.

Here is Leigh's introduction speech and my acceptance speech:

> **Leigh Steinberg:** In 1978, when Warren Moon was being scouted, a number of NFL personnel strongly suggested to me he would have a better chance for success if he would change his playing position.
>
> In certain football circles, there was doubt as to the ability or desirability of an African American to master the high-profile quarterback position, with its emphasis on intelligence and leadership. Warren answered that question with steely resolve. "Never," he said. "I was born to play quarterback. No one's going to stop me from fulfilling my dream."
>
> That moment played a critical role in reshaping NFL attitudes and opening the door for future generations.
>
> Warren followed his dream to Canada, where his brilliant play on the field led in 1984 to a three-league, twelve-team competition for his services that resulted in Houston making him the highest-paid player in the history of the National Football League.

After seventeen seasons with his dazzling performances on the field—that's eight straight Pro Bowls—his dignified bearing off the field, Warren's steely resolve showed the stuff that dreams are made of.

He wore number one for a reason.

Years later I sat in the living room of a young African American quarterback who was preparing for the draft. There were the usual trophies and family pictures in that living room, and there were two other pictures. One was Martin Luther King; the other was Warren Moon. The young athlete told me, "I looked at it every day. It gave me hope and inspiration."

I used to call Warren Yoda, that *Star Wars* repository of eternal wisdom. His circle of family, friends, teammates is extraordinary. Everyone relies on Warren for his sage advice, his support, his generosity. He's a rock, a father to all.

He could have been student-body president of the National Football League.

Warren's impact as a role model has been enormous. He's worked tirelessly to help people who can't help themselves. He established a scholarship fund at Hamilton High School in Los Angeles, at the University of Washington, and his Crescent Moon foundation.

I sat in a banquet hall where an emcee asked every college graduate whose scholarship Warren had paid for to stand. One by one they stood, until an entire room was filled with college grads whose scholarships Warren had paid for.

One young medical student walked up to me and said, "You know, I had no idea how I was going to get to college, much less become a doctor. Thank God for Warren Moon."

Here we are, two old Hamilton High grads thirty years later and 70,000 yards later standing in the shadow of the Hall of Fame. Warren Moon is about to make history as the first African American quarterback in the modern era to enter the Hall of Fame.

And because of his courage and perseverance, he won't be the last. From the Rose Bowl to Edmonton to Minnesota to

Seattle to Kansas City to our office in Newport Beach, I've been honored to walk the road and dream the dream with you. My partner, my best friend, I love and respect you for the way in which you've held on to your dreams and ideals and touched the lives of every person you've met for the better. Ladies and gentlemen, it's my extreme pleasure to present Mr. Warren Moon.

Warren Moon: Thank you very much. Wow. Just sitting up here listening to everyone speak, talk about their feelings about today is really giving me a heavy feeling inside my heart and inside my mind.

I want to thank Leigh Steinberg, who is one of my closest friends, a great business associate, a guy that's made me millions of dollars through his negotiating style, but also for helping me and instilling in me his philosophies about giving back and using your status as a professional football player to make a difference in communities of where you live.

I've tried to do that each and every place I've stopped along the way, hoping to make our society just a little bit better. Hopefully I've been able to do that.

I want to thank the city of Canton and the Hall of Fame committee. You guys have been unbelievable this weekend, treating not only me but my family and all my friends and relatives that have come from all over this country, treating us first class. The hospitality, the warmth that you feel everywhere you go in this city, I want to thank you all for everything you've done for me and my family. Thank you very much.

It is an extreme honor for me to be standing up here today. Given where I came from, what was thought of me in my early days, and to be up here with these guys, a lot of 'em who I rooted for as a young kid. A lot of 'em were my heroes. And now for me to be standing up here as a part of them, I am deeply humbled and deeply honored to say that I am part of this family, the most esteemed family of any professional sports Hall of Fame in the history of sports.

I thank you guys for having me. I thank you for letting me be a part of this group. I'll do whatever I can to instill the honor and keep the integrity of these great young men behind me.

They are the game. They are the guys that have made the NFL great. And for me to be a part of that, it's something that is really hard for me to believe each and every day. I've tried over the last six months since my nomination to wonder if I even belonged in this club of people because I have held them in such high regard for so long.

But sitting in that luncheon yesterday, getting a chance to shake hands with a lot of those guys that I rooted for, a lot of them I got to know over my playing career, I really am starting now to feel like I belong. I will make sure I come back to Canton each and every year for this induction ceremony, because that's how important it is.

We're a family, and families support one another. I'm a part of this family. I'm going to support everything that it does.

Football for me has been a journey. It was a journey that started some forty-four years ago. Make that thirty years ago for me. Playing at Baldwin Hills community park in the Pop Warner association at ten years old. I played on some teams that were very, very talented, or either we had coaches that just didn't understand personnel.

On my first team there, I played with another guy who is a member of the Hall of Fame, James Lofton. We were both on the same team together. James being a defensive end, and me being a linebacker. That tells you what kind of talent we had on our team, or that tells you our coaches just didn't know what the heck they were doing [smiling].

One of my coaches is out here today, councilman from Los Angeles, former police chief of Los Angeles, Bernard Parks, a guy that really instilled the values in me at a very young age of what being a policeman was all about. They showed us the same types of discipline they learned in the police academy. They taught us hard work. They taught us to be dedicated. That's why we had so much success at such a very young age.

Then I went on to high school where Jack Epstein, my high school coach, came up to me one spring and told me, "Young man, you're going to be my varsity starting quarterback next year." That's after the year before, as a sophomore, I hardly ever got on the field because I had another coach that didn't believe I could play the position.

So I want to thank Jack Epstein and Ron Price, my two high school coaches, for believing in me at such a young age and giving me the opportunity to play quarterback at the high school level.

It was tough for me to get a college scholarship because, again, it seemed like I was always having to try and prove myself at that position. But knowing me, a very stubborn young man and a very confident one at the same time, I wasn't going to let anybody tell me that I couldn't play the position; it was just a matter of finding someone that could give me that opportunity.

Don James at the University of Washington gave me that opportunity to play major-college football. He saw something in me that a lot of other people didn't see. He stuck with me through some very, very tough times at the University of Washington early in my career. I thank him so much for his confidence in me, for his dedication to me. I was able to persevere and move on and have a pretty successful college career.

Don James, I know he's in Africa right now on safari that he planned a year ago, but I know he's here with me today. I want to thank you, Coach, for giving me that opportunity to play major college football.

After college, there just wasn't a good feeling about me going to the National Football League, by the things that I was hearing. I was not really invited into the pro-football combine. I had no coaches come out and give me individual workouts. It was just pretty much a foregone conclusion that quarterback was not in my future in the National Football League but changing positions was.

Again, as a young, stubborn, and confident player, I was going to play quarterback, and I was looking for somebody that was going to let me do that. The Canadian Football League came along and gave me that opportunity. Hugh Campbell, Norm Kimball, again, they saw something in me that a lot of other people did not see. I want to thank the Edmonton Eskimos football organization, Hugh Campbell, and all my tremendous teammates that I played with up in Canada for a tremendous six-year experience that I will never regret doing.

A lot of people always ask me, "What would have happened if you had come to the National Football League instead of going to Canada?" I never looked behind. I always looked forward. I always take advantage of the opportunities given me. That's what I did when I went to Canada.

The Canadian people were so refreshing, so supportive of me. I had six of the greatest years of my life up there with those guys. I will never regret making that decision. So thank you, all of you people north of the border. Thank you, Canada.

A lot of guys would love to play their career with one football team. I'm no different. Troy Aikman had a chance to do that. Harry Carson had a chance to do that. Rayfield Wright had a chance to do that. I ended up playing with five teams throughout my professional career, and over twenty-three years of professional football. But, you know what? I am so privileged to have played in all five of those places. I've played in five great football cities that had great football fans.

You're talking about Edmonton. Those of you that have never been there before, we sold out every week, very rabid fans. It's known as the City of Champions. The Houston Oilers, everybody knows about the Astrodome. Love ya, Blue, the House of Pain. On to Minnesota, the Metrodome, one of the loudest places to play in the National Football League.

Everybody knows about the twelfth man and the intensity up in Seattle at the Kingdome. And then ending up with the Kansas City Chiefs, one of the best football environments you could be in for a player. Eighty thousand strong, all in red every week. A great football environment for any player to be a part of.

I want to thank Bud Adams, the owner of the Houston Oilers; Ladd Herzeg, the general manager at that time; and Mike Holovak, player-personnel director, who gave me that opportunity to come back to the National Football League and show what I could do. Those guys had tremendous faith in me at a time when a lot of people were not so sure if I could make that transition. But Houston gave me that opportunity. There was a lot of pressure on me when I went down there.

But they eventually gave me the tools to be able to do the things that I was able to do, along with some tremendous teammates and tremendous coaching.

I want to thank Jerry Glanville; Jack Pardee, offensive coordinator; quarterback coach June Jones for helping turn my career around in those early days, and then Kevin Gilbride, my offensive coach and quarterback coach who is here today as a member of the New York Giants for really taking my career and taking me to the next level. I really want to thank you for all the efforts that you showed me as coaches, to make me the best player I could be.

Then I moved on to Minnesota, where Dennis Green didn't think I was done at the tender age of thirty-eight years old. He gave me that chance to play football, along with Jeff Diamond, their general manager. I had a chance to be with Brian Billick and also Ray Sherman. We took that offense to some new heights.

Then on to Seattle at the tender age of forty-one, where again, Paul Allen, Randy Mueller, Dennis Erickson gave me the chance to play some more football, along with Bob Bratkowski, also Rich Olsen, as my coaches on the offensive side. We were able to do some good things in Seattle in the short period of time I was there.

Then at the tender age of forty-three years old, I went to Kansas City because I wasn't finished playing professional football. My body said, "Keep playing." My heart said, "Keep playing." So I kept playing.

Gunther Cunningham, Carl Peterson, the great Lamar Hunt gave me an opportunity to play for the Kansas City Chiefs. I had coaches like Jimmy Ray, Tom Clements, and also Tom Rossly that gave me the opportunity to keep playing the game and still showed me some things in my twenty-second and twenty-third year of playing football.

I want to thank all those coaches, all those owners, and all those general managers that had faith in me.

We had many, many great players on all those teams that made me the player that I am today. There's no question about it. A quarterback is only as good as the people around him. I was so blessed to have great talent around me that made my job just a little bit easier. I want to thank all those players that are here today. I want to thank all those players who are out there and couldn't be here today. A little part of this induction has to go to you because, like I said, I couldn't be here today without the support of the guys around me.

A lot has been said about me as being the first African American quarterback to go into the Pro Football Hall of Fame. It's a subject that I'm very uncomfortable about sometimes, only because I've always wanted to be judged as just a quarterback. But because I am the first and because significance does come with that, I accept that. I accept the fact that I am the first.

But I also remember all the guys before me who blazed that trail to give me the inspiration and the motivation to keep going forward, like Willie Thrower, the first black quarterback to play in an NFL game; like Marlin Briscoe, who is here today, the first to start in an NFL game; like James Harris, who is here today, the first to lead his team to the playoffs.

Then on into my era with Doug Williams, the first black quarterback to go to the Super Bowl and be most valuable player. Like Randall Cunningham, one of the most exciting players during our era. Like Vince Evans, who played twenty-plus years of professional football. All of us did what we had to

do to make the game a little bit better for the guys coming after us.

I only played this game not for just myself, not just for my
teammates, but I always had that extra burden when I went on
that field that I had a responsibility to play the game for my
people. That extra burden I probably didn't need to go out on
the field with, because I probably would have been a much better player if I didn't have that burden. But you know what, I
carried that burden proudly.

As I looked at young people all along my route as a professional football player, they always told me, "Warren, you got
to represent. Warren, you got to represent. Warren, you got to
represent."

Well, I'm standing here to say that, I hope I did represent
while I played in the National Football League.

When you play the game for twenty-three years, a lot of fine
people pass through your life. I wish I could acknowledge them
all, but I can't. But family is so important to me that I have to
acknowledge my family.

I was born and raised in a family that had six women. My
dad died when I was seven years old. My mom took care of six
of us. I have five sisters that were the loves of my life. They
were my biggest fans. They let me get away with my night to
wash dishes every now and then, my night to cook dinner every
now and then, because my mom made me do those things.
They were just huge fans of mine throughout my whole professional career. I want to thank all of my sisters, Gail, Carolyn,
Natalie, Patsy, Kim, and Renee, for being supporters in my life.
I love you all.

I have four of the best kids I think that any father could ever
ask for. They are all in college. They're all very polite. They're
all very good looking. I think they're all going to be very
successful.

But the thing I love about them the most is, as a father, as a
professional football player, it takes you away from home a lot.
You miss a lot of things. As I moved around the National Foot-

ball League, my family stayed in Houston. So I missed out on a lot of things in their lives. Those are things that I can never get back.

But I always asked them, "How do you feel about me going here to play?" They always told me, "Dad, just follow your dream." I want to thank you all for letting me follow my dream. I love you all very much, and I only wish the best for you, and you know that.

I also want to thank the mother of my children, Felicia Fontanelle. She was with me when I was a junior in high school. You couldn't ask for a more supportive, a more loving wife that kept a family together throughout all those years of my professional career. I'm so happy that she's happy in her life right now. I'm so glad that she's here today because she's as important a part of my career as anybody that's passed through my life. Thank you for being here, Felicia. I'll always love you.

And to my cornerstone, the lady that made it all happen for me, my mom, Pat Moon. The way she kept our family together, the way she provided for us, I never in one day during my life thought I was poor because of the way she provided and made sure I had everything that I needed, whether it was for school, whether it was for sports—whatever it was, she made it available for me.

Mom, you're the most important person in my life, and I don't think you always believed that because of the busyness of my career. You are that. You will always be my rock. You will always be the person that I look to when things are tough. You'll always have those words of wisdom that you've had all my life. I will always love you more than any human being possible. Thank you for being my mother. I love you.

Finally to my wife, Mandy, who even though she came into my life after my career was over, I am looking so forward to the journey that we have ahead of us. I think we have a very promising future. I love you being in my life right now. I look forward to spending the rest of my life with you. I love you, and thanks for being here.

I know I've gone over my time, but everybody else has. Quarterbacks just seem to do that. It's been a great experience being here this weekend. I love professional football. I have a passion for professional football. I'm a fan of the game. To be included with these guys back here, besides my four kids being born, this is the happiest day of my life.

I want to thank you all for being a part of this. I want to thank all my family and relatives that came from so far around the country to be with me, to share this momentous weekend. Thank you much, and God bless all of you. Thank you.

16

Not Perfect

B y no means am I perfect. I'll be the first person to admit it.
Unfortunately, we seem to focus on the mistakes of an individual as much as we focus on their triumphs—I know I'm the same way—but that really has left a blemish on my professional legacy that I'm not proud of. Both privately and publicly I have expressed regret and remorse for exposing my four children, Chelsea, Jeffrey, Blair, and Joshua, to this inexcusable behavior, and it is something for which I will always hurt on their behalves. But while it is not something I can change, it is something I can work to ensure never happens again.

I guess you could say that the problems began with the much-publicized domestic abuse incident on July 18, 1995, with my wife at the time, Felicia, who, you'll remember, I met at Hamilton High School and was married to for nearly twenty years. But the truth is they started long before that.

My entire family was struggling during those last few years in Houston. We all dealt with a lot of things in that town that we didn't always discuss enough, and Felicia and I both kept a lot of things inside. Some of the stress she was feeling came from the way the family was treated in the stands—there were often horrible comments thrown out that not only hurt her but bothered the kids. She didn't really tell me about much of it because she didn't want to upset me.

And it wasn't just confined to the ball games. Our kids would come home from school and tell their mother about things that were being said to them that peeled away at their self-esteem. Kids can be kids, and they tend to tease and do all those things when Dad doesn't play well or when the team doesn't do as well. I know I'm not the only guy that ever faced this; I'm sure the children of every quarterback in every city, when their team loses, are going to get teased at school about what happened on Sunday. The children of professional athletes are in a difficult position. In some ways, they are viewed as living on a pedestal, and some kids are always looking to knock them down if they can.

A lot of that played in to the problems that we had in our life and in our marriage. Felicia was bottling up the things that were bothering her and started shopping just to feel a kind of release. I wasn't talking to her about the things that were eating me up inside and instead, just got angry that she was spending money without taking the time to understand what could be driving her to look for a way to vent her frustrations.

This was all compounded by our impending move to Minnesota—we had all of the emotional issues from Houston that we hadn't left behind, and all of the added stress of moving and adjusting to a new life in a new place, and we still weren't communicating the way we needed to. We finally decided that I should move out of our home in Missouri City, Texas, for a while so that we could have some space and to help keep us from fighting in front of the kids. We hadn't decided on a divorce yet, but just needed to be apart.

One evening in the middle of July 1995, I came back to the house to get some more clothes and a few other items I needed back at my place. The older kids had left for summer camp in San Antonio, so I thought this would be a good time to take care of it, in case there was an argument.

Sure enough, Felicia and I started bickering over money. I told Felicia that I was in the process of consolidating all our credit cards into one, and I needed to get the other credit cards back. I was standing in the closet, opening drawers and pulling things out to pack, when she came back and threw all of the credit cards at me. I just looked at her and went back to what I was doing. She started getting upset because I wouldn't talk to her and she felt like she was being ignored.

She finally grabbed a candle holder and threw it at me, hitting me in the back of the head as I was bending down to pick up my bag. I stood up, and I guess she saw the anger in my face because she took off running. I ran after her, and we wrestled until I got her down on the ground. I said, "Now you want to talk? Let's talk. What do you have to say? Let's talk." She was screaming and hollering and trying to get up on her elbows, but I kept her pinned down, so her shoulders got bruised.

Unfortunately, we weren't alone. Both our youngest son Jeffrey, who was seven at the time and had a dentist appointment earlier in the day, and the maid were also at home, and they heard all the screaming and yelling. The maid told me later that she got nervous because she had never heard me raise my voice in the eight years that she had worked for my family, so that's when they called 911. Scared and crying, Jeffrey talked to the police.

By this time, Felicia had grabbed her car keys and driven away toward the interstate. I followed her in my car for a short time but then decided to head to my office. She pulled into a Dairy Queen to telephone a friend and, when she returned home, the police had arrived at our house.

The police waited until Felicia came home and had her give an account of what had happened. I don't know how it got written up, but I honestly believe that they made a lot of assumptions based on what they saw and surmised from the circumstances, because Felicia refused to press charges based on the way it was recounted back to her. Officers who responded to the scene said Felicia had scratch marks on her face and abrasions on her neck.

There was a new law on the books in Texas that stipulated that "spousal privilege," which gives a wife the right not to testify against her husband, was no longer honored in domestic-abuse cases in Texas. In the past, a wife could not be compelled to testify against her husband, or vice versa. So Felicia didn't have a choice after she advised police that she didn't want to press domestic-abuse charges against me.

Three days after the incident, I held a news conference in Missouri City and apologized to Felicia in front of our kids, apologized to our families, and apologized to the fans. That same day I was arrested, charged, and released on a thousand-dollar personal-recognizance bond. I pulled into the garage under the police station, and it was something I will never forget. The fingerprinting. The mug shots. We also held a press conference in Minneapolis after the incident and Felicia repeated her desire not to press charges. While I was criticized for having my children at both press conferences, I wanted them there to hear me apologize to their mother and the world. We decided to tackle it as a family, and we vowed to make it together through the ordeal as a family. There was no way to soften it for the children or for our families.

When the case came to trial in February 1996, Felicia refused to testify for the state. She insisted that she did not want to go forward with any charges, but she was told that she was required to do so, and if she refused, she could end up going to jail and losing her children. She was terrified. On the day of the trial, she put Jeffrey in the car and drove off, just to stay out of the courtroom and away from anyone trying to take her child.

When she was called to the stand to testify, however, she said that I hadn't intended to hurt her in any way. Felicia told jurors that she was to blame for the incident and that she denied knowing the source of the bruises and injuries in the police photographs. In fact, she sat right behind me during the trial, and we often exchanged glances and nodded to each other in support.

My lawyer, Rusty Hardin, called Felicia the most compelling witness he had seen in his twenty years of practicing law. He told the media that Felicia was smart and funny and that no one could, after watching her testimony, come away thinking she was anything but a strong, independent woman who thinks and does for herself.

All charges ended up being dropped against me after only thirty minutes of deliberation, but I'd already gotten headlines as a wife beater in the media. Of course, my acquittal was hardly the tabloid fodder that my arrest had been. I insisted that the intense media scrutiny of my case indicates why other players plead guilty rather than fight domestic violence charges in court. I went through it because my wife and I were adamant about what happened. There was no way I was a criminal in that whole process. We wanted that to become public and for the record to be clean. The way the media covered it was as if I had chopped somebody's head off.

Now, in no way can I justify the way that I acted toward her, and I'm not trying to. But Felicia and I have remained good friends even after our divorce, because we have a tremendous respect for each other. I try to point this out whenever anyone tries to paint me as a monster that attacked my spouse.

Once the story hit the national newspapers, everybody was calling me—my mom, and Leigh Steinberg, of course, and it seemed like everyone else I'd ever known. Felicia called me, too. She was very upset about the press coverage and wanted to make sure I was all right and ask if I needed anything.

We talked for a while about what I was feeling and how I remembered how good it felt to discuss my problems with Thelma Payne while I was in college. We decided together that I should try to find someone to fill that role for me in Minnesota, so I called Thelma and she helped arrange for me to meet with a counselor she knew and respected. Felicia was really supportive through all of that.

In the end, I came to realize that our marriage broke down because we weren't communicating and, frankly, hadn't gotten to fully know ourselves before we were married. We were married so young that we didn't really come to realize just who we were as adults, without the other person being right there and being a part of it, and that can really stunt your growth and prevent you from being honest with yourself.

The truth was, we were just very different people and had been trying for almost twenty years to be who we thought the other one wanted us to be instead of who we really were, and it bred frustration, resentment, and anger.

Through my counseling, I came to realize that in any unhealthy marriage, there tend to be some deep-rooted problems on both sides that deteriorate the partnership—except maybe when drugs or alcohol are the culprit. Otherwise, it seems to always be an emotional struggle that is not being addressed honestly through real, meaningful communication.

In the case of Felicia and me, we were two sober, levelheaded people that just had a lot of pent-up stuff we were dealing with, and it got to the point where we exploded. That's kind of what led to our breakdown. I wanted to know what truly got us to that point, and that's why I started the counseling.

Being divorced was hard on me. I'd been with Felicia since I was sixteen years old, and when I was away at college in Washington we were still together, even though we weren't in the same place.

Now, all of a sudden, I was alone.

I'd always thought marriage was a forever kind of thing, so I didn't even think about dating for a while after the divorce. As much as I hated being without someone, I finally realized how important it was to come into my own as a person—not as an athlete or a quarterback or a celebrity or anything else. I needed to get to know myself as an individual, and I had to work through the hurt of my failed marriage in order to make that happen.

The divorce took a while, and during the Super Bowl in 1998 in Atlanta, as the process was coming to an end, I went out with some friends from Minnesota who were in town. I was finally starting to feel a little more comfortable with myself and to get used to the idea that Felicia and I were finished. That evening was one of the first times in a long time that I was really able to enjoy myself out in public.

That was also the night that I first met Mandy Ritter, a former collegiate athlete (softball) at the University of Minnesota.

Mandy was friends with several people in that group, and I was struck with how attractive and fun she was. But I wasn't ready to think of her or anyone else romantically for quite a while. That group of friends really helped me unwind and remember how to laugh and cut loose and let go of the things that were weighing me down—in short, all the things I hadn't done in a long time. They were a wonderful group of people, and we started hanging out more in the coming year because we all lived in Vikings country.

It wasn't until close to a year after we met that I started to realize I might have feelings for Mandy. We started to date, and I was amazed by how much I enjoyed being with her, but even then, I wasn't sure I could imagine settling down with her. I felt like my life was still a bit scrambled.

I had come from a big family, so there was always someone around. And then when I moved out of the family house, I bought a large place on my own so that there would be plenty of room for my kids to run around when they came to visit. But it was pretty miserable to walk into a big, empty house 60 or 70 percent of the time when the kids weren't there.

It was so hard to get used to, and it hurt so badly—but I also knew that I couldn't just remarry in order to have someone in my life. That wouldn't be right, and it wouldn't be fair to anyone involved. But Mandy was special.

We dated for five years before we married in 2005 in Hawaii. I wanted to talk to Mandy's mother, Bonnie Ritter, in person to ask for permission to marry her daughter, but the ring had burned a hole in my pocket. So I telephoned Bonnie and asked for her permission, and she was great. In a span of fourteen months, I had a wonderful wedding in the middle of the Pacific Ocean and a spot on center stage at football's greatest shrine, the NFL Hall of Fame, with family gathered to watch.

While I came from a large family, Mandy's parents divorced when she was six years old, and she lived with her mother and a younger brother. We hung out as friends initially, and we tried to arrange our schedules to meet each other in different cities before we had to go back to our real lives. Mandy got to see me on the football field late in my career with Kansas City, but it wasn't enough to *really* impress her.

Mandy, who turned thirty-three in 2008, was smitten by my personality and smile. But she also admitted—with her great smile—that an older guy like me (I am nearly twenty years older than Mandy) wasn't in her profile as marriage material. She also wasn't afraid to make fun of the mustache I wore for many years, either. Not even our cultural differences—Mandy is white—impacted our relationship and how we felt for each other. We hit it off and had so much fun when we were together. It was as if we were soul mates.

Mandy and I had our first child, Ryken, in February 2007. Mandy picked out the name, which is a combination of her brother's name (Ryan) and her mother's maiden name (Gerken). Since my four children with Felicia are now young adults, this is the second go-around for me with children. I really didn't know how I'd react, and I know Mandy was nervous about what kind of dad I'd be. But I have to say I've really, really enjoyed it.

I get up early every morning because I am on the go so much, so the morning is daddy time with Ryken. I feed him and change his diapers. It is the quality quiet time that I didn't get to spend with my other children because of football. It was difficult to go away each season, especially later in my career when my children were teenagers. That's when they start to challenge you a little more and start to think they're grown, so I learned that it's important to communicate and reach out to each other.

I don't intend to be a long-distance father to Ryken. I want to be there each step of the way.

Of course, Mandy quickly reminds me that we will have our challenges, because Ryken was born in February, between the Super Bowl and Pro Bowl. Talk about perfect timing for a quarterback! Twenty-four hours after Ryken's birth, I dropped Mandy and Ryken off at our home and headed to Hawaii for my commitments at the Pro Bowl. Mandy, of course, wasn't thrilled to be dumped off at home with her newborn child, but she understood and supported me.

While I missed many of those proud-papa moments that help balance some of the more-trying events that came with raising my four older children, I plan to enjoy my daddy time with Ryken.

But as I chose to title this chapter, I'm not perfect; I've experienced bumps along the way and have learned from them.

Earlier in my playing career with the Minnesota Vikings, in 1995, I reached an out-of-court settlement with a team cheerleader who had sued the Vikings and me eight months after she had been fired by the team. I knew the cheerleader, and I had actually been her and her husband's friend, but she claimed in her suit that I made unwanted sexual advances toward her in the team hotel on a road trip. I was adamant in my denial because I knew I had done nothing wrong, but my attorneys advised me that I didn't need the unwanted publicity. The team's internal investigation into the allegations resulted in the club determining that the woman filed the suit out of revenge for getting fired.

And even as my life was getting back on track, and I was discovering a new kind of happiness and confidence I'd never known, I made some really bad decisions in 2007, when I was arrested twice on suspicion of drunk driving. In April of 2007, I was arrested under the suspicion of driving under the influence, but the charge was later reduced to first-degree negligent driving, and I was sentenced to forty hours of community service, an alcohol-awareness class, and a $350 fine. The same thing happened eight months later, in December of 2007. It was humiliating. I was so angry with myself that I had been so stupid and irresponsible, and even more upset for the embarrassment I had caused Mandy and my children.

I also embarrassed the Seahawks organization, and I thanked Seattle owner Paul Allen, CEO Todd Leiweke, and president Tim Ruskell for their patience and for not jumping to conclusions. They pride themselves on running the organization with high character and high integrity and I did something that tarnished that. It's not something I feel great about but I am determined to do everything in my power to try and change my tarnished image.

I mean, what was wrong with me?

I enrolled in a clinical evaluation, and they showed that I did not have a dependency on alcohol. That was good news in one sense—it meant that I wasn't an alcoholic, which had always been a fear of mine, given my father's history of the disease. But it was bad news in another sense, because it meant that I had just made some truly terrible decisions with no excuse. As part of my sentence, I served five days of electronically monitored home detention. I certainly understand the dangers of drinking and driving. On the same day of my second arrest, former New York Yankees catcher Jim Leyritz was charged with DUI manslaughter and DUI property damage after the SUV he was driving was involved in an accident that killed a thirty-year-old woman.

My mistakes in my life have really opened my eyes. On and off the football field, you have to be held accountable, and anyone can make these mistakes. It really knocks you down a few notches and lets you know that you are no different than anyone else. There might be fans out there who are happy to see professional athletes and high-profile people stumble and fall. But I believe good things can come from learning from your mistakes. I am definitely more careful now, and I wouldn't wish this kind of trouble on anyone.

As I told the press at the time, I view myself as someone with high integrity and high character, but my actions certainly didn't reflect that standard, and it's something I am deeply sorry about.

I know I am on my last chance with the Seahawks, and I know what will happen if I misstep again. It's three strikes and you are out. While I am not going to base it all on just my job, it's something that I don't want to go through again.

I am not about to let that happen.

17

More Relaxed

Through my recent decision to attend therapy, I have learned why I am able to put the bad things in the back of my brain, lock them up, and move forward. I always rationalized in my mind that I enjoyed a challenge, and there have been a lot of "challenges" I have experienced in my life.

Some were because of my skin color and my determination to play quarterback. I always felt that I had to prove myself, had to make sure that everyone, from the coaches to my teammates to the people in the stands—*everyone*—knew that I was the best man to lead the team. That got exhausting both mentally and physically.

Every week, every game I punished myself so that there could be no doubt, but every week those same nagging feelings got to me. When I was younger, I watched guys like Jimmy Jones at USC and Roman Gabriel, who was a quarterback for the Rams, and I'd think, *You aren't just playing to prove kids like me right; you're playing to prove everyone else wrong.* I'd feel that every time I'd see them call a play or complete a pass or (God forbid) have an unsuccessful drive. It hurt to see that because it meant so much more to me than just moving a ball down the field.

When I took the field as a black quarterback, then, I didn't feel like I was just playing for myself and my team. I felt like I was playing for every little Warren Moon who was out there in the stands or watching at home on TV and thinking, *I want a chance to do that.* And I was playing against every coach who had a child like that on his team who he didn't trust to play the position, or any fan who chalked up a team loss to the black quarterback not being able to shoulder the responsibility. I knew there were kids and coaches and fans who thought that way because I'd been that child and I'd met those coaches and fans. And I especially resented that last inference—if there was anything I knew how to do well, it was how to shoulder responsibility.

So that plagued me throughout my entire career. For me, every play, every snap, every pass, every tackle had all of that history behind it. It was a lot to drag around with me because while it made every minor failure seem that much worse, it also tempered every victory, because I just felt like there were still people out there who weren't satisfied or who didn't believe I could do it. If I screwed up, I deserved to be booed—but I wanted it to be for my poor play and not for my skin color or what I represented.

It wasn't until I really began to come to terms with the emotions that were driving that nonstop push to prove myself that I was able to relax a little and accept that I *had* succeeded. It was so freeing to finally feel myself accept the success I'd worked so hard to create.

That realization made me come to grips with emotion in general. I had denied myself the luxury of expression for most of my life. When my father died, I didn't ever give myself a chance to grieve. Instead, I stepped my seven-year-old self right into the man-size hole he'd left, and I took over his role in the family to the best of my ability. I probably didn't enjoy childhood as much as I should have, but that was something of my own doing—I wouldn't allow myself to enjoy it because I didn't think it was what was being asked of me.

This became the way I dealt with anything dramatic. Instead of letting my feelings out, I forced myself to have a stoic response. It seemed to me that emotion didn't solve problems but action did. I was always so concerned about what it meant to be a man, since I was missing that presence in my life during the formative years, and my image of a man was one who protected, provided, and directed. I didn't feel it was possible to do those things when emotion got involved.

Unfortunately, that kind of approach to life doesn't mean that a person is without emotion; it simply means that the emotion isn't expressed. I was channeling it into unrelated venues, like sports or organizing my house. And some of it combined with that constant need to prove myself, which ended up coming out as anger. I didn't know how to feel sad, and I didn't want to know. Sadness can't accomplish anything. Anger, frustration, confusion, passion—these are emotions that are charged with energy, and I think I turned to those subconsciously when I was trying to suppress other feelings.

I was always afraid of showing weakness because I felt like my family depended on me. First, it was my mother and sisters; later, it was Felicia and the kids. I felt needed, and I *needed* to be needed. I knew my place and my role when people were relying on me. I knew I could trust myself to step up and take care of things.

It's funny how open I am to talking about my counseling now, when I was so closed about it at first.

After Thelma arranged for me to meet with a therapist in Minnesota in 1995, I made sure that my appointment was always the last one of the day. That way, there would be no one in the waiting room when I arrived, and I'd have to come in the back door anyway. I didn't want anyone to see me. I was terrified that the press would find out and splash it all over the headlines. To me, it was so humbling to admit that I needed help, and to actually talk to a stranger about my problems. I thought that was showing weakness, something I had fought all my life to avoid doing.

My sessions were twice a week, on Tuesdays and Fridays. On Tuesdays we would delve into more serious issues and Friday would be a day for blowing off steam before Sunday's game. We talked a great deal about where I had come from and what it was that made me *me*. That was my most pressing question because after my marriage broke down with Felicia, I realized that I didn't really have an identity separate from her. I had football, but I didn't have a personal life with a clearly defined sense of self.

The more I came to understand who I was and why I was feeling the way I was, I also came to understand more about Felicia as an individual, as well. I came to realize that she was going through many of the same questions that I was going through. As our children were getting older and starting to look toward college, she was struggling with the questions, *Who am I now that the children don't need me in the same way? Am I Felicia Moon, or do I even know what it means to be Felicia?* She didn't know what her next goal would be, and I think she had a kind of growing void that she was trying to fill with other things while she sorted that out.

She'd really had a rough childhood and viewed me as something of a protector once we started dating in high school. It was a role I was happy to take on, but it didn't set us up for the healthiest relationship because we were both carrying notions of each other to the marriage, but didn't have a clear sense of ourselves. Our identities were entirely wrapped up in what we represented for the other person. I think if we'd known that going into it, our marriage would have had a much better chance of making it.

I thought that this kind of insight was so important that I went back to counseling in Los Angeles before I asked Mandy to marry me. I didn't want to enter into another commitment without being absolutely comfortable with who I was by myself. Without that, I couldn't give my life to Mandy completely. Because I now have the necessary knowledge and comfort about my own life, I think our relationship is incredibly strong and healthy. I've always been so glad that I took the time to get myself sorted out before I entered into another marriage.

But beyond coming to understand more about myself, I felt that the counseling gave me an insight as to how I relate with my children.

For example, Joshua, my oldest son, struggled in school because he was diagnosed with attention deficit disorder. He was such a good kid but he had trouble concentrating. The doctors recommended putting him on Ritalin, but Felicia and I agreed that we didn't want him medicated. I thought about how important talking with Thelma Payne had been for me when I was younger, so we decided to try counseling for him, and it made such a difference in his life. Suddenly, he wasn't getting into trouble at school because he was turning his energies to special jobs the teacher gave him, like looking after the classroom hamster.

As I watched him learn to control his excitement and desire for activity into something productive, it reminded me of my own childhood and how I had invested all of my emotions into sports and my responsibilities at home. I used to think that I was very different from Joshua because I had kept my emotions so suppressed while his were so close to the surface, but once I understood what was behind a lot of that energy—a need to feel responsible and engaged in his surroundings and focused on something—I realized that this was very similar to how I was as a kid.

Joshua didn't share my drive for athletics, though. He was an incredible swimmer, consistently getting times in the backstroke that had him ranked nationally in his age group; but he didn't stick with it as he got into high school. He still swam for awhile, but not with the vigor he'd previously had, and even though he received some scholarship offers from several small colleges, Joshua eventually decided to let the swimming go.

It really bothered me at first that he could be so nonchalant about his sport. I couldn't understand how he could have so much energy and such a desire to be active—and not channel it into an area where he clearly excelled. When I was his age, everything in my mind and body ached to be playing sports. I came to realize, though, that so much of my drive came from a desire to rise above where I was. Football would be my ticket out of the old neighborhood, into college, and maybe even on to a professional career. It was a way out for me. My children didn't grow up poor; they never had to deal with the fear of whether we could make rent, buy groceries, or pay the light bill that month.

Don't get me wrong—my children had to work. I think the big thing parents need to emphasize is having their kids set goals and making them work for the things they accomplish. That's the way it's going to be in the real world—they're not going to be given anything out there. If you work, you should be rewarded; but if you're not going to work for something, you shouldn't get it. It's just that simple to me. I'm proud that I was able to provide a worry-free life for my children, but I never wanted them to fall into the trap of feeling "privileged."

. When Joshua decided not to pursue athletics, I was confused and a little disappointed, but I wasn't going to force the issue. Sports had given me hope for a better future; my children were able to look to other things for fulfillment because the drive for them to rise above their circumstances just wasn't there, because it didn't need to be.

Joshua searched for a while to find himself. He transferred colleges several times and tried to figure out just what it was that he wanted to do with his life. He started on a modeling career and did a little acting, but that didn't really click for him, either. Eventually, though, he met a wonderful young lady who got him back into church, and he began working for the online services of a chain of Christian bookstores owned by her mother. Doing that, Joshua got his focus back and his priorities straight and realized his love for public relations. He's now going back to school in order to get his degree so that he can work in sports marketing.

It makes me so happy to see how Joshua took the time to really figure out who he was before he started thinking about marriage. It took him a little longer than some people to find his identity, but I know from experience just how important it is to see that journey through before committing your life to someone else.

Chelsea is next in the birth order and she is the one who is definitely the most like me. I didn't need the counseling to understand what made her tick, but it was fun to recognize so much of myself in her as I came to realize who I was and what drove me.

She is just very focused and so organized. Chelsea is very well-rounded and much more intense than her siblings, but she also tends to keep a lot of her feelings inside. That's clearly something she inherited from her dad! She tends to internalize her emotions, but instead of letting them eat away at her, like I did, she manages to harness them into a fierce, smart energy that is perfect for her chosen career as a lawyer.

She certainly had some challenges along the way: She found out she was pregnant just before her high school graduation. I was devastated. I felt like it was my fault because I had been away a lot during that year, while she stayed in Texas with her mother; plus, the divorce was in full swing at that time. I felt as though I had let her down and set her and her child up for a struggle just like I had witnessed growing up. I had visions of Chelsea as a young single mother, trying to raise her child and manage a house and hold down a job—and it scared me. I'd worked so hard to get my family out of that scenario. When she first told me she was pregnant, she knew how disappointed I'd be about what it might mean for her plans, so she told me, "Dad, I'm going to go to law school, and I'm going to graduate. I promise." I have to admit that I had my doubts.

It turns out I was completely wrong, though. She and her boyfriend got married and had the most wonderful little baby boy, named Trey. They have a very happy family and are both really involved with their son, and now I realize that I wouldn't want it any other way. I should have recognized that Chelsea was enough like me to not be held back by the odds stacked against her. She graduated college *and* law school, both with honors, and has found that she can juggle all the responsibilities in her life just fine.

With Blair, I found that even the therapy couldn't explain everything; for example, how can two girls have the same two parents and be so completely different? Where Chelsea is all about drive, decisions, and action, Blair takes her time. She thinks about everything a hundred different ways before making a decision and even then is willing to retrace her steps and start over again.

This was definitely true when it came time to choose a college. Blair was an incredible athlete and was offered a scholarship to play volleyball for several major Division I schools. She signed with Georgia Tech and played with the Yellow Jackets for one season in 2002 before she decided the program wasn't right for her. So she transferred to Houston Community College and then signed with Tulane and played volleyball for her final two seasons in 2004 and 2005.

Blair's personality really confused me at first because it was so vastly different from my own. Once I make a decision, I want to commit, stick to it, and see it through. I can't understand exploring it from a dozen angles and still being unsure as to which way is best. I eventually came to realize, though, that Blair is just like her mother. Felicia handled things in a similar way, worrying about it all and wanting so badly to make the right choice that she sometimes couldn't even make a choice at all.

Blair's indecision doesn't stem from anything negative, though; it comes from her naturally sweet disposition and her desire to make everyone happy. Even though she is an incredibly tough competitor on the volleyball court, Blair is the kindest, most loving person you will ever meet. She has recently worked as a personal assistant for actress Jessica Alba.

Finally, there is Jeffrey. As much as my counseling enabled me to understand how I could relate to my children, Jeffrey is still a wonderful mystery to me.

He is quite a bit younger than the other three, so whereas they had each other to keep company—and to try to outyell—Jeffrey didn't really have a playmate or competition to be heard. I think that's a big part of what made him the quiet, gentle young man he is.

When he was little, we lived on a lake in Texas, and he would take his fishing pole down to the end of the dock and just fish by himself for hours on end, all day long if we let him. He'd be so happy, just sitting out there quietly. It was the cutest thing in the world to watch. He was just one of those kids that just didn't need to be around a lot of people.

Sometimes it worried me a little bit that he wasn't being open enough with his emotions. I didn't want him to keep them bottled up inside, but it never seemed to bother him. He is able to deal with his feelings in a way that I could never manage, and I admire him for that.

But as different as we are in some aspects, Jeffrey definitely inherited my drive. He was a very gifted soccer player and played football for a while, too, redshirting in his freshman year at Tulane. During that first year, though, he decided, "I want to be a veterinarian." And that was that. It was his goal and he was going to chase it with everything he had. He realized that the science course that would be required of him for that pursuit would be too much to keep up with while playing football, so he gave it up and pursued his career instead. Jeffrey transferred to the University of Texas, San Antonio, and is planning to apply to the vet school at Texas A&M.

Of course, part of me would have loved to watch him out on the gridiron, but when I think about his future, I am so proud I could just burst. I'm so proud of all four of my children, and I am so grateful for the experience I had with my therapy that enabled me to relate to them in a unique way, and to understand their personalities both in how they are similar to me and how they differ.

When I consider how much of a difference therapy made in my life—how it helped me deal with unresolved issues from my childhood and professional hang-ups and emotional issues and pent-up frustrations and in coming to know myself and relating to my children and setting the groundwork for my new marriage—it saddens me that there seems to be such a stigma tied to it among men in the African American community.

Why are black men so reluctant to go to counseling? I obviously was at first. I didn't want anyone to know I was seeking help. I thought it was a sign of weakness because I was admitting I couldn't handle it all on my own. Maybe that keeps some men away. Maybe it seems "soft"—like it's about hugging and crying instead of being strong and unshakable. But as I quickly learned, it's actually incredibly hard to face your fears and to honestly tackle your issues. Maybe it's just viewed as a crazy snake-oil treatment that people like to peddle as a cure-all that doesn't really help anyone. I can definitely say that one's not true. It turned my life around and made me a fuller person, not because it solved my problems, but because it made me realize them and take them on myself.

It's amazing how much better I feel and, according to those people who have known me the longest, how much happier I seem in recent years. My sisters have noticed the difference in my confidence. A couple of them have pointed out that I always tried to sound put together and educated when I spoke with the media. I think I did that because I wanted to put my best face forward so people would take me seriously. But in doing that, I wasn't allowing my full personality to come across. I feel the freedom to be a little silly now, to allow myself to crack jokes. I've realized that I don't have to prove that black quarterbacks can be successful. My statistics can back that up. I can let go of that chip on my shoulder.

Leigh always cracks up when I do my turtle imitation, tucking my head into my neck and making a ridiculous face. It's just a dumb little thing I do to make him laugh, but it's a looseness I never had before. He was agonizing about some decision recently and without thinking, I just turned to him and said, "You may ask me. I am Yoda—mature and wise. Sound judgment I have." Again, it's just a dumb little joke, but it's a new side of me that I finally feel I can allow to exist.

It's not like I never laughed or cracked jokes. I've been known for my quick smile. I like to observe people, too.

I went to a movie with good friend Lorenzo Romar and a few other guys in the early 1980s. The movie was called *The Hand*, and it was about a guy who lost his right hand in a car accident. The hand was not found at the scene of the accident and returned by itself and followed the guy around and murdered anyone who angered him. The movie started at 7:30, but there were still people walking in after the movie had started and looking for open seats. Under my breath I'd say, "The movie started at 7:30." As more people walked in, Lorenzo and others around us also started to say, "The movie started at 7:30." It got to be like a little joke. Pretty soon, you didn't want to be the next person who walked in late, because everyone in the row let you know it.

It's been a long journey for me, and certainly not an easy one. But I know that I am now a complete man—something I was always so concerned with as a little boy. I have a successful career, I have a family I dearly love, and I have a life that I'm no longer afraid to live. I am proud of myself as a man, as an African American, and simply as a person. I've come a long way from where I was just a few years ago, believing that I could never show any kind of emotion, and letting that repression eat away at me.

I can cry now, and it's cleansing. There's a lot in those tears—a lot of pain and a lot of strength. I'm proud of those tears.

18

Field Generals

Keeping the history of African American quarterbacks in the NFL alive is important to me. I was fortunate enough to be there when we started writing it. I wanted to preserve our legacy as best I could, but I needed some help doing it.

After attending a memorial banquet in 2001 that honored Joe Gilliam, a group of us decided that something had to be done. Along with Doug Williams, Randall Cunningham, James Harris, and Marlin Briscoe, we started the Field Generals, an organization founded by and consisting of NFL African American quarterbacks who are dedicated to teaching and preserving the history of the African American quarterback.

All of us did what we had to do to make the game a little bit better for the guys coming after us. We wanted to have a better line of communication with guys who are in the game. Our intent wasn't to tell them how we helped make it possible for them to get where they were, but to be a sounding board for them so they could share their experiences—so that we might be able to help them.

While the issue of how black quarterbacks are treated will continue to be an ongoing topic, it has been great to watch major changes as they unfold. And it really never unfolded better than in the 1999 NFL draft, which was considered monumental for African American quarterbacks and should be accompanied by a drum roll:

Donovan McNabb of Syracuse was picked by the Philadelphia Eagles in the first round with the second pick overall, which at the time was the highest draft pick ever for an African American quarterback. McNabb was joined by several other African American quarterbacks, including Akili Smith of Oregon, selected third overall by the Cincinnati Bengals; Daunte Culpepper of Central Florida, selected eleventh overall by the Minnesota Vikings; Shaun King of Tulane selected in the second round by the Tampa Bay Buccaneers; and Aaron Brooks of Virginia, selected in the fourth round by the Green Bay Packers.

And even more strides have been made since then.

In 2001, Michael Vick was selected as the number-one overall pick out of Virginia Tech by the Atlanta Falcons. It marked the first time that an African American quarterback was selected as the top pick. The number of African American quarterbacks on NFL rosters by season's start in 2006 was twenty-four. JaMarcus Russell of LSU was selected first overall by the Oakland Raiders in the 2007 draft, and Vince Young of Texas was drafted third overall by the Tennessee Titans.

While numbers have increased when it comes to African American quarterbacks in the NFL, let's put it in perspective. Heading into the 2009 season, there were ninety-six African American quarterbacks drafted in NFL history, according to the Black Quarterback historical Web site. The first African American quarterback who retired from the NFL was Charlie "Choo Choo" Brackins after he played one season with the Green Bay Packers in 1955.

At least now as a radio and television analyst for the Seattle Seahawks, I can watch McNabb one week, Young the next. It's exciting for me to watch the changes I and the other Field Generals helped bring about.

Little by little, NFL teams began to view black quarterbacks as franchise players. In 1990, the University of Houston's Andre Ware, the first African American quarterback to win the Heisman Trophy, became the first black quarterback in twenty-one years to be selected in the first round of the draft.

Until recently, black starting quarterbacks in the NFL were a rarity. In fact, in the 2005 NFC championship game between the

Philadelphia Eagles and Atlanta Falcons—when McNabb and Vick played against each other—it was the first time in NFL history that black quarterbacks faced each other in a conference championship.

That kind of meeting will remain a big deal until the system changes, until black quarterbacks are accepted in the league even when they are not stars, until they can hold clipboards, get released and latch on to other teams as backups, until they are booed for reasons other than their skin color.

Of course, many have said I served as inspiration for countless young black players who are determined to follow in my footsteps. Current-era quarterbacks like Steve McNair, Culpepper, and McNabb have thanked me for helping prove the prejudices wrong and beginning a path for their own success. Look around the NFL. McNabb is a superstar. While Vick's legal problems knocked him from that superstar pedestal, there was no denying his talent. Byron Leftwich, Aaron Books, McNair, Culpepper, and Young, who led Texas to the 2005 national championship, all had been starters during their careers.

As important as the "now" is, the "then" was just as important.

I never would have had the opportunity to accomplish what I did if black quarterbacks such as James Harris, Joe Gilliam, and Marlin Briscoe—my own heroes—hadn't been there to inspire me and show me how it can be done. They were the true trailblazers, athletes who had to deal with racial discrimination in its fiercest form.

When the NFL presented the Man of the Year Award to me in 1989, the idea of a black man playing quarterback was still a big deal, a relatively new concept. And it was only a year earlier that Doug Williams had become the first black quarterback to play in and win the Super Bowl. I was nearly in tears watching him.

When Doug won the Super Bowl, I was a little envious. I wanted to be the first black quarterback to win it, but I was so happy for him at the same time—not only for what he did for himself but for what he did for all the African American quarterbacks.

He answered that question that everyone always asked, They're good, but can they win the big game? All those many doubts that owners and coaches had were resolved by Doug. He went out there and proved he could lead his team to victory.

It took some time, but we were changing the minds of NFL owners. Slowly but surely, they were coming around. Some owners had more reservations than others.

Historically, as a quarterback, you are not only the leader of your team, you are the leader of your organization. You are the face of the organization, and you are the face of that city. Peyton Manning is the face of the Indianapolis Colts. The quarterback position is the most visible of any position in any professional team sport. Suddenly, it was more common to have a black player as the most important person in your organization—an organization that had traditionally been owned by older, white men. It could be kind of hard for a lot of them to swallow.

Throughout my playing career, race was always an issue I was uncomfortable with acknowledging publicly. I wanted to be judged only on my performance as a quarterback. Many times I felt the best way to ensure that standard was to leave "black" out of it completely. Others have made it an issue, however, such as outspoken conservative Rush Limbaugh on Donovan McNabb.

In September 2003 Limbaugh declared on ESPN's *Sunday Countdown* that McNabb, despite five trips to the Pro Bowl, was overrated by the press simply because he was black. "The media has been very desirous that a black quarterback do well," Limbaugh said. "There is little hope invested in McNabb, and he got a lot of credit for the performance of this team that he didn't deserve." Three days later, amid a storm of controversy, Limbaugh resigned from the show.

In a 2007 interview on *Real Sports with Bryant Gumbel*, McNabb told interviewer James Brown that African American quarterbacks faced added pressures because there are fewer black quarterbacks—and because some still don't want black athletes playing the position. "There's not that many African American quarterbacks so we have to do a little extra," McNabb told HBO. "Because the percentage of us playing this position, which people didn't want us to play . . . is low, so we have to do a little extra." Two weeks into the 2007 season, five of the thirty-two teams (15.6 percent) had black starting quarterbacks. McNabb later said he felt that African-American quarterbacks were graded more harshly and that the media was tougher on him than on white quarterbacks such as Carson Palmer in Cincinnati and Peyton Manning in Indianapolis.

I never publicly said it was discrimination when I had to spend a year at junior college before getting a major-college opportunity from Don James at Washington. I never publicly blamed my skin color when I wasn't drafted in the National Football League, pushing me across the border into the Canadian Football League for six years. During the opening of my acceptance speech into the Hall of Fame, I didn't mention race when I spoke about my lack of major-college opportunities coming out of Hamilton High School in Los Angeles.

But that's not to say I didn't know what was happening. I understand the significance of my induction into the Hall of Fame, and I embrace it. Race affected my career but not my success. I took a very unconventional route to the NFL, where I had to reestablish myself. The way I did it was different because of the other things I had to overcome that didn't have anything to do with football.

I'm glad I was able to make the impact that I did, especially for today's younger players. The NFL is different now, and more people are benefiting through the struggles and effort I put into my own career. When we started to see these guys selected in the first round benefiting, when you had McNabb, Smith, Culpepper benefiting, that's when progress was made. In 2004, for example, all three National Football Conference Pro Bowl quarterbacks (Culpepper, NcNabb, and Vick) were African American. You started to see a lot of other guys get drafted later who might not be guys who can play right now at the elite quarterback level.

My criticism of the unspoken system in the NFL was always that they wouldn't draft you if you weren't good enough to play right away, and because they wouldn't help you develop. Would they draft you in the third round, knowing maybe you wouldn't be the guy right now but they would groom you for later on? Doug Williams could play right away in the NFL, so they drafted him in the first round. For me, I was a project. They said I first needed to go to Canada to be groomed and then come back and show them I was ready to make an immediate impact. That's the way I always thought it was up until the late 1990s, when teams began investing in black players for their future.

Doug Williams, after his success in the Super Bowl, is a prime example of some of the attitudes that existed in the NFL in the late 1980s. He had a record-breaking performance in football's biggest game as the first black quarterback to start. Two seasons later, following injuries and serving as a backup for Mark Rypien, he was out of the league. An injury to McNabb or Vince Young alters the landscape where you have seven black quarterbacks and now there are two—with no one in the wings to replace them. That door can close very, very quickly. While the NFL—and all sports—is based on performance and more African American quarterbacks are being selected in the draft, you must always keep your foot in the door, or it can and will close.

Many of the younger guys would be faced with these challenges if we hadn't dealt with them earlier. If Troy Smith, the Heisman-winning quarterback from Ohio State, had come out when I came out, he would be in Canada. The guy was 25–3 as a starter in college with a national-championship appearance. At least Troy Smith had an opportunity to get drafted when he was selected in the fifth round of the 2007 draft by the Baltimore Ravens. The point is, he still got drafted and has a great opportunity to play quarterback.

Now, the guys coming into the league as quarterbacks are being judged solely by coaches and owners who think they can play or don't think they can play. There are enough player-personnel directors and scouts who have played the game and understand the priority given to winning instead of color. There are enough African Americans in those positions, too, who are now judging all these players the same way.

The Field Generals' role while we were playing was a little different than most players back then—and even now. Then, when we got an opportunity, we had to take advantage of it. By taking advantage of that opportunity, hopefully our accomplishment in some way enhanced opportunities for others. That was our role.

It would be great if all the young guys knew our stories, knew what we achieved and accomplished, it would be great, but it's not that way. Many younger players don't know much about Marlin Bricsoe or Doug Williams or James Harris, and Harris is currently the senior personnel executive for the Detroit Lions.

Harris, in fact, was the first black player to start a season at quarterback and was also the second black player to start in any game as quarterback in the modern era for a professional football team behind Marlin, who was the first in 1968 with the Buffalo Bills. In 2000, three of the twenty black quarterbacks on NFL rosters played for the Jacksonville Jaguars under Harris's watch in Byron Leftwich, David Garrard, and Quinn Gray.

Players not knowing our history is something we have no control over. We always have hope that the accomplishments and our struggles can benefit someone along the way. Personally, I always felt fortunate that I got an opportunity that others didn't get. This is what the Field Generals are all about, building on past achievements for future opportunities.

I still feel for some of these guys whom I knew could play but who never got the chance, because they were precluded from playing a position based on race and preconceived notions.

It hasn't just been about Field Generals all the time in every league. The CFL, which has been good for black quarterbacks, has had its own discussions on race and quarterbacks. Damon Allen—the most prolific passer in professional football history—has been a focal point for this discussion.

Allen, another successful black quarterback in the CFL, has a somewhat similar story to mine. He was an accomplished high school quarterback, who had the opportunity to play that position at California State University at Fullerton—not exactly a major force in college football. But, he did have a successful career in college but did not get a call from the NFL, so he went to Canada to play.

As a quarterback, it's hard to think of someone who has been more productive on the field than Damon. He holds the record for most career passing yards. But, besides that, he's third all-time in the CFL for rushing yards, and fifteenth all-time in any professional league—323 yards behind NFL Hall of Famer Marcus Allen—Damon's older brother. In the CFL, when Damon speaks, you listen.

In 1993, while I played in the NFL, Damon Allen used the CFL's Grey Cup to talk about black quarterbacks and how they weren't appreciated enough. It took a lot of guts to use the biggest game in that league as a medium for his message. He knew many people didn't see things the way he did. Many owners, league administrators, and fans did not share his point of view. But he felt he needed to speak out on the issue. He saw what he understood to be a flaw in the CFL's system, and wanted to correct it—not because he had any grievance with the league, but because he appreciated what the CFL had offered him and enjoyed being involved with the CFL.

He used the Grey Cup and media surrounding the game to shed some light on the subject by explaining how black quarterbacks were judged by a harsher standard, even in the CFL, where they had long been welcomed with open arms. When you make claims like this, you know you have to play a great game—and you better win.

He did and he did.

Allen won the 1993 Cup with Edmonton after his interview. He also won in 2000 with the British Columbia Lions and then the 2004 Grey Cup with Toronto. Previously, he won it in 1987.

What Damon was trying to point out was not whether or not black quarterbacks are given opportunities to play professionally—in the modern era, they do have those opportunities. The point was that there are different standards, based on skin color. To get the equal opportunities, you had to prove more as a black quarterback then as a white quarterback—that's just how things have developed. But as long as Damon and others like him were willing to work against it, it would eventually change.

Now even—fourteen years later from when Damon spoke out—in 2007, Donovan McNabb continued to question the two sets of standards for black quarterbacks and white quarterbacks.

Donovan has been in the league for nearly a decade. He has played in a Super Bowl. He has been the face of a franchise in a city, Philadelphia, that's not afraid to criticize its professional athletes. He has seen success, and he has seen failure. Who hasn't seen both? But McNabb has an interesting perspective on the subject, because a few African American quarterbacks had gone before him and had proven they were successful on the field. He didn't necessarily have that kind of pressure following his play. But he has felt other pressures, similar to what Damon Allen discussed.

Some people dismissed what Donovan said, saying he's too sensitive, he has no proof, it is just the Eagles organization, fans, and media. People pointed out that there were seven black quarterbacks starting in the NFL heading into the 2008 season. And there would have been eight had Michael Vick not been convicted of running a dog-fighting operation.

Like McNabb, many do assume the role of franchise player for their teams. How about JaMarcus Russell? He was the number-one pick in the 2007 NFL draft, taken ahead of Notre Dame quarterback Brady Quinn. Doesn't that indicate things are changing and for the better? Yes, there are more black quarterbacks in the NFL. But it moves beyond numbers, it's an attitude—a disposition—from team management and fans toward black quarterbacks.

As McNabb suggested, it's about attitudes, and never being quite good enough in the eyes of many. Many times, we have to prove more—to earn it more—to have that opportunity and be deemed successful as a quarterback. Our bar is set higher for the same reward. Black quarterbacks are expected to do more—whether it's openly admitted or not. Given identical situations, they need to be more accomplished than their counterparts to earn the same amount of respect.

I believed this inequality existed years ago. And true to the testament of Damon Allen and Donovan McNabb, I believe it still.

It was interesting watching the Tennessee Titans—formerly the Houston Oilers—defend themselves on how they dealt with their franchise quarterback, Steve McNair, who signed with Baltimore in 2006. The organization has a history of signing and starting black quarterbacks—beginning with me and continuing with Steve McNair and Vince Young—which is their wonderful contribution to the league. But the story can't end in a signature or a two-year contract for a player. In reality, they have to take the next step and treat their players equally well.

McNair led the Titans to a Super Bowl and was known as a warrior throughout his career. He played through injuries and sacrificed his body. Yet, following the 2005 season, he was asked to work out some place other than Baptist Sports Park with the team during the Titans' off-season conditioning program, for fear that an injury would make the team liable for the entire amount of his $5 million salary cap hit for 2006, which would limit the team's ability to sign their 2006 draft picks.

Every player gets into some kind of dispute with the organization from time to time in their careers. Just like any other player who commands a large contract, I had my disagreements with team management over the course of my career. Spending ten seasons in Houston provides more than enough time for a dispute to arise. But to ban a quarterback from the workout facility after you tell him to seek out employment elsewhere speaks volumes. Many people will question those types of actions and the core message you're sending as an NFL team.

After being involved with the pro game for so long, you begin to figure out where the inconsistencies exist. Why it might not be explained solely by racism, after a while you begin to wonder why some people don't get the opportunity to play, or why some get treated a certain way—why one person is successful, and another person is not.

As a player, you're measured statistically in every way possible. Yardage, completions, completion percentage, yards per completion, yards per attempt, yards per play, interceptions thrown—there are endless statistics and measurements for players. It's easy to tell when you aren't being as effective as the next available guy and are therefore replaced. Having easily weighed and compared statistics makes it easier to discern who is a better or more effective player—and let the better player play.

Now people are zeroing in on the head coaches.

There was much to cheer in the ascent of Tony Dungy of the Indianapolis Colts and Lovie Smith of the Chicago Bears, the first black head coaches to compete in the Super Bowl. Pittsburgh's Mike Tomlin, born in 1972 and the third-youngest head coach in any of the four major North American professional sports, is the tenth African American coach in NFL history and first in Steelers history. With Pittsburgh's victory in Super Bowl XLIII on February 1, 2009, Tomlin became the youngest head coach to lead his team to a Super Bowl victory. He's also the third African American head coach to participate in the Super Bowl and the second to win it. But coaching is more difficult to measure, because the next available guy may not have a win-loss record to go by. But the recent increase in black coaches in the NFL owes much to "the Rooney Rule," named after the idea's patron, Pittsburgh Steelers owner Dan Rooney, which compels owners to interview black candidates for coaching jobs. The Rooney Rule was implemented in 2002, after the late Johnnie Cochran and Cyrus Mehri pressed an antidiscrimination suit against the NFL, which at the time had only two black head coaches.

The first African American head coach in the NFL was Art Shell, who was hired in 1990 by the then–Los Angeles Raiders. Shell and seven other blacks who have coached in NFL's modern era, heading into the 2008 season, have a combined winning percentage of just under 55 percent and have made the playoffs in twenty-nine of their fifty combined seasons.

And then you look around and think, *Wow, 80 percent of the league is black, and you have five or six black head coaches, and a couple of them have been recycled.* It's not like they are brand-new hires. The situation is even worse in the executive box—there were three black general managers following the 2007 season.

Prior to the start of the 2008 season, black quarterbacks such as Aaron Brooks, Daunte Culpepper, Byron Leftwich, and Quinn Gray no longer had NFL jobs. All had NFL starting experience under their belts, but all were free agents at the start of the season, leaving some to wonder if it was a simple matter of economics, or a race issue, or if some quarterbacks may have been blackballed.

ESPN analyst Shaun King, a former Tulane and NFL quarterback, was quoted in published reports that "*Blackballed* might be too strong a word. But if you really are objective, the facts point to it must be something. It's outside of normal when you look at the way that some of the quarterbacks are recycled. If you look at the rosters right now—and I don't want to call specific guys' names, but if you look at the rosters in the National Football League and then you ask yourself based on accomplishments alone—how is an Aaron Brooks or a Daunte Culpepper or a Byron Leftwich or a Shaun King, for that matter, not somewhere?"

All but King and Brooks signed by the 2008's season's halfway point—Leftwich signed with the Pittsburgh Steelers in August, Gray signed with Kansas City in October, and Culpepper signed a two-year contract with the Detroit Lions in November 2008. In his retirement from pro football, Brooks announced plans to be a land developer.

As I said in William C. Rhoden's book, *Third and a Mile*, there's no denying this era of players has a lot more power than we did. When I was in the league, there were five other African American quarterbacks, at most. There was always the possibility you could be tossed out. In some ways I wanted to speak up. In other ways I wanted to hide. As soon as someone came up and asked, "When did you stop being a black quarterback?" I was like, "Man, I don't want to deal with that right now. Everything's going well. I don't want to talk about it."

But now we must talk.

Progress has been made but the struggle continues for total acceptance of African American quarterbacks as not just athletes but as leaders and the faces of their respective teams and organizations. When Joe Gilliam died of a heart attack only days before his fiftieth birthday, it was his legacy that helped give birth to the Field Generals and our commitment to teaching and preserving the history of the African American quarterback.

19

NFL's Hidden Secret

There were a lot of football games over the years where *boom!* I got hit in the head and immediately felt dizzy or saw stars. There are plays and parts of games that after having taken a hit to the head, I really can't recall with clarity. I know there are twenty-five minutes of a Pittsburgh Steelers game that I don't remember—that part of the game just never came back to me. It's lost forever.

Like most players, though, I tried to shake off the grogginess and continue to play. Knowing what we know now about concussions, that wasn't a wise decision.

I was diagnosed with six concussions during my twenty-three-year professional career in the CFL and NFL. But I probably had more than that, starting in Pop Warner football when I was eleven years old. I've learned so much more about concussions in recent years. It's a very serious injury, and if you go back out there on the field with a concussion that you don't know about, it can lead to very serious brain injuries.

I have not experienced any long-term effects, but I always look for little signs and make sure to get examined regularly. Mounting knowledge and increased awareness have greatly improved the managing of head injuries while also convincing players they must not take risks.

While it's not a new issue for the NFL, it's a new issue for the league to acknowledge that there is a need for continued dialogue concerning concussions. For many years it had long been a tricky subject for the league, which used to operate more in theories and remain behind closed doors on the issue. But thanks to a revolution in the recognition of head injuries and the consequences they can hold for athletes, concussion denial seems to be on the way out. It's now in the open and being discussed.

Most players never want to admit they were "dinged" or had their "clock cleaned" or "bell rung" after a big collision. They want to pop up, dust themselves off, and show their opponent they are okay. If a player is helped to the sidelines, most make the emotional decision when asked if they want to return to the game. They pull themselves together and get back on the field. That's not a good thing. We've learned more about the harmful effects of concussions in the last five years than we did in the previous fifty.

The key is how to be smarter and safer.

I was never knocked out per se, during a game. I was knocked dizzy at times. And that's what most people think, in order to have a concussion a player has to be knocked out cold. Usually when that happens, the prognosis can be worse than a concussion. I've gotten knocked silly a lot, but I was diagnosed with six concussions, so who really knows how many I have sustained throughout my career?

Believe it or not, most of the concussions I suffered were from my helmet slamming against the turf. It had nothing to do with the hit that I had absorbed. The playing surface has a lot to do with preventing, or in my day, causing concussions. The turf I played on the majority of my career was one of the reasons that I had those concussions. It was basically carpet on concrete, with a thin piece of rubber between the two. That's not nearly enough to soften the impact.

It's great to see that manufacturers are trying to improve the quality of helmets, coaches are continuing to stress the proper techniques of tackling, and the league is adding rules to prevent helmet-to-helmet blows. While all these things are designed to prevent concussions, you will never get rid of them. It's impossible to eliminate concussions, which often result from a rapid sideways motion of the head. No equipment modification or technology in sight is going to change that fact.

Concussions, like first downs, are part of the game, and they will continue to happen.

That being said, awareness is the big issue with concussions nowadays, and the NFL is developing league-wide protocol for the treatment of concussions, waiting periods, and symptoms for anyone who gets a head injury. A concussion, because it is by definition a mild brain injury, should be taken seriously.

Every team in the NFL now gives players a neurocognitive test—a battery of memory and concentration exercises before the season. If the player takes a hit to the head during a game, he can be benched until his scores return to the baseline. The league's concussion policy also has set up an anonymous "whistle-blower" system that enables players and doctors to report anyone's attempt to override the wishes of concussed players or medical personnel.

Perhaps the most important change in the managing of head injuries is an individualized approach, since no two are the same. In the past, a blanket approach was used. A football player whose symptoms subsided within twenty-four hours might be allowed to play the next week, or a player whose symptoms disappeared within a few minutes might be allowed to reenter the game.

The Center for Disease Control says there are more than 300,000 sports-related traumatic brain injuries in the United States each year, and there is fear that unreported cases number several times that amount, because the signs and symptoms of concussions are poorly understood.

Proper testing is important and guesswork needs to be taken out of the prognosis and the recovery time. The more information and concussion analysis that is shared, the safer the game becomes.

That way a player's career doesn't have a Pittsburgh Steelers moment in it like mine does.

I am the national spokesman for the Sports Concussion Institute in Los Angeles. The institute's director is Dr. Tony Strickland, who, ironically, also attended Alexander Hamilton High School at the same time I did in the early 1970s.

Tony didn't play football, but he was an accomplished baseball player with a ninety-mile-per-hour fastball. It's funny how our paths have intertwined. It was Dr. Strickland's research that got me and my business partner, Leigh Steinberg, also a Hamilton High alum, involved and led our national charge to discuss what is happening with concussions among athletes.

At our second summit in April 2008 in Marina Del Rey, California, SCI had top neurologists from all over the country come in and talk about the research they had compiled on head trauma. Orthopedic surgeons, trainers, team physicians, equipment companies, turf and helmet manufacturers, all the different components that will help prevent more concussions, attended. The NFL was also represented after not appearing at the inaugural conference in 2007.

SCI, with the help of Leigh and me, put this brain trust together to encourage conversation, to share ideas, and to keep this important research progressing so that concussions can be better understood and players can be educated. We especially need to inform parents, teachers, administrators, and coaches at the youth level of the signs that can determine if a player has a concussion and how to treat that player.

As I said, I had my first concussion when I was eleven years old. Fortunately, my mom was a nurse at the time, so she kind of knew the signs to look for postconcussion; she knew to watch out for nausea and headaches, and to make sure I didn't fall into a deep sleep that night, she woke me up every hour.

There are a lot of parents who wouldn't know that type of information or where to reach out for it. That's the kind of instruction we are getting out to parents now. The brain continues to grow and enlarge until the age of twenty-five. That's why children are the most at risk for suffering concussions.

In December 2007, in an unprecedented statement of commitment to athlete safety and well being, the California Interscholastic Federation requested that 100,000 high school athletes in the state of California be provided concussion-management services.

Other smaller states like Hawaii have introduced such testing, but athletes in California represent the largest group ever to take the neurological exams. Leigh and I are building a similar relationship with the foremost academic research institution, the University of Pittsburg Medical Center, and Dr. Mark Lowell, who developed IMPACT, the software for baseline testing.

But even kids, like their NFL heroes, fib to get back into the game. Playing hurt and shaking off injuries is a hallowed tradition, even at the youth level. In an October 2008 *Sports Illustrated* article, Kenneth Podell, director of neuropsychology and the Sports Concussion Safety Program at the Henry Ford Heath System in Detroit, told the magazine that "concussions don't show up in brain imaging. A lot of times it's based on self-reporting of symptoms, and it's believed about 15 to 20 percent of athletes fake having no symptoms to get back into the game."

You have so many more kids wanting to "get into the game" and playing contact sports today. You've got all the extreme sports, like skateboarding and rollerblading. These kids need to have the proper safety helmets to help prevent concussions. Mixed martial arts is another sport where the force used by the fighters is staggering.

Plus, there are so many more women and girls involved in sports. The concussion rate for women is four times higher then for men. I didn't realize it, but a lot of it is because of neck size. Most women have longer necks than men. Their necks aren't as muscular, either. That's your shock absorber when it comes to head collisions. You look at most football players, they seem to have no necks, because they have built up those muscles so much. Most women don't have those neck muscles, so when they take a blow to the head, they can get a concussion much more easily. It is things like that that people aren't even aware of.

We are vigorously extending our message concerning concussions to all youth, girls and boys. They are the ones most vulnerable to what's called second-impact syndrome. You get one concussion, then another one before the first one has gone away. But there are other issues as well.

One, a concussion is called the stealth injury. It's not like a shoulder, knee, or ankle injury, where you can visibly observe the athlete hobbling or struggling. Two, the actual number of athletes who have suffered concussions may be larger because a concussion is difficult to recognize and poorly understood. And three, the cultural competition that was ingrained in all of us sometimes doesn't let athletes actually acknowledge when a concussion has occurred. If you are pulling yourself out of a game and you are not hobbling or visibly injured, it's difficult for some individuals to understand why you are not playing. It's about sucking it up, doing what you need to do, putting it out there on the line for the team.

Since the professionals who manage the athletes have a very poor understanding of what a concussion is, how do you expect the athlete to make the distinction between a concussion and "a ding"? Well, both a "ding" and your "bell rung" are concussions by definition. They are simply on a continuum like everything else, from being a momentary alteration in awareness to actually being knocked out.

Think about how NFL players have changed physically over the years. They are bigger, stronger, and faster. When a player, say twenty years ago, was a 250-pound guy on the line, he was considered a behemoth. The physics of the game have been altered so significantly, you now have multiple guys who weigh well over 250 pounds, 300 pounds for that matter, and can run like tailbacks and tackle with the force of a train. Players are six foot four, six foot five, and they can fly and lay you out. The physics have simply outstripped the gains that have been made in protective equipment in helmets and pads.

As long as there's football, clocks will be cleaned and bells will be rung.

The NFL has faced criticism after reports of several former players who ended up with brain damage before their fortieth birthdays. Those players often took little or no recovery time following a concussion. A second concussion before the first is healed can cause serious, if not extensive damage.

In 2007, a study conducted by the University of North Carolina's Center for the Study of Retired Athletes showed that the rate of diagnosed clinical depression among retired NFL players strongly correlates to the concussions they sustained. The study also found that retired NFL players faced a 37 percent higher risk of Alzheimer's than other U.S. males of the same age.

The study was based on a general health survey of 2,552 retired NFL players. It corroborated other findings regarding brain trauma and later-life depression in other subsets of the general population, but ran counter to longtime assertions by the NFL that concussions in football have no long-term effects.

The study, which appeared in the journal of the American College of Sports Medicine and was detailed in the *New York Times*, found that of the 595 players who recalled sustaining three or more concussions on the football field, 20.2 percent said they had been found to have depression. That is three times the rate of players who have not sustained concussions. The NFL is conducting its own study on concussions. Results are expected to be published in 2010.

Former New England Patriots linebacker Ted Johnson, who retired in 2005 after ten years in the NFL and winning three Super Bowls, has said his significant depression and cognitive decline had been linked by a neurologist to on-field concussions.

Johnson, who told the *New York Times* that he "shouldn't have to prove to anybody that there's something wrong with me," is among a number of athletes who have agreed to donate their brains following their deaths for study of the long-term effects of concussions. Johnson hopes Boston University's Center for the Study of Traumatic Encephalopathy can help clear up the debate on the issue.

Concussions can be tough to diagnose, and deadly.

A neuropathologist in January 2007 claimed that repeated concussions likely contributed to the suicide of former Philadelphia Eagles player Andre Waters. Other deceased football players found to have the type of brain damage commonly associated with boxers as a result of their football careers included Mike Webster, Terry

Long, Justin Strzelczyk, and my former teammate with the Houston Oilers, John Grimsley, who died of an accidental gunshot wound. His wife allowed scientists to study his brain for the long-term effects of head injuries. Postmortem tissue from Grimsley showed evidence of chronic traumatic encephalopathy; investigators at Boston University link the condition to his past history of concussions.

During a segment that was broadcast on Canadian television in November 2008, it was reported that three of my former teammates with the Edmonton Eskimos—lineman Bill Stevenson, York Hentschel, and David Boone—may have suffered undetected concussions in the late 1970s and early 1980s that may have contributed to their premature deaths.

The segment looked at the issue of head injuries in football and life expectancy among players in the Canadian Football League. Stevenson, Hentschel, and Boone played with me on our Eskimos team that won five consecutive Grey Cups from 1978 to 1982.

Stevenson, an offensive tackle, died in 2007 at age fifty-five after falling down stairs while drunk. Hentschel, a member of our famed Alberta Crude defense, died in 2006 at fifty-two of organ failure after years of alcohol and drug abuse and depression. In 2005, Boone shot himself at home in Point Roberts, Washington, after years of profound depression.

Dr. Jim Adams, who was a trainer with the Eskimos during our dynasty years, told the television station that he wasn't aware of any particular head-injury problem at the time with the aforementioned players, but is now convinced their troubles after football related to head trauma.

It's so sad.

Studies have shown that in cases where athletes had three or more concussions, they were five times more at risk for early onset Alzheimer's disease, three times more at risk of significant memory loss, and four times more likely to have severely elevated depression. I am in the Hall of Fame, but I look at a bunch of these guys—it's a Who's Who of the best players who have played the game—and it's sad.

Former Baltimore Colts great John Mackey suffers from frontotemporal dementia, which makes him particularly protective of personal possessions and suspicious of anyone who tries to control his actions. And there are many others who walk around and they don't even know where they are. You see guys like Mike Webster and other Hall of Famers who were in such bad shape physically and emotionally that they committed suicide.

Steinberg, who put on two similar conferences in the 1990s before our first concussion summit, has represented clients such as former 49ers quarterback Steve Young, whose career ended in a flurry of concussions. Steinberg has often described a moment in 1993, when he saw quarterback Troy Aikman after the Dallas Cowboys had beaten San Francisco in the NFL title game. Troy didn't know where he was, and he even asked Leigh if he had played that day and if he had won. Leigh told Troy that, yes, he had played and, yes, he had won, and that the Dallas Cowboys were going to the Super Bowl.

Ten minutes later, Troy asked Leigh where he was again.

There's really a lot of work being done and different people are admitting that, yes, concussions probably had something to do with some of these effects, some of which can be debilitating. Finding the best methods to deal with concussions is just as important as the game itself for me.

Last year the NFL held a medical conference on the subject of concussions. It was attended by team physicians and athletic trainers from every NFL team and by active players and medical representatives of the NFL Players' Association. The conference reviewed the current medical and scientific research and included presentations by doctors and scientists from within and outside the NFL. It's good to see that NFL commissioner Roger Goddell is making a very strong statement that the safety of players takes precedence over competition.

What the NFL learned and implemented in its concussion treatment was forcing a player who has suffered a concussion to gain rest. For an NFL or college player, three days of complete rest are usually required. For a high school player, seven days are usually required.

The NFL outlined a summary of key factors in deciding when NFL players can safely return to the same game or practice. These points were highlighted. The player should be completely asymptomatic and have normal neurological test results, including mental status testing at rest and after physical exertion, before returning to play. Symptoms to be taken into account include confusion, problems with immediate recall, disorientation to time, place and person, anterograde and retrograde amnesia, fatigue, and blurred vision. If an NFL player sustains a loss of consciousness, as determined by the team medical staff, he should not return to the same game or practice.

Here's an excerpt from the NFL player concussion pamphlet:

What is a concussion? It's more than a "ding." Concussions are caused by a hard hit to the head. The hit is typically from another player's helmet, shoulder pad or knee, or from a fall to the ground. The effects usually last a short time, but it's important that they are treated properly and promptly by you, your team doctors, and your athletic trainers.

You shouldn't decide if it is just a "ding." Instead, you should report any symptom from the list below to our medical staff. The most common symptoms are imbalance, headache, confusion, memory loss, loss of consciousness, mood change, vision change, hearing change, fatigue, and malaise (don't feel right).

There were many games where I took a big hit, and "boom," I didn't feel right. It's about being honest with yourself.

Football is important.

But life is more important.

20

Busy as Ever

When I retired from the NFL, my life actually seemed to get busier.

I remain heavily involved in football, doing radio-television work for the Seattle Seahawks and management for Leigh Steinberg in our sports and entertainment agency. I travel the country from my hometown in Seattle as a motivational speaker.

I also try to stay involved with the various community groups and philanthropic causes I support, as well as keeping up with the business ventures I'm involved with, or looking to start. Basically, it just never slows down for me—and I wouldn't know what to do with myself if it did.

One of the neat things about playing in the NFL for as long as I did and enjoying the success I did, is that it exposed me to so many different things, and I took advantage of it. When Steinberg first recruited me out of college, he talked about my second career before my football career had even started. That was the thing that made me want to go with him.

All every other agent talked about was negotiating my contract and my career. Leigh started talking about a second career and how football was a stepping stone to your second career by taking advantage of the opportunities that you made while you were playing.

I took that to heart, and so I did a lot of different things throughout my years playing the game, hosting television or radio shows, involvement in commercial real estate, or getting projects like the concussion seminar together. I did a lot of different things, including fund-raisers and volunteering my time for charity. I developed a lot of great relationships from everything that I have done, but I also learned a lot about different subjects.

One thing that I especially love about my life now is seeing how much the game has changed, even in the relatively short time since I left it.

It's such an honor for me to be friends with guys like Kordell Stewart, Andre Ware, and Donovan McNabb. Stewart last played in the NFL in 2005 but in late 2008 expressed interest in trying to make a comeback. Ware is now part of the Houston Texans' radio-broadcast team after playing both in the NFL and CFL. I look at what they've done with their careers, and it makes me really proud to know that I was a part of the first wave to pave the way for them to really make their marks. I've had a chance to talk with Daunte Culpepper and Michael Vick, too—just the fact that, off the top of my head, I can name five black quarterbacks who are either playing now or were until just recently is truly amazing.

I'm also so impressed with how many of them handle themselves. McNabb, for example, is such a class act. When all of the controversy was raised a few years ago with the NAACP getting upset at Rush Limbaugh's suggestion that McNabb was treated more gently by the critics because of his race, McNabb refused to enter the fray. He took the high road and let his performance on the field be all the response he needed to give. As someone who struggled with letting negative comments get to me, I can really admire how he handled that situation.

As much fun as it is to get to watch these talented young men prove that African-American quarterbacks have a place in professional football, there is one area of the game that I feel has not moved forward: team ownership. As of 2008, there are still no NFL teams owned primarily by African Americans, and this is a statistic I would like to change. Two former NFL players—Deron Cherry of the Kansas City Chiefs and Ray Childress, a teammate of mine with the Houston Oilers—own a small part of two teams: Cherry with the Jacksonville Jaguars and Childress with the Houston Texans.

It's not easy for anyone to purchase a team, of course, when tens of millions of dollars of capital is required upfront. There have been prospective African American buyers in the past who seemed like they might be able to strike a deal, but something has always fallen through at the last minute. A not-so-private wish of mine is that I will be able to be one of the first black franchise owners—and I'd especially love it to be in the Los Angeles market. There's been talk about bringing a team back to L.A. for a number of years, but it's obviously a tricky business, and so far nothing has come of it.

I think that having an African American team owner isn't just a neat "first"; it's also the key to getting more people of color in management positions within the NFL. I just hope that I can be a part of it. I would love to be able to put a team together. I would love to be a vice-president of football operations, the person who is responsible for the product on the field. As I think about that, it's probably something that I need to get more involved in from a personal standpoint. I really follow the game and even though I am with the Seahawks in a broadcast role, I am always talking and picking the brains of management and scouts about how they go about doing things.

Running or owning a team is something I would like to do.

I guess I've really never known what it was like to not be busy from the time I was a kid. Even when I was still playing, I'd always find myself involved in a lot of things outside the game, and a number of those efforts have had lasting effects.

For example, as a player I was very concerned about the state of the NFL's retirement plan. I can't think of a single career that is more physically grueling on a person's body, week after week, year after year, than professional football. People think of athletes as being in great shape, and it's true that we do try to focus on weight lifting and cardiovascular health, but all of the hits and tackles are punishing to even the fittest guys.

There are former players who at age thirty have the joints of a seventy-year-old, not to mention having experienced multiple concussions and countless sprains. Because of this kind of pounding day after day, the average career in the NFL is less than five years—which was hardly long enough to get vested in the system, let alone conducive to keeping people healthy to live long enough to cash in on the pension. As a result, a lot of guys were destroying their bodies and then couldn't get any kind of benefits afterwards. This just seemed wrong to me and a lot of other players, so we started organizing talks, then protests, to demand changes to the retirement system.

The problem with the system is that it's too hard to qualify for the money that's sitting there. If I am critical of anything, it's that the NFL Players' Association hasn't changed the protocol to get it done. I think there is almost a billion dollars sitting out there, but it's just sitting there, not being used. Our pension plan is not the greatest, but most guys don't live long enough to receive their pension; studies have shown that the average professional football player dies by the age of fifty-eight. You've got to make it to sixty-five in order to get your pension.

Gene Upshaw was the executive director of the National Football League Players' Association until his death in August 2008 from pancreatic cancer. Gene had alienated many retired players after comments he made in response to 325 former AFL and NFL players' receiving minimal retirement benefits. I was critical of Gene for not having a number-two person by his side to be prepared to step into his role when he retired. In late 2008, the executive director position remained vacant following Gene's death.

It's difficult to think of retirement as a player, but it was especially worrying as the trend was moving more and more toward it being a young man's game. Teams increasingly demand more and more out of their young quarterbacks rather than allowing them several years to learn the ropes.

In the late 1990s, a lot of veteran quarterbacks were talking about retirement: Dan Marino, John Elway, Steve Young, Jim Kelly, Troy Aikman, and myself all left the NFL within about two or three years of each other. Because so many guys with such high stats left at the same time, there was a rush to start recruiting young quarterbacks high in the draft, and a new kind of pressure was put on them to lead their teams to the same kinds of numbers right away that we had managed to achieve over the course of our careers.

Quarterbacks have to know their offense, inside and out. They have to know all the different formations, motions, and personnel groupings that go with that offense. You can have one play, but if you change the formation or you change the personnel grouping, that play becomes something totally different, and a lot of people's roles in that play change. Young quarterbacks have to learn all of those things. It just takes a while before you get all those pieces together in your head and feel comfortable behind the center.

I talked to Matt Hasselback (Seattle Seahawks quarterback) about it, and he said it took him about four years before he really felt comfortable with what he was doing in his offense. There were guys like Trent Dilfer who played in the league a long time, but it was the same thing. It took Trent a long time before he really felt comfortable. But once you get it, you get it. All of a sudden it clicks, and you start seeing those guys have success, and it's hard to stop it if you know what you're doing. If you don't know what you're doing, it looks ugly.

Young, heralded players such as Tennessee Titans quarterback Vince Young have had to struggle with outside pressures as well. Young was quoted by NFL.com after his first season in 2006 as saying that he thought long and hard about retiring because it was crazy being an NFL quarterback, and football wasn't fun anymore. In September 2008, Young disappeared for more than twenty-four hours after spraining his left knee and being booed in his home stadium during his team's 17–10 victory. While Young called his disappearance no big deal, his emotional well-being was such a concern to his coach Jeff Fisher and the quarterback's family that Fisher asked Nashville police, a crisis negotiator, and a psychologist for assistance in finding and dealing with the twenty-five-year-old.

I was asked to reach out to Vince by a Titans team employee, but we never connected. If I had, I would have wanted to know what Vince was dealing with at the time, because I heard so many different things about what was going on. Was it only football-related? Was it something emotional that we didn't know about? When suicide is mentioned, like it was in the stories surrounding Vince, this issue can't be just about football.

Struggles among young quarterbacks can also be physical. The result is often a young man allowing his body to take hits and be sacrificed in a way that will likely only allow him a few years of playing before the rough treatment on the gridiron takes its toll.

We didn't necessarily see this trend coming in the late 1980s, when this retirement program argument really came to a head, but our argument was obviously a timely one. I was very active with the effort to push for improvement for quite a while, and I am happy to say that the pension plan has improved a great deal over the past decade. And now I am one of those retired guys I was fighting for!

It was also interesting to watch the developments that surrounded Brett Favre's retirement following the 2007 season with the Green Bay Packers, to his return in 2008 with the New York Jets. Bottom line, I think the Packers wanted to go with the younger guy in Aaron Rodgers, much like when the Oilers traded me to Minnesota after I was named all-pro in 1993. The Packers gave Brett the choice to come back, but he chose to retire and Green Bay moved forward. Then Brett changed his mind and wanted to play again. I don't think the Packers didn't want Brett because they didn't like him as a player, I just think psychologically they went in another direction. That happens in football.

I've found some other ways to stay involved with the league.

While I tried to mentor younger players during my career through experiences on the field, I've tried to do the same and offer advice to current quarterbacks, such as Ben Roethlisberger of the Pittsburgh Steelers. I attended Roethlisberger's pro-scouting day at Miami University in Oxford, Ohio, and spent time with Ben. When the opportunities arise, I still enjoy getting out and playing catch with rookies during training camp.

I have provided color commentary for the Seahawks and Titans, and I've done some commentary for Westwood One's broadcast of Sunday night games, too. But I have to admit that one of my favorite things during football season is Fantasy Football. I am a huge fan and probably spend way more time tracking my teams than I should. Together with Erik Kramer, who also played in the CFL before his career as an NFL quarterback, I have done some episodes of Ultimate Fantasy Football for Fox Sports Net, and we always have a blast.

I also participated in the *Pros vs. Joes* television reality show, which matched male amateurs against professional athletes (many of whom are retired like myself) in athletic competition. I really didn't know who watched the show, until one morning at three A.M., I received a text from Brad Johnson, my former teammate at Minnesota, who played in Dallas in 2008. Brad said I had way too much free time. Of course, I busted Brad's chops for taking the time out to watch.

I've owned a number of business ventures over the years, from my own personal chain store—we made chocolate-chip cookies, an embellishment of a recipe I learned from my mother—which was later purchased by nationally renowned Mrs. Fields Milk Chocolate Cookies; to a nightclub-restaurant in Newport Beach, California, that I currently co-own with good friend and Kansas City tight end Tony Gonzalez; and my work with dear friend Leigh Steinberg, our sports and entertainment agency in Newport Beach.

One of our initiatives at Leigh Steinberg Sports and Entertainment is the Sporting Green Alliance. The concept is to take sustainable technologies and integrate them into stadiums and arenas throughout the sports world. These innovative technologies will drop the carbon emissions and reduce energy costs. They will also turn the stadiums and arenas into educational platforms, where the literally billions of fans that come to games can see a waterless urinal or solar panels for the first time and hopefully think about how to use these concepts in their own homes and businesses. We are going to "green" up sports franchises with green forests and Saturday morning cartoon shows featuring green sports superheroes fighting polluters. We consider the environment and fighting global warming key to not being the first generation in America to hand down a degraded quality of life to our kids.

Leigh and I plan to host a flag-football event at the Sundance Film Festival to benefit the Sporting Green Alliance. It will pit former NFL greats such as Ronnie Lott, Bruce Smith, and myself against movie stars. This is an example of the fusion of sports and entertainment that our company is working on—the development of content for motion pictures, television (reality shows), video games, the Internet. Or I could host a television show that features professional athletes retrofitting single mothers' homes.

I started the Quarterback Club and was its first president. The group includes Bernie Kosar, Boomer Esiason, and others and provides marketing for players. It was a real breakthrough in player empowerment and autonomy. We once produced a commemorative collector tin of myself for the Children's Miracle Network. In Sacramento, Leigh and I and the late Bill Walsh lobbied the California legislature for tighter restrictions on supplements used by high school players and better steroid enforcement. Of course, my career has also remained a topic of conversation since my retirement. There are some who will say that my passing statistics in the Canadian Football League (21,228) shouldn't count toward my overall professional total (70,553). Hugh Campbell, my former CFL coach at Edmonton, calls that thinking arrogant at the minimum and a tad of racism at the maximum. Hugh has called me as good as any quarterback he has seen. What we did together in Canada was special. What I did in the United States was special.

Together, it was football.

The thing that keeps me occupied the most right now, though, is working with the various organizations I sponsor or support. I've really been fortunate over the years to work with some amazing groups.

After working in a support role with various philanthropic causes for a number of years, I decided that it was time for me to start a foundation of my own. In 1989, the same year I was voted the NFL Man of the Year, Crescent Moon Foundation was created to provide college scholarships for deserving young people from the cities that were home to me: Los Angeles, Houston, Minneapolis-St. Paul, and Seattle.

Education has always been a big concern of mine, and I was lucky enough to have caught a scout's eye and been offered an athletic scholarship. Most kids, though, aren't going to have the chance to be a quarterback or a three-point shooter, or an entertainer, or a movie star—and some seem to think this is the only way out.

For students growing up in inner-city areas or with single parents, or in disadvantaged school systems, there aren't a lot of opportunities or money to take advantage of special programs. And, of course, there are always a thousand pressures to drop out or give up or to just become another part of the cycle of poverty. But if you are educated, you have a chance. You can get out of the old neighborhood, and you can get the tools to stand on your own two feet.

I decided that if I was able to provide college tuition for students coming out of high school who wanted to continue their studies but didn't have the means to pay for it, I could really have an impact. Students are required to meet certain academic requirements and have to be involved in their communities—the goal is to help improve lives, after all—and they have to have a desire to put in the work to be successful. That's probably the single most important criteria.

The foundation also does work with camps for children suffering from sickle-cell disease, which helps to provide them with a fun time away from hospitals and not thinking about the pain that the disorder causes. I've also worked with the Urban League, Ronald McDonald House, American Heart Association, Cerebral Palsy Foundation, United Negro College Fund, Special Olympics, Cystic Fibrosis Foundation, Juvenile Diabetes, the United Way, and March of Dimes. I also hold an annual Bowlathon for charity in Las Vegas, and Eva Longoria and Tony Parker have helped make it a success.

It's also important to cultivate and develop our young leaders. The Wharton School of the University of Pennsylvania has helped the Field Generals—our nonprofit organization dedicated to teaching and preserving the history of the African American quarterback—form leadership strategy. UCLA's School of Business also wants to be involved in developing a similar approach. Our goal is to identify and work with kids who want to be in this curriculum, who have leadership aspirations and want to make a difference. That's what makes it appealing to me, when these kids want to be there and everyone is on the same page.

Many times when I speak at clinics, I quickly discover that some kids attend for the wrong reason. They are simply not interested or were forced to attend by their parents. It's neat to connect with kids who are motivated to get better at what they are doing. I am sure they've heard a lot of people talk, but it's another voice. I've had success, and it validates my message. Hopefully, they think that if Warren Moon says it, too, there must be something to it.

The same goes for my motivational speaking. Be it sales representatives, surgeons, CEOs, or college students, I share my views on the importance of strong mentors and the accountability that each of us has to those we touch in life. I also talk about how sports relates to business, making good decisions, and having the perseverance to succeed in a competitive and sometimes hostile environment. I really enjoy the Q&A aspects of my appearances, because when you get to answer a specific question and interact one on one, you have an opportunity to really make an impact.

I am very plugged into my church, too, though it is something I rarely talk about publicly. My faith is extremely important in my life, especially as I struggle to overcome certain things; but it's also a very private thing for me. My mother always made sure that Sunday school was an unquestionable part of our weekly routine and insisted that we recognize the source of every blessing in our lives. I still thank the Lord every time something happens, and I pray through the difficult times. My faith definitely gave me strength to get through the most challenging periods of my life, but it's just not something I tend to talk about in spiritual terms. It's more of an inner faith than a platform for me.

It might sound a little melodramatic to say so, but it really has been wonderful, overall, to see the fruits of my labor be realized both on the field and off.

It's also humbling to think about the honors that have been given to me: serving on President Bush's media advisory committee in 1990, being recognized as the Houston Firefighters' man of the year, receiving the Superstar Award from the National Urban Coalition for helping students' futures. In 2006 I was honored in front of the L.A. City Council and Mayor Antonio Villaraigosa with these words: "Your achievement is not just about blacks, it inspires Latinos or anyone else told they can't do something, are disqualified because of ethnicity, skin color, religion." The appreciation of my success and the ability to overcome barriers has really made the past few years special.

I've been recognized by a lot of different organizations that I played for, but, of course, the Hall of Fame is the pinnacle. Everywhere I go now, anywhere I am introduced, it is a special feeling to have that, the NFL Hall of Fame, connected to your name. Everything that I went through, both the good and the bad, it was all worth it. I've been asked if I would have been a different person if my father hadn't died when I was seven years old. That's a great question, and I honestly don't know.

I wouldn't say I'd want anybody else to go through what I did, but in some ways for me, it made me a stronger person.

I think, if people do know my story, maybe it will help them as they go through things that might be similar to what I went through. I think it will make people appreciate a little bit more just how difficult it was for me to play the game. It wasn't "just a game," where I had to go out and practice every day to get better. I think a lot of people have wondered who I am. I played the game with very little emotion. When people see me today, they think I was so cool and so calm. Of course, they also saw my skin color.

They just never knew what was going on inside of me.

Acknowledgments

What makes the Warren Moon story special is that for so many years he made it a point not to share it with others. At the risk of sounding like he was ungrateful—or worse, fearful—Warren dulled the nerves that had been sliced raw with years of challenge. To be able to tell the story, Warren had to unleash the emotions that he had so bottled up . . . and he had to ask dozens of friends and former colleagues to share stories some had never mentioned.

To do this required help and time from many people.

Warren's family and friends helped tell his incredible story, starting with wife Mandy, who was at Warren's side during that snowy, Detroit afternoon car ride in 2006 when Moon was informed he had become the first African American quarterback inducted into the NFL Hall of Fame. Warren's family, specifically his mother Pat; sisters Renee Moon, Kim Odom, and Natalie Paul; and daughter Blair, made themselves available for hours of interviews, as did his youth coach, Bernard Parks, a former chief of the Los Angeles Police Department and current member of the Los Angeles City Council, and other coaches such as Jack Epstein and Hugh Campbell who helped shape Warren's magnificent career.

Childhood friends such as Lorenzo Romar, the men's basketball coach at the University of Washington, and NFL players and pioneers such as Doug Williams, James Harris, and Tony Dungy, who retired in 2009 as the head coach of the Indianapolis Colts, also offered wonderful, emotional insight into Warren's remarkable journey.

This book couldn't have been possible without the help and vision of Warren's longtime friend and agent Leigh Steinberg, literary agent David Vigliano, editor Kevin Hanover, and business partner Jeff Buchanan.

Research help came in a big way from respected colleague William C. Rhoden, a sports columnist for the *New York Times* who authored acclaimed *Third and a Mile: The Trials and Triumph of the Black Quarterback*; John McClain, the veteran columnist of the *Houston Chronicle* who has known Warren since his playing days with the Houston Oilers and is a member of the Pro Football Hall of Fame Selection Committee; Peter King, senior writer and good friend from *Sports Illustrated*; Len Pascarelli, NFL football writer for ESPN; Bill Hyde, vice president of community relations with the Tennessee Titans; team officials and personnel with the Seattle Seahawks, the Minnesota Vikings, and the Kansas City Chiefs; the sports information office at the University of Washington; and employees with the Pro Football Hall of Fame and the Canadian Football Hall of Fame.

Newspapers, magazines, and Internet sites that also helped in research included *Sports Illustrated*, ESPN, *The Sporting News*, Yahoo Sports!, *Pro Football Weekly*, *USA Today*, the *Los Angeles Times*, the *Seattle Times*, the *Seattle Post-Intelligencer*, the *Everett* (Washington) *Herald*, the *Bremerton* (Washington) *Sun*, the *Tacoma News-Tribune*, the Associated Press, the *Houston Post*, the *Dallas Morning News*, the *Kansas City Star*, *American Way* magazine, the Black Athlete Sports Network, the Canton Repository, and the *Akron-Beacon Journal*.

That list also included Canadian newspapers such as the *Orilla Packet & Times* in Ontario, the *Hamilton Spectator* in Ontario, the *Calgary Herald*, the *Edmonton Sun*, the *Toronto Star*, and *The Globe and Mail*.

Closer to home, key members of our writing and research team also included the amazingly disciplined Jim Henry, who kept this train on the tracks, and the gifted Tiffany Yecke Brooks, whose ability to turn a phrase is uncanny for her age.

To all of you, thanks for making the telling of this story possible.

Index